Brian Ó Concúbair
Trá Lí
5 Samhain 1999

THE RIVER SHANNON

The River Shannon

Text and Photographs
by
Maeve Henry

The Conna Press

1996

First published 1996 by
The Conna Press
P.O. Box 5097,
Dublin 7, Ireland

A CIP record for this
title is available from
The British Library

ISBN 0 9528521 0 1

Typesetting, book layout
and cover design
Tony Moreau

Colour scanning
and film output
Lithographic Plate Plan Ltd.,
Grenville Place, Dublin 8.

Printed by Betaprint.
Unit 2a, Newtown Industrial Estate
Clonshaugh, Dublin 17, Ireland.

Contents

List of Maps

Chapter One

IN THE NORTH-WEST LOOP OF COUNTY CAVAN, looming steeply above the borders of Fermanagh, lies the Cuilceagh mountain range, in the foothills of which the River Shannon has its source. It extends for three miles across the countryside, rising to three peaks - Cuilceagh in the east, the crest of which is dominated by a large burial cairn with a smaller one a short distance away, Knockatona towards the centre, and Tiltinbane on the western rim. Its summit is a set of tablelands, deep and wide, topping a series of slopes marked by rocky outcrops, interspersed with patches of bog, marsh, and arable fields - a rounded contour making a dark green and brown elevation which merges into the cloudy grey strata of the skyline.

To designate it as 'mountain' is largely an exaggeration, since Cuilceagh, the highest summit, stands at just 2,188 feet, yet it is the highest in the oval girdle of peaks which here encompass parts of three counties - Cavan, Leitrim and Roscommon, to form a spectacular landscape of hill and valley, plateau and slope, river and lake.

The rolling heights of Tiltinbane and Knockatona, extending to the Cuilceagh crest and beyond, rim the northern boundary with, on the east side, Ben Beag, leading to the Bellavally Gap, to Ben Breac, Sliabh na Cille, Munter Eolus, Ben Croy and Knockabell, and continuing into the sharp dominant outline of Sliabh an Iarainn in the south. Opposite them, in the north-west, the Corry Mountains run southwards to merge with the Arigna hills which extend into the Kilronan range of County Roscommon.

This ridged and lofty palisade which overlooks and surrounds the district of Glangevlin, from which the headwaters of the Shannon flow to join Loch Allen, its first great lake expansion, is capped by impervious rock materials – by Millstone grit, Yoredale shale, and sandstone, beneath which multilayers of carboniferous limestone reach down into the bowels of the earth floor. Coal seams are found on Ben Croy and Sliabh an Iarainn, which also has deposits of iron ore, from which it is named, while in the west, the Corry Mountains, and especially the Arigna hills, are pockmarked with the sites of coal mines, ancient and modern, the last of which ceased to function in 1990. All of these elements combine to make a meagre top soil devoid of the basic nutrients necessary to maintain a rich flora and fauna.

• • • • •

Yet even in this bleak and inhospitable terrain, ancient archaelogical sites and signs show that people lived in the area from pre-historic times. Various names are used to describe the earliest tribes - Parthalonians, Formorians, Fir Bolg, Tuatha De Danann, and lastly, the Milesians, a tribe already known in the history of European development as the Celts.

Cuilceagh Mountain

Two colonisations are deemed to have occurred between 6,000 and 3,000 B.C. The first in the Mesolithic, or Middle Stone Age, consisted of bands of nomads who existed by fishing and hunting, who travelled from Northern Europe, through Britain and Scotland to Ireland, entering the country at Antrim in the north-east. From here, they spread southwards along the east coast, and westwards towards the Atlantic Ocean. These people lived at the margins of forests, hunted birds and wild beasts, and used boats carved out of tree trunks, or made from the skins of animals, to enable them fish and cross rivers and lakes. Caves and underground passages provided living places, and it is possible that the crannóg, or lake dwelling, originated at this time. Their tools were made of flint – axeheads, arrowheads, scrapers and boring implements.

The second colonisation occurred in the Neolithic, or late Stone Age, bringing pastoral groups of people from Western Europe and the Iberian peninsula, who settled along the Atlantic seaboard, making homesteads and establishing the first communities. They were farming folk with efficient tools, able to fell trees, clear spaces, sow crops, such as, wheat and barley, and domesticate animals – cattle, sheep, pigs and goats. Some of their largest settlements were made in Mayo, Sligo and Donegal, areas adjacent to North-west Cavan, which, in time, they occupied as they spread eastwards. They made pottery, food vessels and urns and later, with the discovery of metals, of copper and gold, and an amalgam of copper and tin which ushered in the Bronze Age, crafted tools, weapons, and ornaments. These skills were

The State forest of Burren

The Giant's Grave within Burren Forest

developed farther in the Iron Age. Expert in metal crafts, the Celts mixed with and eventually dominated the native tribes, giving them a legal system, a common language, and a religion, known as Druidism.

Antiquities belonging to this long period are to be found in North-west Cavan, close to Glangevlin and its surrounding districts. These artifacts usually take three forms - firstly, areas of habitation, such as, caiseals and stone and ring forts; secondly, elaborate burial places for single and multiple graves, and thirdly, the crafting of pottery, as well as metal tools, weaponry and ornaments.

On the western slopes of the Cuilceagh, the State Forest of Burren contains a cemetery-type group of graves, court, portal and wedge forms. A single grave, the Giant's Grave, is the best known. Moneygashel, nearby, has the remains of three caiseals, originally there were seven enclosures surrounded by stone circles or walls. Farther east near Ballyconnell, the townland of Killycluggin has the residue of a stone circle, a decorated stone and two slabs, Kilnavert, close by, a wedge-type grave, stone circle and standing stone, and Lissanover, also adjacent, a circle of stones. Such circles stand on small hills in this area, sometimes with burial chambers inside them. At Cohaw near the centre of the county, there is a large court grave with five burial chambers, and a similar though smaller one at Drumavrack. Close to Loch Allen are single court graves and wedge graves at Curracloona and Kilnagairns Lower.

Objects known as 'grave-goods' were often found in the ancient burial chambers giving an indication of when they were constructed. Such objects included flint arrowheads, stone tools, food vessels, shards of pottery, ornaments and metal implements, pointing to the different periods of craftmanship.

But, perhaps, the best known artifact in this area is a part of the Black Pig's Dyke, an ancient earthwork which exists in sections over four counties, from Leitrim to Armagh, and is said to be an old frontier of Ulster. It runs for up to two miles along the banks of the River Shannon between Dowra on the Cavan border and Loch Allen.

Crannóga, or lake dwellings, another visible reminder of ancient habitation, have been found in Cavan, on the islands of Loch Oughter in the River Erne, and also on Loch Allen, and are said to have been begun in the Bronze Age, though they continued to be built until medieval times.

Apart from the megalithic signs of ancient eras, there is in the townlands of Glangevlin and Loch Allen, a very rich vein of folklore relating to the pre-historic peoples who inhabited these areas, particularly the tribe of the Tuatha De Danann. Legend has it that they made a headquarters at Derrynatuan, a district through which the infant Shannon flows, and also at Lios an Iorrus, west of Loch Allen. On the slopes of Sliabh an Iarainn, many large rock formations mark another of their legendary centres; one standing stone

Caiseals at Moneygashel

Grave at Kilnavert, Cavan

is known as 'the King's Stone.' With them is associated the widespread belief in 'the little people,' the fairies and the leprechain, a belief that lasted well into modern times.

The epic tales of the Fianna have left their traces on these mountain slopes also. A prominent rock called the Brevagh Stone is associated with Finn McCool, their warrior chief. A number of standing stones on the hill of Shantemon, east of Cavan town, is called 'Finn McCool's Fingers,' while his burial place is said to be at Sheebeg, a hill with a pre-historic mound on its summit some miles east of Loch Allen.

The old pagan practices and beliefs brought by the Celts, with their worship of natural forms, also have their place here, traditionally considered to be the last refuge of druidism in Ireland. Crom Cruaich and his sub-gods, a group of large graven images, sited at Magh Sleacht near Ballyconnell, were the chief idols of Celtic Ireland. St. Patrick, it is said, while travelling to Glangevlin, stopped at the spot, overthrew and destroyed them.

But all such practices were not so easily shed. An ancient sports' ground called 'the Playbank' sited on a slope of Sliabh na Cille, used to host an assembly of people on the last Sunday of July, Domnach Deireannach, also named Bilberry Sunday, to usher in the harvest festival, well into recent times. There were athletic contests, feasting, music and dancing, and the picking of bilberries. The celebration was held in honour of Lu of the Tuatha De Danann, the God of Light, after whom Lughnasa, the month of August, is named.

• • • • •

The foothills of the Cuilceagh are peaty, with thin infertile soil. Rivulets abound here, streaming from summit, outcrop and slope. They bicker over scarps of rock, stone and shale, gouging out gullies and ravines, depositing sediment of pebble, clay and gravel ripped from the hilly flanks. They carve runnels in thin substrata and often sink underground to seep through the soft limestone sponge like invisible canals only to reappear on the surface of the land lower down the slopes.

Many such embryo streams combine to form the source of the River Shannon, our greatest waterway and one of the basic natural shapers of our landscape. It is 214 miles long, including the 60-mile estuary which merges with the Atlantic Ocean at Loop Head in County Clare. Its navigable waters, with 15 lakes and tributaries reach 1,130 miles, while it drains up to one-fifth of the area of the country, an immense region of 6,060 square miles.

The Shannon has its source, not in a tiny spring on the summit of the mountain, or in a robust little stream making a spillway over a stray outcrop of rock in riffles and cascades, but in a deep wide pool at the foot of Tiltinbane. The most westerly point of the Cuilceagh range, Tiltinbane is half a mile in width and 1,949 feet high. The pool known as Lug na Sionna, or the Shannon Pot, is over 15 feet deep, though its real depth has yet to be determined. Fuelled by two springs which erupt in its centre, it is in a constant state of inner agitation as it receives an unceasing flow of the underground water which seeps from the subterranean limestone sponge of the mountainside.

On a June day, Lug na Sionna wears a peaceful rural and scenic aspect. Approached by a narrow path at the end of a newly constructed tarmac avenue, debouching off the Learga (Blacklion) Road, it is surrounded by rough pasture in which browsing cattle gaze at intruders with curious though unalarmed eyes. The surface of the pool dimples beneath the blue and white of the sky, its broken reflections emblemed by twisting skeins of grey cloud and the winged rhythms of flying crows.

Its length and breadth are difficult to determine. On all sides it is ringed with lush vegetation. Ancient trees of hawthorn, bramble and sally, their trunks encrusted with grey lichen and clumps of warped moss, stretch crooked branches over the waterway. Saplings emerging from old roots in the soft mire of the banks, trail in its shifting eddy pools. Dense thickets of fern and briar make an impenetrable hedge on one side while a wealth of wildflora - marsh marigold, buttercup, cow parsley and flowering rush - lend bright tints of colour to the soft grey-green mosaic of the countryside.

It is only in the first weeks of winter when the vegetation is dying away, its rotting stems wilting into the moist dank earth, when the leaden-black trunks and spines of the trees stand bare and desolate, that the pool can be seen as it actually is. Then it reveals itself as an oval stretch of water, about forty feet long and twenty wide. The water is peaty brown in colour, clotted with wood debris, opaque and dirty, its surface spattered with withered leaves, crushed twigs and stems. Only the rains which at this time of year are coming with greater frequency can scour its expanse of this autumnal waste.

In the background, the summit of Tiltinbane, rearing its bare crest against a dove-grey bank of cloud, seems alien, mysterious and remote. There is no apparent connection between it and the pool, no winding rivulet, no mountain lake or emergent spring gushing over rocky scarps. The waters that feed the pool flow largely underground, through a mass of limestone, seeping into its unresisting fabric, carving a spillway through holes, caverns and ravines.

Carboniferous limestone, the basic rock of much of our soil, is uniquely different from other natural clays which are purely mineral in origin, such as sandstone, quartz and mica. It is composed of calcite slimes formed from the shells and skeletons of aquatic life, corals, clams and snails, indicating the presence of ancient seas flooding the land in past aeons of existence. This factor makes limestone the most soluble of all types of rock and the element to which it is most vulnerable is the acid contained in rain water.

It is through this giant pouch of limestone that the infant Shannon begins its downhill course. Almost imperceptibly, it emerges from the western corner of the pool about four feet below the lip of the land. At first sight, what seems to be a deep ditch or gully meets the eye. On scanning its depths, however, one sees a watery channel about three feet wide carved in the soft dark slime through which a rivulet, clear and golden brown in colour, moves silently away from the pool. Almost immediately it is joined by a tiny runnel of water trickling from the hillside. Its banks are high and grassy and in summer are clothed with woodland scrub and wild flowers - buttercup, dandelion, daisy and wood anemone – interspersed with clumps of fern and brown dock. In late autumn as this vegetation dies away, the rivulet becomes highly visible. Its narrow channel has filled with dark turbulent water gushing from the pool. Its current is slow, the gradient gentle rather than steep, on this, its first essay across the ridge of the hillside, the depths of which are already incised with underground streamlets, the surface mired by rough patches of marsh and swamp.

In the townland of Derrylahan, 500 feet above sea level, the stream has begun its course. It has acquired an identity and a name – Sionna. Yet the origin of the word 'Sionna' is by no means certain. Two possible explanations have been put forward. The first suggests that it derives from the Gaelic term 'sean abhainn' or 'old river' and the earliest reference to its existence is very old indeed, going back to the 2nd century A.D. when the geographer, Ptolemy, mentions it under the title 'Senos.' The second explanation rests on a poetic and tragic tale embedded in Irish folklore. It describes how Sinann, a princess of the Tuatha De Danann, in an eager quest for knowledge and in defiance of a sex taboo, plunged into St. Connla's Well in which the salmon of wisdom lay. The well erupted in a wild spate in which Sinann was swept away and drowned as the foaming torrent flooded into and created the river which now perpetuates her name and memory.

On the lower slopes of the Cuilceagh, however, the river is still in its incipient stages, still a very narrow stream giving no hint of the momentous journey it has begun. Only eighteen miles to the west the long

Tiltinbane, the western peak of the Cuilceagh range

Court Grave at Cohaw

Graves at Kilnagairns Lr.

Rock form on Sliabh an Iarainn

Sheebeg, legendary grave of Finn McCool

Lug na Sionna, or the Shannon Pot

Lush vegetation overcrowds the Shannon Pot

The emerging Shannon

The Shannon trickles down the hillside

Shannon Bridge

low curve of Sligo Bay offers an open gateway to the Atlantic Ocean but the stream veers southward and maintains this direction for its entire course.

Trickling gradually down the ridge of the hillside, the soft unresisting soil yielding to its persistent pressure, it expands to a width of five feet. The banks remain steep and in the summer months are heavy with weedy vegetation and a sprinkling of wild flowers - meadow sweet, dog roses, wild rockets and marguerite. They are also very uneven with muddy dykes made by the forays of cattle and spits of soft ooze forming on the verges. Clumps of rush appear at intervals and an isolated section of reed. Though free from mature trees for the most part, willows bestride the stream where the banks have dwindled in size and hazel saplings take root in the watery slime. The channel is weedy, the current obstructed at intervals by logs of wood and broken twigs. Pools and eddies occur, sweeping and swirling around small boulders.

Passing into the adjoining townland of Lattoon, the stream reaching a shallow depression, had expanded across both banks into a small lake. But the expansion was impermanent. Drought, evaporation, and the irresistible pull of the current drained it of running water. Tussocks of grass and clumps of spike rush began to grow in the soft mud, trapping clay and gravel in their roots to make unwieldy hummocks. Adding to this process was the wilting vegetation of autumn and winter, the mass of brown rotting leaves, the withered stems and branches, the perennial debris of the fields. All found a resting place here, turning it into puddles of squelching and decaying verdure, covered by a thin layer of grass and patches of moss. Now a swamp and treacherous underfoot, it is known locally as a 'blind loch'.

But the stream is not baulked by its surrounding quagmire. Its shallow bed is in continuous movement. Its drifting skeins of rocky sediment are in perpetual friction, disturbing each muddy grain, shifting and pushing it in countless minute ways.

Floating in the current, or temporarily impeded, each particle impels motion in a myriad other slivers of stone, clay and gravel, and so changing their form, abrading and diminishing stone to pebble, gravel to fine sand.

Unhindered, it flows increasingly downhill, absorbing water from minute and nameless streamlets, cutting into its gully-like bed, creating its own pools and runnels, forming bends, gouging into banks with slivers of jagged stone to release rock and clay. Its channel begins to widen, bearing in its eddies and swirls increasing amounts of sediment, sharp-edged particles of shale, tufts of grassy loam, gravel and pebble.

The flanks of the hillside slant more steeply and the stream starts to surge forward, its cutting power enhanced. It begins to roll and gush over large shelving slabs of stone and mounds of sand and pebble, caught in the twists and bends. Eddies bubble and foam-crested waves appear as the current sluices past the soft yielding banks, undercutting the lip of the land and depositing in its wake fine sediment to line the stony verges.

Its speed quickens as it falls through a long narrow gorge, rough and irregular with ridges of slab, rock and boulder. Tall overhanging trees, hawthorn, sally and ash, darken its channel on both banks. Abruptly it turns and in a flurry of rapids tumbles downward to its first small bridge.

Flowing strongly after heavy showers of rain, the stream passes beneath the old stone bridge which is forty feet long and possesses one low arch. About a mile distant from Lug na Sionna, the bridge is on the northern arm of the Glangevlin Road, that skirts the hills on the eastern slopes of the Cuilceagh, making a fork at the village of Glan and sending one arm north to Learga and the other south to Dowra. Sited in the district of Lattoon, the bridge is unnamed and in the summer months is almost hidden beneath a canopy of foliage and luxuriant woodland vegetation.

The stream's channel has widened to between ten and fifteen feet and part of its bed is choked with sediment. Slabs of rock, rough gravel and pebble lie discarded on the muddy ooze of the verges to make spits and bars as the current swivels and twists over outcrops of shale, pushing runnels and rivulets in tiny cascades over the raw, terraced build-up of stone. It gouges troughs and fissures around the base of small boulders, as it carries a muddle of pebbles and clay under the bridge to spill out more widely into the channel beyond, where the leafy shroud of trees has given way to bush, scrub and grassy hillock.

A short distance from the bridge the stream divides in a scissor-like movement to form a narrow fork and create its first tiny island. The cutting power of the current has sliced a wedge from the adjacent field, almost thirty feet in length. It is triangular in shape, crisscrossed with grass, fern, saplings and young trees. Beneath it, on the left, is a narrow trough-like spillway, littered with stone and pebble through which a streamlet dribbles and trickles around the tip of the islet where it drains reluctantly into the main channel which is gushing rapidly downhill, its whirls and wavelets capped with scallops of foam.

The banks, with much of the woodland scrub cut away, have become low and open. A sprinkle of flowers – primrose, daisy, buttercup – flanked by rush and fern, shimmer in the thin covering of grass while the broad leaves and pale stems of marsh marigold invade the tussocks on the edges of the stream, their bright cups a yellow glow of colour in the soft muddy haze.

The progression of the stream is twisty and winding, in places broadening to pool formation where the current cuts beneath the unstable banks and sweeps away clay and gravel, at other times narrowing, as it swirls westward to form a large loop out of which it flows strongly to its second bridge, a smaller and somewhat delapidated version of the first. Though the distance between the bridges is less than half a mile, the second, fringed with flowering hedgerows of hawthorn, bramble and ivy, is sited on a minor road set almost at right angles to Glangevlin Road in the townland of Derrynatuan.

Here, the widening channel is layered with rocky shelves over which the churning stream tumbles and gurgles in mini-waterfalls on both sides of the bridge. Below it, the terrain slopes steeply into rough marshy land. Low hedges grow out of deep wet dykes and occasionally outcrops of rock break through the slanting hillocks that ridge the fields.

The stream, cooped in its channel, hardly more than ten feet wide at this point, gushes rapidly downhill between banks of thick rushy growth and some low scrub. It narrows to almost half its width as it reaches large spits of rock jutting out from both banks while a large boulder, lying in the bed, impedes the flow. Swirling around this obstacle, its speed increases as it meets a steep escarpment. It tumbles over the ridge of rock, its fall almost precipitous as it races downhill for up to fifty yards, a torrential waterfall, cannoning against great slabs of stone, sweeping over crag, small boulder and jagged shelf.

Its current is shallow and very fast, its surface black and gleaming as the shifting sunlight picks out slivers of shale, spits of gravel and tossing shreds of foam. The banks are low and largely free of cumbersome grassland vegetation with the exception of the weedy dock, spike rush and a spattering of fern rooted in the mud beside the verges. Jets and rills race swiftly by the shallow clay margins into which they slice and carve, undercutting the edges of the rough pasture fields which in places are fenced with a palisade of boulders. With bubbling splashes, loud gurgles and a continuous murmuring clamour, the water submerges all obstacles as it rushes down the humped uneven slope, the steepest it has encountered since its emergence from the pool.

It drops to a widening plateau and temporarily slows as a makeshift dam put together with boulder, tree trunks and stone obstructs its course, dividing it into three rivulets. The two smaller ones on the left of the channel carve two tiny islets out of the moist loam as they shape new waterways and plunge downhill. The main stream on the right tumbles over the lip of the plateau and races tumultously over a further steep incline to reach the base of the hillside where it is joined by the two smaller rivulets to form

The Shannon flows from the Bridge

The stream in spate

a large pool which appears almost stagnant by contrast with the preceding bustle.

Making a sharp turn, the river proceeds to flow across flat rushy fields in a south westerly direction. There is a shallow slant in the terrain and the current, though slow, remains brisk. Brown peaty water streams through the channel which is ten feet in width and two in depth. The banks are clotted with thick weedy vegetation and in places, broken into dykes and holes from which muddy tufts float, trapping other debris,forming pools and riffles. Great tussocks of rush grow into the water. A bed of tall lightcoloured reeds breaks the monotonous green of field growth,their crumpled heads weaving strange patterns in the quickening breeze. Small trees and saplings grow in the centre of the channel but do not perceptibly hinder the water flow nor does a narrow stone dam which crosses the stream, allowing the current to sluice through freely.

A pheasant darts from a large tussock of rush with a clatter startlingly loud in a silence broken only by the soft splashy drone of the water, and flees in panic to the opposite bank and away into the deserted countryside. There are no houses near these spongy water-logged fields though a sprinkling of sheep and cattle graze on the low hills.

The river's channel and verges are dotted with marsh marigold in beds and clumps, its intense yellow hue the only touch of colour in the prevailing olive and brown of rush and field. Its tendrils are rooted along the muddy ooze of the bottom, its stems trail through the water to enable the flower cups float on

The bridge at Derrynatuan Road

Drumburrin Bridge

the calm surface. Close by and almost unnoticeable, stray tufts of primrose and daisy peer from the hollows of the banks.

The river enters a flatter terrain, slowing, making stagnant pools. Willow scrub invade its channel. Weedy growth chokes the verges as it winds forward reluctantly, the current dwindling to a slack and lifeless meander, its energy apparently spent.

It has come to a pause in its two-mile rush from the hillside pool. Its journey has been largely a silent and solitary one. The only sounds that have vibrated on the air around it are those which it has made itself – the soft lapping of wavelets against stone and pebble, the intermittent splashes over slabs of rock, the gurgles in the narrow fissures between jagged boulders and the ongoing chant of sudden rapids and tiny waterfalls.

Of bird song it has heard none.

Only the large carnivorous birds frequent the marshy fields and the thin soil of the uplands. The raven and the carrion crow may be seen singly or in pairs making regular sorties to the high barren slopes, their dark powerful wings slicing the pale sky.

Nor can the hillside stream attract and hold plant life to any degree. Its speed and constant inner agitation as it swirls around snags, stones and bends,prevent all but the most tenacious from obtaining even a sparse existence. Some types of algae attach themselves to the ooze and clay on the bed of the stream. Tiny strands and patches of moss cling to wood debris and mounds of gravel in quiet runnels. Stonewort and hornwort burrow into ledges and niches and put out runners under water. In the shallow verges can be found dock and nettle, dwarf fern and water plantain.

Similarly, insect and fish life exist in only a very limited quantity in the chilly turmoil of the fast-flowing hillside stream. Some fly larvae drift with the swirling current. Others, like the waternet caddis fly, attach themselves like leeches to the crevices and fissures in stones. In the neutral pools beside crags and boulders, the tadpole and the minnow with strong gripping jaws anchor themselves to the undersides of rocks when the onrush of the current threatens to destroy their slender lives.

But in the sluggish watercourse of the dawdling stream, stimulated by warm weather, these problems of aquatic life have gradually become easier. The soft slime covering its bed has become a peaceful haven

for fly larvae and tiny fish, molluscs and water beetles. The flowers and leaves of the marsh marigold float profusely in the slow current, in patches, skeins and clumps. On the surface tiny pits and dimples are being made by the wings and feet of water insects who live by clinging to the stems of rush, reed and other growth haunting the shallows.

The stream continues to meander towards the south-west in a gentle curve.

The confluence of the Shannon (left) with the Owenmore River (right)

Abruptly, the current begins to quicken as a slant in the terrain urges it forward. It falls rapidly over stone and slab as it approaches a small concrete bridge built on a narrow laneway, a turning off Derrynatuan Road Lower. This is Drumburrin Bridge, sited in the townland of the same name and erected about forty years ago.

In the area of the bridge the stream makes a sharp turn to flow to the south-east. Its channel has widened though it is very shallow with much stone and rock. The current is clear and unfettered, the vegetation on one bank having been cut away while the other bears a section of woodland. Downstream of the bridge, however, a rough dam of rocks and boulders traverses its width. The stream has now passed from thin-soiled rushy terrain to grazing land and meadow where hay is being harvested. In this stretch, the last of its existence as an independent river, its progress is greatly impeded by unchecked vegetation. Bulky swaths and clumps of overgrown reed, grass, rush and fern,invade the channel from both sides, giving it the appearance of a choked ditch or gully. Willow scrub reaches from bank to bank in places, making small sluggish pools around its roots and branches. Lush alder and thorn saplings, a mass of sticks, stems and foliage, trailing in back lies of water, devour air, light and space as they tangle with spreading mops of weed growing from the bottom ooze.

The banks are fenced off in many fields by rows of barbed wire erected up to ten feet from the river margins which are almost invisible at this point. Within this fencing,old tree trunks fling out gnarled branches, saplings push their thin lengths into any available space. Thick scrub and weedy vegetation, grassy tufts and clumps of rush cover the uneven ground while the leafy canopies of mature trees overcrowd the shallow channel which is gradually widening despite formidable obstacles. A heavy ceiling of foliage stretching from bank to bank darkens and obscures the winding channel so that only the trickle and gurgle of the slow current trickling around spit, stone and small boulder, reveal its passage. The water, unable to scour itself of its woodland garbage, has lost the clear limpid qualities of its hillside course. Spattered with mounds of clay and pebble, rocky shelves and stones and an occasional large boulder litter its bed. Its surface is clotted with fallen leaves, broken twiglets and field debris, and it has become brown-scummed, turbid and almost stagnant.

For up to two hundred yards the stream dribbles sluggishly forward in its darkened ravine. When it finally emerges from the grey-green tunnel of trees and weeds, it spreads into a calm tranquil pool between banks from which the vegetation has largely been cut away in a pleasing landscaped effect, giving light and space. Gushing forward freely, its current swirls around an irregular sliver of land which has prodded its grassy way into the channel.

Here, in the fields of Golath, the stream, having travelled down the hilly countryside for two miles, a thin strip of water, carving a stony and deserted spillway, reaches an open space in which it meets the most important tributary of its course – the Owenmore River.

· · · · ·

The Owenmore is, primarily, the river that drains the eastern and central slopes of the Cuilceagh, those of Ben Breac and the valley of Glangevlin. For the greater part of the year, the summits and slopes of the Cuilceagh and its surrounding peaks are rent and scoured by rain. Continuous drizzles and downfalls, ice and frost, batter and gouge crevices and fissures into the hard outer cap of the crests. Through these slits, rainwater laden with acid, percolates, seeps and sinks into the vast limestone maw that lies beneath, dissolving the rock and forming channels and pools beneath the surface of the soil.

The Owenmore rises in the uplands of the Bellavally Hills which are 1,139 feet high, and becomes an amalgam of the streamlets flowing from the surrounding peaks, from the small lakes in the tablelands on their summits and from the underground rivulets that have nibbled their various ways through the vulnerable limestone strata of the mountain slopes.

The Gap of Bellavally breaks the chain of hills on the eastern rim of the Cuilceagh and carries the mainroad from Ballyconnell to Glangevlin and West Cavan. Gleann Gaibhle, the Glen of the Fork, is so named because the road is divided at the village of Glan, the southern arm going to Dowra, and the northern to Blacklion (Learga). Below the gap, the hills rise again to Ben Breac and to the line of peaks farther south.

The road to Glangevlin ascends rapidly from the lowlands. On the right, grassy flanks shoot upwards at a breathtaking angle. They are dotted with the autumnal colours of heather, golden fern, brown dock and a multitude of wild stems and flowerets. A huge triangle of coniferous forest sweeps down with startling suddenness and the black streaks of turf cuttings are just visible in the long grass by the shallow ditches. On the left the land seems to topple into deep valleys, then rise abruptly to form sparsely-clad hills upon which sure-footed sheep wander at will.

Many small stone bridges less than ten feet long occur on this part of the road, bearing witness to the number of streamlets trickling from the slopes. Periods of drought and fine weather show only a narrow runnel of water or a shallow pool to mark their passage. One can then clearly see the depths of the grooves they have gouged out of the hillsides, the rocklike sediment of stone and clay they have torn away from outcrops and escarpments and have swept onward in their torrential flow when swollen by continuous downfalls of rain.

In the winter months the valley of Glangevlin, encircled as it is by a range of peaks, is a sombre and solitary area. There are few houses and the human presence is confined to those of the farmer and sheepherder, and an occasional motorist. Only the larger birds frequent the higher slopes – the raven, the carrion crow, occasionally the red kite and the peregrine falcon – drawn there by the sight of grazing animals. All predators, all avid to feed on the carcasses of dead sheep which have tumbled into gullies or ravines, or have become victims of snowfalls and winter gales.

It is in this area of hill, forest and valley, that the Owenmore. the Abha Mór, or 'big river', starts its five-mile run westward to its confluence with the Shannon. For its first two miles it flows at a short distance from the main road and is often visible from it. If it can be said to have its beginnings on the surface of the soil, it is in a number of streamlets that flow into each other about half-way down the hills of Bellavally, in the townland of Derrynananta. Some of these come from the slopes of the Cuilceagh, streaming beneath the roadway and emerging robustly on the other side to be augmented by slower but continuous dribbles seeping through the boggy soil of the slopes. They fall into a deep narrow trough from which they overflow to pour downhill through a raw dyke of jagged rock, fenced with clumps of rush. Passing into a basin-like declivity where high ridges of earth, rough and broken, block the channel, the stream, racing onward, forms a small waterfall and makes a spillway over slab and rock to reach a hillock farther down where it cuts through soft mire to widen itself to almost two feet. It continues to carve a raw harsh gully down the craggy slope, tearing rock and stone from the thin soil, hacking sharp grooves in the marshy hillside.

It flows behind a wood of conifers where a very small bridge enables it to stream beneath a laneway. No trees, scrub or brush line its route which is crowded with great clumps of rush and other wild vegetation. Through these, trickles, seepages and runnels of water dribble in to widen its channel which increases to five feet.

As it reaches the foothills and flows through grazing and meadow land, it begins to enlarge itself, undercutting the banks which become broken and uneven as large grassy mounds are sliced from the soil and float in the stream. Stone and rock continue to litter the channel. On the banks, hawthorn, willow and bramble scrub begin to appear while nettle, rush and dock, sprinkled with foxglove and thistle, grow profusely.

The Moneen Bridge

Carty's Bridge

The stream begins to widen

The Owenmore Bridge

Streams flowing from the slopes of the Cuilceagh

The confluence of the Bellavally and the Cuilceagh streams

A mound of rock and pebble in the river

Unnamed Cuilceagh stream

The stream falls rapidly to its first bridge and widens to almost ten feet. This small stone structure with one low arch is sited on the Moneen Road which debouches from the main highway. The road stretches across the flank of the hillside for about two miles and has five such bridges from beneath which rivulets, clotted with sediment, tumble down into the valley. The stream flowing fast through rushy field and woodland,its banks partly open, partly lined with clusters of scrub and wild vegetation, has a section of rapids and waterfalls and gradually absorbs all these rivulets, countless rills,dribbles,and a bustling cascading river from the Cuilceagh, the Doon River, itself a channel for the copious waters from the slopes, for the Tamnaigh and Dubhóg streams.It crosses beneath the roadway at Carty's Bridge, a small masonry structure, and flows down the valley to its confluence with the Bellavally stream which can be approached by a laneway and footbridge. Most of these rivulets and streamlets are nameless. Where they are named, they usually take that of the townland through which they are passing – the Moneen River passing through Moneensauran, the Doon River passing through Dunmakeever at the foot of the Cuilceagh.

The stream from Bellavally has now increased its width considerably and continues to do so as it spills down the steep gradient to lower levels,and small tributaries keep on adding to its volume. Its banks are being ground relentlessly, as it wrenches at loose mounds of clay, stone and gravel, rupturing rocks and boulders until they are prised from their muddy sockets and topple into the channel,dissolving the slimy ooze in which the roots of trees lie buried, until they hang precariously from their niches to fall eventually into the swirling watercourse.

In dry weather the bed of the stream is exposed to reveal a floor of stony sediment. Great slabs of shingle stretch widely from bank to bank in many places. The verges are heaped with rock, gravel and slab. Yet the current maintains a quiet momentum, trickling, swirling and splashing down the ravaged spillway of its eroded course.

Making a shallow curve into the countryside, it flows westward at the back of the village of Glan. Its banks are largely free of heavy woodland growth but, in sections, hazel and willow scrub appear. Its

The Bellavally Hills with the Gap of Bellavally in the background

passage is a winding one with many bends and turns. As it reaches the valley floor the current slows, and pools begin to appear in the channel, covering the rough array of sediment. Here, it approaches its second bridge, passing on its west bank a row of tall trees, sycamore, willow, hawthorn and sally which loom over the waterway while branches, twigs and leaves invade it. As it slows to a meander, its width broadens to almost thirty feet.

It is now, recognisably, the Owenmore River, mentioned in the Annals of Loch Cé and the Annals of the Four Masters as the 'Abha Mór,' or 'big river.' The bridge to which it flows is the largest in the area, being 120 feet long with one high arch. It is sited on the road from the village of Glan to Dowra in the townland of Garvolt. Beneath it the current flows strongly over shelving rock and stone, particularly after bouts of heavy rain. In fine weather large spits of sand and pebble are deposited in the bends and verges, but in the cloudbursts a tremendous amount of sediment cannons its way towards the bridge in the flooded waters.

The river passes away from the bridge leaving a wide bulge of gravel and shingle below the arch and crosses into Garvolt Upper, a wedge of land between the two arms of the Glangevlin Road. Its width narrows as it meanders towards the north-west through the ravines and recesses of this largely hidden area, shrouded by tall trees and flanked by scrub and wild vegetation.

Winding a slow passage through meadow land, it carves a channel at the base of a hill which rises in steep, almost clifflike ascent from the left bank and is patterned with the bushy brilliance of whitethorn and yellow gorse, interspersed with straggling clumps of hazel. The right bank is shadowed by massive willows and alders leaning over the watercourse. The river flows on, its current steady but with shallow depths. Rock and stone, fragments of tree trunks, decayed willow branches, appear continuously on the exposed bed. The current forks, gouging an islet from the left bank, leaving a shelf of pebble and slab, around which a narrow backwater trickles to join the main stream, which, finding a lower spillway where young trees are rooted in the muddy verges, widens into a deep pool. Minnows, tadpoles and other tiny fish, dart about in the slow rippling current. A dipper flits between bank-side boulders and insects, weaving a droning flight, skim the water surface.

The banks are often steep, sometimes open but mostly crowded with overgrown clumps of rush, nettle, creeper and fern. They are flanked by meadows, dotted with buttercups, bluebells and purple vetch. A pheasant rises wildly from the long grass and hurtles towards the shelter of tall trees. Skylarks streak into the upper air.

The channel which narrows and widens alternately, but in general, maintains a width of up to thirty feet, degenerates into a maze of boulder and stone with deep mounds of shingle on the verges, by which the current trickles and eddies. As the gradient becomes steeper, it begins to gush forward in a whirl of rapids to reach its first sharp turn, the starting point of a sequence which will totally alter its direction. It forms a wide sluggish pool as a small tributary pours in on the left bank. Shortly afterwards, it makes its second turn and is joined by a streamlet on the right bank. Flowing silently onward, it winds around its third bend, still shallow and laden with small crags, splinters and pebbled stone.

It now enters a smooth deeper stretch where the bulky detritus is no longer visible on the surface. Flat slabs of rock appear below the left bank which is partly free of wild verdure. The long glide continues around the fourth bend between tree and bush-lined banks until an area of stony shingle appears, filling almost the entire width of the river bed. The current flows sluggishly on the left, then increases its speed to reach the fifth turn, making a long slow-moving pool as it curves to reach its third bridge, the small concrete Curravagh Bridge which is sited on a laneway of the same name within a very short distance of the Glangevlin/Learga Road from which it debouches.

The river widens broadly as it streams beneath the bridge. Its banks are treelined though not as heavily as before and the channel is largely clear for a short distance. Despite the changing weather and the onslaught of thunder showers, the river is low and soon great slabs of stone and shingle are uncovered on the verges and intrude across the channel. Trees overshadow the right bank, willow, sycamore and alder. Wild flowers flourish on the bushy left bank – purple thistle, wild roses, and marguerite. Birds chatter and flit through the clustering foliage. The current broadens into a long sluggish pool in which a large mound of clay, wood and dead leaves from which grass and saplings grow, intercept the flow as it makes its final turn to stream in a south-westerly direction.

Though it moves swiftly it leaves large islets of shingle on both sides. Streaming into a wide declivity, it makes a pool with deep banks, bordered on the right by a cumbersome mass of gravel and stone. The trees begin to close in, narrowing the channel. Running into a short deeper stretch where all sediment is covered, the river's natural pattern soon asserts itself. Large spits and wide shelves of stone begin to re-appear. Old branches and broken tree trunks clog the watery verges around which the current trickles and swirls, cutting a narrow backwater at the left bank.

Curving southward, the river leaves an island of stony debris which obstructs the channel and slows the current to a restricted passage at the right bank. Below the island the speed of the current increases as it widens to its normal size. Here, the river is deeper and surrounded by woodland. The channel widens to make another turn. A tree grows in the river, trailing in the current where a large pool has formed. Downstream of the bend the pool formation disappears and a long stretch of slabs and boulders straddle the channel in this wild stretch of waterway through which the current trickles slowly but steadily. Banks are steep, trees and branches fall across the channel, great boulders divide the stream which gurgles and splashes around obstacles.

As it winds through this stony labyrinth, it reaches deep shelving rock over which it pours in a small waterfall and rushes forward on a lower level between rocky verges and pebbled spits to tumble down a second jagged shelf and sluice around a wide heap of boulder and clay. A solitary house, a derelict farmer's cottage, appears on the open left bank which is here quite shallow and beneath which a small pool has formed. The river alternates between quiet pools, great spates of boulder and tiny islets around which the current pursues its way.

It flows into a stretch where the boulders are largely on the verges. Its channel widens and deepens as it spurts swiftly on. The banks are partly free and partly lined with tree and bush. Meadows flank them on both sides. Streaming on, making a wide slow glide deep enough to cover the sediment in the channel, the current slices into the soil, cutting off islets of grass and sapling, shaping eddies and backwaters, leaving spillways and pools in its wake.

The river curves as it winds continuously towards the southwest. It becomes shallow and sediment appears again on its surface. The maze of slab and rock recurs at intervals. A small circular wall has been built into the channel to impede the current yet it travels swiftly. The banks have become steep, uneven and partially open though other sections are clotted with creepers, old tree trunks and looping branches.

As it streams through meadow land it begins to narrow between encroaching masses of trees – ash, hawthorn and willow beneath which mounds of weed, rush and wild flowers proliferate. The current slows to a trickle as it becomes saturated with grasses, seeds, falling leaves and the general waste of the mown fields. Slowly it flows out of this dark stretch, passing open weedy banks to reach the end of its sprawling five-mile journey from the hills of Bellavally. Here, at its meeting with the Shannon, the river attains an almost scenic quality by contrast with the raw harshness of its course. It sweeps around a broad spit of gravel and sand on its right bank on which tufts of grass, golden fern and young willow grow, giving

Curravagh Bridge

Boulder and stone in the river

it a garden-like aspect. On the left, cutting into the bank, it severs a narrow wedge of soil that juts into the channel and behind which a small pool gurgles and swirls. Wild flowers and grasses grow profusely in the niches and crevices of the bank, bringing colour and brightness to the soft misty greyness of the fields.

Flowing onwards, it forms a long sandy spit in the mouth of the confluence. The dividing current swirls around at both ends, undercutting the banks and widening the channel as it rolls forward to meet the dark sluggish stream of the Shannon, made narrower by the small triangle of land intercepting its course. The Owenmore has come almost face-to-face to join a smaller and slower stream, but one which will change its westward direction completely.

The confluence of the Owenmore River and the Shannon in the backround

Chapter Two

AS THE STREAMS MERGE, they turn and spread into a wide pool out of which they flow in a southerly direction, cutting a course at the base of a low wooded hill. Rounding the slope, the river passes into a scenic area of tree and bush, flowing between shallow grassy banks. Almost immediately, it begins to broaden its channel with astonishing vigour while still remaining at a very low level, its bed visible and littered with stony sediment. Attacking the banks on both sides, gouging at the friable limestone fabric, prising off shards of rock and tree stump, it carves away segments of the soft marl and extends its channel

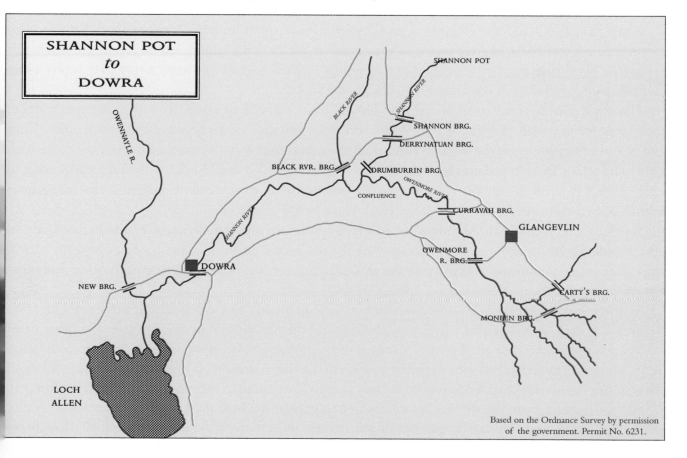

SHANNON POT to DOWRA

Based on the Ordnance Survey by permission of the government. Permit No. 6231.

to upwards of forty feet. A short distance below the confluence, it reaches a long cement footbridge known as the 60-pound, or Murphy's bridge,where it expands still more. This crossing over the widening river is reached from a laneway which curves around the base of a hillside and leads to Glangevlin Road.

As it streams away from the footbridge, it receives a tributary on the west bank, the Black River. A small fast stream, up to ten feet wide, it rises in a loch some miles west of the Shannon Pot, passes beneath a short road bridge in Doobally and winds south to Derrynatuan where a second bridge enables it to flow rapidly into the nearby Shannon.

Now a wide,fast-flowing river, the Shannon enters a patch of woodland so crowded, it looks almost like a section of forest in its wild untamed growth. Tall trees − ash, willow, birch and alder − line both banks. Angular pouches of foliage combine to shut out the light. Overarching branches cast strange shadows on the swirling foam-capped wavelets. The current is rapid but not more than a foot deep. The banks are low and unstable with masses of leaves hanging down to dabble and clot the water. In places, the stream gushes just beneath the lip of the land, forming pools and shallows alternately, undercutting the roots of trees, contouring its channel in wide determined sweeps or gouging fissures and dykes in rapid spurts around spit and stone.

The amount of sediment the river has carried from the hills is everywhere apparent. Boulders bisect the watercourse, at times singly, at times in bulk. The slowed current, unable to move them, must swivel and twist at their bases, or pour over low spurs on the jagged ends. Beds of clay, pebble and splinter, have formed at bends and snags above the level of the current and will remain there unless dislodged by heavy rain or winter floods.

A tree has fallen across the channel,its roots loosened and rotted from the supporting socket of soil by the erosive edge of the acid river water. In the centre of the stream a sapling has begun to grow where a crude raft-like structure of clay, boulder and stone has lurched together to form a tiny islet where twigs and foliage dip and shift in the almost stagnant pool at its base.

The sun begins to shine strongly and light blazes on the palisade of wood. The morning mist starts to melt away. Stringy coils of white vapour shrink and break and slide down between the dark trunks. Glints and beams of sunshine gild the serrated margins of the foliage and etch the crooked lines of the twigs with gold. The splash, bubble and gurgle of the river is all-pervasive. No small birds shriek their alarm notes to each other. No small mammals are rooting in the undergrowth, or squirrels leaping and chattering from branch to branch to forage for food. It is a bleak place to live.

Yet there is a sudden startled movement in a tree-top on the opposite bank. A hooded crow bounces and wobbles. It has been plucking and devouring the red berries of the mountain ash. Now with a harsh squawk of anger and unease, it pivots into the air with a furious clap of its wings,and darts off to find other harvests.

At times the river seems to be almost unmoving, seeping silently past its low banks, harbouring all kinds of sediment, rock, stone, pebble and clay, dead leaves and the rotting stumps of fallen trees. At other times it is bouncing robustly over all obstacles, gliding swiftly southwards, sweeping wide at bends to form pools at the outer verges and gravel spits in the narrow turns. Its depth remains shallow and unvarying while its bed can be clearly seen with tendrils of moss and crowsfoot writhing in the swirling and confused current.

Soon it emerges from the shroud of trees into open grassland where wild vegetation crowds its banks. Waist-high weeds and bulrushes, patches of tall nettles and creepers, flourish unchecked. Blackberry trailers and runners of thorny briar lean in all directions like a wickerwork of spikes, while fallen twigs clutter the dense undergrowth which is sodden with moisture and ridged with slabs of loose jagged stone.

Daisies shine like minute stars in the bright sunlight. Dandelions wave their cotton-puff heads over the creeping ivy leaves and the purple-red flowerets of the marsh thistle. Over all are the wet earthy smells of the farmlands, of cattle whose sunken hoof-prints are embedded in the thin soil, tinctured with the familiar scents of the fields. The needs of agriculture are everywhere asserted from Lug na Sionna down the hillside to the more open plain, and barbed wire fences frequently bar access to the river banks, not only to prevent cattle from wandering across the countryside, or into the river, but also, unfortunately, to deter nature's enthusiasts from approaching too closely.

Access is difficult all along the upper Shannon, an area which in itself forms a unique scenic trail. It needs pathways and placenames, road signs and maps of local detail, all of which would be a boon to the hiker and naturalist.

The river reaches a more sloping terrain, narrows its channel and becomes deeper as it passes beneath the Metal Bridge, a small railed structure on a minor road which links those of Glangevlin and Derrynatuan with the main road to Dowra. An ornamental bridge in contrast to the low stone structures of the hills, it is rustic and pretty, with clustering trees of hawthorn and alder dribbling their yellowing mounds of foliage over the passing stream.

Making wide sorties westward in large arcs, the river flows through the townlands of Corratubber and Cashelbane. It is surrounded by fields of rough pasture in some of which cattle graze. A weedy rutted pathway hugs its banks, bordered by an overgrown hedge burdened with scrub, briar creepers and low bush. Waving tufts of grassheads, clumps of flowering rush, and gorse spikes tinted with saffron and brown, heather, withering stalks of dock, jostle each other in autumnal abundance.

Skirting the farmlands, its banks becoming higher, the river flows fast as it streams beneath a delapidated footbridge and moves south into a large basin-like arc which curves westward. Then, veering slightly to the north-west, it turns sharply and flows in a zig-zag course to the bridge at Dowra. Its shrouds of trees have been recently cut down, making it more visible but less scenic. Though it has travelled for seven miles from Lug na Sionna and has reached the boundary of County Cavan, the Shannon is still very much the hillside river. It has broadened to a width of forty feet in the vicinity of the bridge, is very shallow, its bed littered with boulder, gravel, wood waste and stone.

Dowra bridge, a masonry structure with three arches, dates from the 1860s, and is the first major bridge on the Shannon. Eighty four yards long, its narrow elongated shape divides the village into three small housing areas which spill away from the ends of the parapets. It forms a road link between the four villages of the area. The short main street leads north to Learga (Black Lion). The road to Drumkeeran moves west of the bridge, and exiting from the east end are two roads, one going north to Glangevlin, the other south to Drumshanbo.

Dowra, the first village on the River Shannon, dates from the same period. A small village with about six hundred inhabitants, it has the District Court, supermarkets and pubs, and is a sales centre, especially for sheep. It is not visibly impressed by its position on the country's longest waterway. Apart from the bridge which reaches well beyond the river banks and is closed off for the most part, as if to discourage scenic pathways and landscaped areas, so that the spaces surrounding them are unkempt with litter and wild vegetation, only a wall map indicates the passage of the famous river.

Streaming away from the bridge, the river narrows and deepens. The exposed bed so evident upstream with its floating debris of rock, clay, twig and pebble gradually disappears from view. A short distance downstream, it makes an abrupt turn to flow westward. It has now passed into County Leitrim, into a flatter terrain of pasture and farmlands. Its banks are largely open, unconcealed and shallow, with only occasional stands of trees or low scrub, but are often cut off by barbed wire fences. Cattle graze in the

The 60 – pound footbridge

The Black River

The boulder-strewn river with overhanging trees

The Metal Bridge

The Shannon flowing to Dowra

The bridge at Dowra

Dowra Village

The Owennayle River

The Owennayle (right) joins the Shannon

The Owennayle flows under New Bridge

The Shannon enters Lough Allen

fields which frequently dip to the water's edge and houses peer from their sheltering arbours of trees.

Clumps of spike rush and reeds root themselves in the muddy shallows. Thistles and nettles invade the damp tussocks and ripe grassheads droop over their twisted blades. A small straggling bush leans perilously over the channel, its bared roots denuded of the sustaining ball of clay which has been eroded by the acid content of the sluicing stream.

From above comes the hoarse cawing of crows as they navigate the air currents and descend to ravage the fields for beetles, worms and mice. A grey wagtail skips delicately from twig to stem, darts above the wavelets and skilfully plucks flies from the air. Magpies forage on the banks, fly along its curves or streak in a startled flurry of wings into the distance to re-appear again when the human presence has passed.

The river continues to veer westward in shrunken twisted loops curving around slender peninsulas, inlets and spits of land. Less than a mile below Dowra it flows south to meet its second western tributary, the Owennayle River.

Flowing from the hills of North Leitrim, the Owennayle, a fast narrow stream, has unusual scenic qualities in its upper reaches. Pouring down the craggy slopes in two streams, it passes beneath a small delapidated bridge about a mile west of Coolegrein post office which can be reached from the Dowra/Drumkeeran road at Newbridge Church. The river tumbles into a wooded gorge, a hundred feet deep and forms a spectacular waterfall, the first of eleven such falls as it rolls down through a semi-forest region towards the foothills. Access here is difficult and only on foot.

As it reaches lower terrain, its banks are partly lined by tree and bush, partly by open fields. In some of its stretches it is full of sediment, clotted with boulders, stone and wood debris. But the current trickles rapidly through these obstructed areas and becomes wider and deeper as it passes through farmlands and swirls beneath three small bridges to reach the Dowra/Drumkeeran road. It is known as a trout stream and in the hollows and pools gouged out by its brisk current, beneath the ledges formed by rock and stone, fish habitually make their lies.

The river's flow has already slowed as it reaches the fields of Lower Kilduff and streams under New Bridge. The stone bridge is short with one low arch; the channel beneath it, almost as wide, stretches to between ten and fifteen feet. In fine weather, mounds of stone, pebble and clay are deposited close to the sides of the bridge as the current bends to the south-east. Wild plants root themselves in the gravelly ooze – silverweed, water celery and hemlock. Bulky sediment, such as boulders, slabs of rock and rotting tree stumps are absent from the smaller river.

The Owennayle narrows as it leaves the bridge to stream in a south-easterly direction through woodland in which cattle graze. Much of the wood has been felled but large stands of trees remain, buttressed by thick unwieldy hedges and deep wet gullies.A rutted animal path follows the course of the river. The current has deepened and no trace of sediment can be seen on its surface. It is slow-moving, the water brown and opaque as it winds between steep banks of malleable clay through which the grazing cattle have gouged out shallow trenches and dykes in their constant thirst-driven forays to the water level.

Riffles, runnels and eddies swivel around weed-covered clods and tussocks cut from the muddy verges. Pools, shining like small mirrors, have formed at their ragged edges, and clusters of yellow flowers cast bright tints on the dull green undergrowth. Barbed wire fences appear and a more modern contrivance, the electric fence, is in place and is drawn across the field beyond which the two rivers meet.

The Shannon receives the Owennayle on its west bank less than a mile from the bridge. At this point the Shannon's depth has increased. It is broad and fast-flowing, its sediment concealed on its bed, its shallow banks almost fusing with the surrounding fields. There are few trees, but a mass of soft flowering vegetation, trailers, twigs and foliage, obscures its approach as it flows in a south-westerly direction. Then with a sharp, almost right-angled bend, it veers south-east taking the smaller river in its flow and absorbing its waters imperceptibly in the strong swift current.

It streams through the townland of Kilgarriff and for a further mile twists and curves repeatedly around narrow wedges of farmland, passing as it does so a section of an ancient historic earthwork called the Black Pig's Dyke. After a final bend, it straightens out and flows directly for about one hundred yards to its first large lake expansion – Loch Allen.

It has travelled a distance of up to nine miles and fallen three hundred and forty feet from its source in County Cavan.

The Shannon enters Loch Allen near the centre of its wide northern boundary and slightly to the east. Its width has visibly broadened to almost fifty feet as it approaches the lake, influenced probably by the latter's tidal flow. Its depth is between two and three feet. It passes on the right by a promontory of mature deciduous trees at the base of which is a smooth area of rock and clay. On the left, a sandy beach, formerly woodland, but cleared almost completely of its trees and vegetation to make a picnic and bathing area, is long and wide and comparable in size with some coastal beaches.

The island of Inishmagrath, its woods protecting the ruins of an old church, its fringes lapped by a slim shallow channel of water, is but a short distance away while above this picturesque and solitary expanse of sand, trees and shifting wavelets, the peaks of Sliabh na Cille and the hills of Ben Croy brood solemnly in their green and brown isolation.

• • • • •

A sombre but beautiful body of water, Loch Allen divides County Leitrim at its narrow waist into two large irregular shapes – the northern section which is mountainous with rivers and deep valleys, the southern a terrain of farmlands, low hills and small lakes.

A natural creation of the Ice Age, Loch Allen was formed by the meltwater of dissolving glaciers which deposited not only enormous pools and spillways in the ravaged course of their dissolution, but drifts of clay and gravel, rock and stone, as well. It lies in a valley surrounded by mountain peaks, craggy slopes, uplands of bog and heather, barren escarpments and outcrops of sandstone and shale. Cuilceagh mountains in the north, leading to Ben Breac and Ben Croy in the east, continuing into Sliabh an Iarainn in the south-east and faced on the west shore by the hills of Arigna and Corry – all affect its dark waters.

Shaped like a triangle, its base is the broad northern margin, its apex, the narrow southern tip. It is seven miles in length and three in width at its widest point, with an area of 3,500 hectares.

The margins of the lake are irregular and are largely composed of poorly-drained rushy soil based on broken shale and grit swept down from the surrounding peaks by countless streams. Deficient in limestone, the waters of the lake lack a plentiful supply of the nutrients, phosphorous and nitrogen, necessary for a rich flora and fauna. They have a high iron content brought to them by the copious cascades pouring down from the most dominant range, Sliabh an Iarainn, or the Iron Mountain. In the 18th century, iron was mined and smelted in this area, the smelting process depending on oak and beech woods to provide fuel for charcoal. When eventually, the supply of timber was exhausted, the smelting works could no longer function, the mines were abandoned and the industry ceased to exist. But the lake water retained the mineral's dust and particles in its depths.

LOCH ALLEN

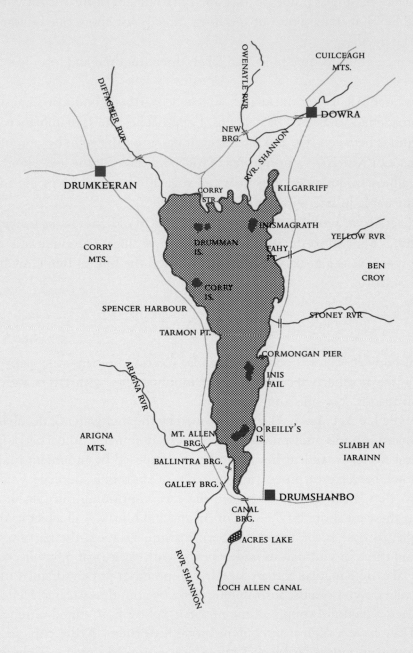

OWENAYLE RVR

CUILCEAGH
MTS.

DIFFAGNER RVR

DOWRA

NEW
BRG.

RVR. SHANNON

DRUMKEERAN

CORRY
STR.

KILGARRIFF

INISMAGRATH

YELLOW RVR

CORRY
MTS.

DRUMMAN
IS.

FAHY
PT.

BEN
CROY

CORRY
IS.

SPENCER HARBOUR

STONEY RVR

TARMON PT.

CORMONGAN PIER

ARIGNA RVR

INIS
FAIL

ARIGNA
MTS.

MT. ALLEN
BRG.

O'REILLY'S
IS.

SLIABH AN
IARAINN

BALLINTRA BRG.

GALLEY BRG.

DRUMSHANBO

CANAL
BRG.

ACRES LAKE

RVR SHANNON

LOCH ALLEN CANAL

Based on the Ordnance Survey by permission
of the government. Permit No. 6231.

The Island of Inishmagrath

The Yellow River flowing to Lough Allen

The Stoney River

Amenity area at Cormongan Pier

Canal lock at Lough Allen

The Arigna River at Mount Allen Bridge

Squalls churn the surface of the lake

The Shannon, though the largest, is but one of the many streams that tumble from the flanks and slopes of the hills into this great natural stillwater. Sizable rivers, absorbing many smaller streams, flow in on both shores. The Yellow River drains the lower slopes of the Cuilceagh and Ben Breac and hurtles down to the lake in storm and gale, an enormous amount of sediment, of rock and stone. The Stoney River in the south-east is similarly a channel for the waters that gush over the barren crags of Ben Croy and Sliabh an Iarainn.

On the opposite shore the Diffagher River streams from the hills of the north-west while the Arigna River empties itself into the lake in the south-west. It flows from the Arigna hills and passes beneath the main road to Drumkeeran at Mount Allen Bridge. Coal mines have been worked in these hills for the past century and a half but the last was abandoned and closed in 1990. The mines fuelled the powerhouse sited on the west shore of the lake and owned by the Electricity Supply Board but this also has been closed.

Despite its spacious area and the enormous volume of water which cannons down the hillsides to swell its flood plain, Loch Allen has not been navigable to cruisers and large boats since the 1920s, a factor which diminished its tourist value to the surrounding countryside. The only Shannon lake so disadvantaged, its problem of low and variable depths was directly linked to its being used as a storage reservoir by the Electricity Supply Board for the hydro-electric works at Ardnacrusha on the lower Shannon, a scheme begun in 1925 and largely completed in 1929. At this time a project to drain the lake and deepen its bed was carried out in order to supply a greater level of water power. The lowering of the lake levels affected its margins and islands. Narrow sandy and shingle beaches bared by the receding waters, stretch along its southern shores. A colony of crannóga or lake dwellings was exposed, and many areas around the islands became shallow.

There is a number of islands of varying sizes, a few distinctive ones and others mere jumbles of rock and wild vegetation. All are uninhabited. Perhaps the best-known is Inishmagrath close to the mouth of the Shannon which has ancient historical and religious associations. It contains the ruins of an old church said to have been built by St. Beog in the 12th century. The level of the water surrounding its tree-lined shore has become so low that only a narrow channel separates it from the beach by which the Shannon enters the lake. Inis Fáil, also known as O'Connor's Island, narrow and wooded, is the largest, while, in the southern section, O'Reilly's Island, with lowered water levels, attracts fish which thrive in the shallows.

Because of its deficiency in limestone, Loch Allen is not a rich feeding ground for fish. Submerged plants, pondweed, algae and mosses lie in the bottom ooze to which shrimps, snails and the larvae of the mayfly attach themselves. Minnows, tadpoles and sticklebacks add to this relatively meagre fare. On the stony margins, dock, clubrush and bur-reed, provide shelter for the adult sedge fly and mayfly and a flush of grasshoppers, all used as bait. In late summer, the mayfly hatch, though limited, attracts trout to the surface, particularly in the shallows of the southern lake, close to the islands and the power house, and near the mouths of tributaries – the Shannon, the Arigna, the Yellow and Stoney Rivers. Good stocks of pike, bream, tench and roach, provide fishing throughout the season, from May to October.

Birds are few. The heron and the swan, mainly the latter, can occasionally be seen. Small birds, the thrush, magpie, wren and blackbird, flit and scurry through the nearby hedgerows and low bush. In winter, when the midland Shannon is an enormous wetland sheltering thousands of geese, gulls and waders, the number making its way to Loch Allen is low, small groups of ducks and swans, and a scattering of curlew and lapwing.

The contours of the lake as it drifts languidly around its islands and indents its shores with small inlets and bays, can give spectacular scenic views but its spacious coves and placid sheen can also be deceptive. When the water level is low, treacherous shallows occur in the narrow southern section, while rocks form a hazard across the northern shore. Weather conditions on the lake are apt to be changeable and difficult. Violent gusts of wind funnelled through the valleys from the bleak slopes whip across its length and breadth. Squalls and storms churn and convulse its surface, making it dangerous for small boats. Though belts of mature trees line the shore at different points, they afford little protection.

Public access to Loch Allen is available at many places on the east and west shores, especially in the southern section where main roads skirt its margins and narrow strands encircle it. At the amenity area of Cormongan on the road to Dowra, where there is a pier and at Corry Strand on the north shore, there are facilities for sailing small boats, for water-skiing, bathing and fishing. Fahy Point, reached from a side-road near the Yellow River, has a large beach area, but few amenities. On the west shore, side-roads off the main Drumkeeran road, lead to Ballintra Bridge where access to river and lake is open, to Strabraggan's narrow undeveloped beach, to Tarmon Point at which are a graveyard and the ruins of an old church said to have been originally built by the O'Rourke clan, once chiefs of this area, and to Spencer Harbour farther on.

At present a change of policy has taken place in regard to this fine expanse of water so under-utilised and undeveloped. The navigable arm of the shallow upper Shannon, the Loch Allen Canal, constructed at Battlebridge with a length of four and a half miles which enables pleasure boats to reach Acres Lake on the outskirts of Drumshanbo, is being restored to its original function of flowing directly into Loch Allen, a facility withdrawn from it in the 1920s. Passing beneath Canal Bridge, a quarter of a mile from Drumshanbo on the road to Drumkeeran and close to the margin of the lake, it is being furnished with double locks, intended to regulate the water levels of both canal and lake.

Cruisers and large boats will at last be enabled to enter the lake and explore its many bays, islands and fishing areas with the consequent erection of jetties, mooring places and amenities not available at present. Hopefully, this development will bring about a general upsurge in the prosperity of the surrounding areas so long and so frustratingly delayed. This welcome facility is expected to be in operation by 1994/1995.

Canal Bridge

Lough Allen with the Arigna and the Corry mountains in the background

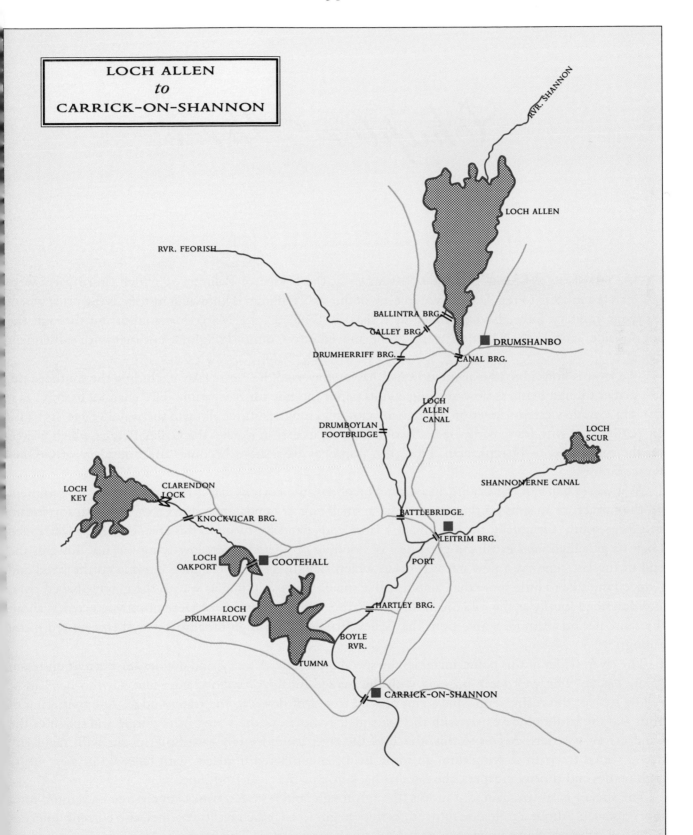

LOCH ALLEN
to
CARRICK-ON-SHANNON

RVR. SHANNON

LOCH ALLEN

RVR. FEORISH

BALLINTRA BRG.

GALLEY BRG.

DRUMHERRIFF BRG.

DRUMSHANBO

CANAL BRG.

LOCH
ALLEN
CANAL

LOCH
SCUR

DRUMBOYLAN
FOOTBRIDGE

SHANNONERNE CANAL

LOCH
KEY

CLARENDON
LOCK

KNOCKVICAR BRG.

BATTLEBRIDGE.

LEITRIM BRG.

LOCH
OAKPORT

COOTEHALL

PORT

LOCH
DRUMHARLOW

HARTLEY BRG.

BOYLE
RVR.

TUMNA

CARRICK-ON-SHANNON

Based on the Ordnance Survey by permission
of the government. Permit No. 6231.

Chapter Three

THE SHANNON STREAMS OUT OF LOCH ALLEN at the bridge of Ballintra at which sluice gates were erected in 1937 to regulate the water levels of the lake. Ballintra is known in history as the place where a French military force, having landed at Killala in 1798, on the Mayo coast, advanced through the countryside, crossed the Shannon at this point, moved into County Longford, but met with subsequent defeat.

The river is now a broad expanse of water, having traversed the entire lake, excluding the southern tip. Its current, though brisk, is slow-moving and its depth too low for navigation. The channel narrows as it flows in a south-westerly direction through meadow and rough pasture rolling to the water's edge. Its banks are partly lined with trees, partly open. Two miles from its exit, it reaches the Galley Bridge which is sited on the main road to Drumkeeran. From this point, its west shore becomes the boundary of County Roscommon.

As it passes beneath the bridge, its channel broadens, the current is fast-flowing, leaving no sediment on the surface, or in spits on the verges. It has a small gust of rapids, then slows to a strong steady stream as it flows south. Originally, the river made a large wide bend westward in this area, creating a lake called Loch na gCailligh, and causing a great deal of flooding on the adjacent, low-lying terrain. Towards the end of the last century, a new cut was made which straightened the channel, eliminated the bend and reduced the lake to little more than a pool with a small rivulet wending its way to the newly-shaped river, and described locally as the 'old Shannon'. Here, too, is the footbridge of Derrintunny, erected at about the same period. Almost a mile from the Galley Bridge, it is a high broad pathway between red metal railings.

The river, wider at this point, increases the speed of its flow. A tiny island divides the current upstream of the bridge. The west bank is heavy with the massed foliage of willow, alder and hawthorn. Flags of yellow iris dot the rushy verges and stems of wild rose drift down to the water's edge. The twittering of birds and the rustle of leaves vie with the soft squelchy noises of the water – the gurgle and splash of the wind driven wavelets. Access to this stretch of the river is moderately easy. Stiles occur with regularity over a rutted towpath straying through rushy fields, encumbered in places with tall wild grasses, waist-high nettles and thorny creepers, the familiar backdrop to the river landscape.

The stream narrows again as it moves through rough land between banks largely free of verdure for a short distance. About a mile downstream, as trees begin to encroach on its channel, the current quickens as a small tributary flows in on its west bank – the Feorish River. This clear limestone stream, noted for its catches of trout, rises in east Sligo, and flows through the stubby neck of north Roscommon to reach the Shannon in the area of Drumherriff Bridge. About ten feet wide and slow-moving, it makes pools and riffles as it flows through farmlands. Weeds trail in the water and grazing cattle have broken muddy dykes in the banks. Falling into a stretch of rapids, it broadens its channel before emptying itself into the larger river.

In the past, a wooden bridge crossed the Shannon on this stretch. Frequently damaged by storm, causing hardship to people and animals, it was eventually removed and replaced a short distance downstream by the large masonry bridge of Drumherriff with five arches, which, spanning the river, also connects a network of minor roads.

On the approach to the bridge, the banks, steep and wide, are encumbered with large hillocks of slab, boulder and stone, encircled with thick swaths of wild vegetation and low bush, giving a look of antiquity to the area, and adding to the patina of age which the long stone structure, clearly in need of repair, already has.

Downstream of the bridge, the banks begin to be shrouded in tall trees, a massed huddle of sally, hawthorn, ash and alder, through which the river flows slowly for about a mile to Drumboylan where a wooden footbridge crosses the watercourse. Close to the footbridge on the Leitrim bank of the river is the island of Inis na gCon. A small irregular patch of land cut away from the surrounding fields by a narrow stagnant stream which seeps out of the Shannon, rounds the island and joins the main river a short distance downstream, it is clotted with brushwood and growing trees, has a derelict farmhouse and is grazed by cattle. Local folklore affirms that St. Patrick crossed the Shannon by the ancient fording place at this point and that the stones he walked on were removed to the island when the river was being dredged. Legend also says that O'Sullivan Beare, the Kerry chieftain and his followers, crossed into County Leitrim at this ford, reaching the end of his heroic journey to the home of the O'Rourke clan of West Breifne.

As the river flows out of this solitary lagoon which is fished for perch, bream and trout, it begins to widen, its current quickens as it makes large S-bends to the south. Lush grasses and wild flowers fringe its waters which tend to flood in periods of heavy rain. The banks are still tree-lined but not so densely as before and one can see a patchwork of green fields as it streams towards Battlebridge. This stretch of the river, broad and uncluttered, with a brisk current, is one of the most prolific fishing areas on the upper Shannon. With hatches of mayfly, it is rich in trout as well as coarse fish, rudd, eel, pike and bream.

The name 'Battlebridge' is given both to the townland and to the road bridge over the Shannon which is sited in beautiful woodland surroundings a quarter of a mile west of the village of Leitrim. A masonry structure, old and weatherbeaten, it has three arches which are largely obscured and crowded with deposits of clay, rock and gravel upon which weeds, grasses and thin saplings grow on both sides of the bridge.

The river, wide, shallow and rocky, streams beneath, entering one of its loveliest stretches between avenues of trees and low, green rushy banks. A family of mute swans float in the shimmering water, dipping thin necks in the stream, ruffling their pillowed feathers as they make playful darts at each other with brilliant orange beaks.

Battlebridge is a milestone in the development of the Shannon. Here, barely one hundred yards downstream of the bridge, the river, flowing strongly and deepening its channel, reaches the required navigational depth for large craft, a minimum of four to five feet. As if to underline this point, two blue and white cruisers, like huge waterbirds, brood and shift at their moorings on the east bank.

Here, too, the Shannon meets its first canal – the Loch Allen Canal. Constructed on the east bank of the river at the point where it becomes navigable, it dates from 1819/20 and was built to bypass the shallow section of the river and enable cargo boats to sail to Loch Allen and transport coal from the Arigna mines

The Shannon leaves Loch Allen at Ballintra

The Galley Bridge

Drumherriff Bridge

Footbridge at Drumboylan

Battlebridge

Cruisers at Battlebridge

to river ports downstream. Allowed to close in 1932, it was re-opened in the 1950s as far as Acres Lake near Drumshanbo, a well-known fishing and amenity area.

The canal, beginning with lock and basin, and running parallel with the Shannon for part of its course, passes under its first road bridge, sited beside the river bridge, and streams into woodland to which a

Loch Allen canal basin

The Loch Allen Canal

Leitrim Village

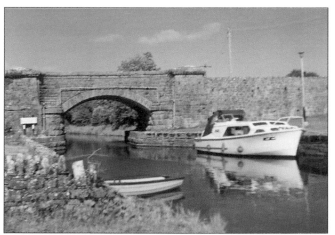

The Shannon/Erne canal at Leitrim Bridge

The Shannon/Erne canal at Loch Scur

The Shannon/Erne canal at Ballinamore

towpath provides access. Its banks are lined for much of its way by trees, alder and willow, vying for space with ivied hawthorn and holly. On the open grassy plots, creepers of wild rose trail in profusion. Clumps of rush, flagged yellow iris and buttercups spatter the verges. It winds its way northwards for about a mile, passes a lifting bridge, and some distance farther on, its second road bridge and second lock, in the pleasant scenic area of Drumleague. A third road bridge, that of Drumherver, crosses its channel half a mile away at the end of a wide leafy pathway. From here it streams slowly to the wooden jetty at Acres Lake, having traversed four and a half miles of countryside. The canal has now been restored to its original position as a waterway to Loch Allen.

Leaving Battlebridge, the Shannon sweeps southwards towards the village of Leitrim which it bypasses on the west by less than a quarter of a mile. Here, it meets its second canal, the Ballinamore/Ballyconnell canal as it was first known. This begins at a small island in the Shannon and veers eastward to stream beneath a bridge in Leitrim village, a small stone structure with one arch, having mooring quays alongside.

Constructed in the middle of the last century, the canal stretches from its junction with the Shannon for over thirty seven miles to reach Upper Loch Erne, via the towns of Ballinamore and Ballyconnell. It was intended to be a commercial waterway between the rivers, Shannon and Erne, and the provinces, Connacht and Ulster. In the event the project was a failure, due principally to competition from the railways which at that time were proliferating all over the country. The canal was abandoned in 1869, scarcely ten years after its opening. It fell into neglect, became weedy and silted up and finally unusable except for a short stretch downstream of Leitrim Bridge which could be explored by dinghy.

In 1990, however, a scheme, partly funded by the EEC, was begun with the object of dredging and developing the waterway for navigation by cabin cruisers and pleasure boats. It entailed essential repairs to locks, bridges and banks, sometimes outright replacement, and the provision of towpaths, amenity areas, wild life havens and mooring quays. Work was completed in 1994 and the re-named Shannon/ Erne canal adds a new and welcome dimension to the Shannon's fishing and cruising waterlands.

Streaming to the right at its confluence with the canal, the Shannon winds through low open fields, a patchwork of rush, grazing lands and tangled scrub. It narrows its channel to skirt a group of derelict farm buildings, enshrouded by trees. Known as Port, this area was once a ford of some importance, protected by a castle which has long since disappeared. Flowing torpidly past fields set with young conifers, between banks cluttered with overgrown reeds and vegetation, there is no landmark to break the grey-green monotony of the scene until, almost a mile farther on, the stark contours of Hartley Bridge pencil the skyline.

Built on a secondary road, debouching from the Leitrim/Carrick-on-Shannon motorway, the bridge is modern in design and dates from the 1930s. It curves in a high and wide arc from bank to bank, is constructed of reinforced concrete and supported by a concrete framework. Totally different from the low – arched stone bridges of the last century, it fails to merge as pleasingly with its environment, preserving a distinctive touch of urban rather than rural life. Open fields, unlittered with rush and weed waste, roll away from the encircling shallow banks to fuse into the hills beyond. On both sides of the watercourse, eddying pools bring small mounds of pebble and clay to the fringing verges. Skeins of crimson and yellow flowers – campion, speedwell and dandelion – trail along the margins. A scatter of farmhouses top the low hills and cattle graze beside the sheltering hedges. In the pools and back lies of this stretch of river, bream, rudd, perch and pike are plentiful, making it a popular fishing venue where access is unhindered on both banks.

As the river streams away from Hartley Bridge the open fields gradually disappear, concealed behind dense growths of reeds on both shores. Moist luscious mounds of vegetation, linked with alder and hawthorn scrub, reinforce the barrier of reeds, cutting off access to the banks, to give an aura of isolation to the narrowing watercourse. Almost a mile from the bridge, the river enters the townland of Tumna on the Roscommon shore. In this calm rural backwater, where a cluster of farmhouses break the line of low hills above the west bank, the Shannon is joined by a major tributary – the Boyle River. This broad and placid waterway leads to the Shannon's first sequence of scenic lakes, and stretches for over six miles to Loch Key in north Roscommon.

The Boyle River rises in Loch Gara and flows by Drum Bridge, from which it is navigable, through the southern section of Lough Key to emerge from its eastern shoreline in a broad leisurely stream. The lake, a beautiful but small expanse of water, dotted with a mosaic of islands, is three miles long and two wide. It is overlooked on its northern margin by the heathered ridges of the Curlew Mountains, a backdrop which highlights the scenic charm of its waters and surrounding woodland. On its south side, a large Forest Park, fringes its inlets and bays, giving shelter to the small boats that seek its coves and islands, to fish for trout. The Park is well-timbered with oak, beech and cedar, and provides an endless source of interest to the visitor, – nature trails, herds of deer, a bog garden, camping and caravan sites, boating facilities and a restaurant.

As the river flows out of this much-endowed watercourse to turn south, it is edged by thickets of reeds on one side and the high leafy canopies of mature trees on the other, bending beneath an abundance of foliage and casting serrated shadows on the sparkling waterway. Clusters of wild flowers and waving clumps of fern pattern the grassy banks. In the undergrowth robins, wrens and blackbirds flit busily in their incessant hunt for insects while tiny mammals, the mouse and the shrew, claw interminably through the woodland waste.

Very soon the river reaches Clarendon Lock, opposite which is a small busy weir, with at times a strong hazardous crossflow, designed to maintain the level of the water, the depth of which, at this point, is between five and eight feet. Downstream, past a pleasant pathway, chequered with diamonds of light and shade and sheltered beneath a weave of branches, Knockvicar Bridge comes into view – a stone structure with three arches, a pleasant amenity area and a quay, favoured by boat people who wish to moor overnight.

Passing under the bridge, the river enters a stretch of open fields and low scrub, and a short distance later, expands into Loch Oakport, a small, secluded and picturesque sheet of water, surrounded for part of its margins by tall woods, weedgirt shallows and islands of waving reeds jutting out from its low verges. Birds haunt the reed beds – water rails and reed buntings – the long yellow-green stems shaking and quivering beneath their weight and their light quick rustlings. Luminous rows of bubbles follow in the wake of mallards and coots as they swim purposefully away from the banks, and swans dawdle with scarcely a movement on the faintly rippling water.

The river streams on to its third stone bridge at the village of Cootehall. Over the short journey from Knockvicar it has moved in slow gentle curves, now it expands to the size of a small bay at which mooring quays for large craft have been erected. As it winds onward it narrows greatly to pass through a constricted channel between wooded banks to enter its third lake, Loch Drumharlow.

A smooth sheet of water with one tree-fringed island, Inisatirra, the lake narrows at both ends and curves and widens in the centre, reaching almost to the main road to the town of Boyle. The verges are shallow and dotted with tiny pools and inlets, lined with mounds of stone and pebble. Small promontories of reeds stretch far out into the water. Groups of houses can be seen on both shores, laid well back from the reedy banks and soggy fields, their white walls shimmering in the sunshine. In the background are the misty blue ridges of the Curlew and Arigna hills while the deep purple summit of Sliabh an Iarainn continues to dominate the flat rolling landscape.

This restful and solitary expanse of lake and river attracts birds. Coots and water hens probe in the

Old houses at Port

Hartley Bridge

The Boyle River at Knockvicar Bridge

Clarendon Lock

Loch Oakport

The river at Cootehall

shallows. Swans float lazily by the reed beds. A flock of foraging crows dip their gleaming ebony wings a if about to glide to the surface, then curve sharply upwards to fly to distant fields. Soaring above th rippling waters, a wave of adventurous gulls spiral and dive, their turbulent wings flapping without pause A cruiser slips quietly down the navigational channel, passing an orange buoy which tilts drunkenly in i

Cootehall Bay

Cootehall village

ast drifting wake. Above it, the
hin black wires of the great
elephone poles on both
anks, spanning the neck of
he watercourse, wink and
litter in the bright air.

Here, too, on the west
ank, are the ruins of the
ncient church of Tumna. A
arrow rectangular area in the
djoining field fenced by a low
vall, it is surrounded by thick
rass and woodland creepers.

The Boyle River joins the Shannon

Two small roofless
buildings are inside,
weed-filled and
stony, in one of
which a ragged
wind-beaten tree
grows. A graveyard
within the wall
holds a single slab-
type grave, said to
be the burial place
of a nun, St.
Eadaoin.

Loch Drumharlow

The lake, like the Boyle River which is noted for catches of trout and bream, is an interesting fishing area. It has hatches of sedgefly and mayfly. Trout haunt the pools and ledges beneath the verges of the island, Inisatirra, and in the shallows of inlets, as well as at the mouth of the river as it enters and leaves the lake.

Slipping imperceptibly onward, the river has barely fifty yards to go to its junction with the Shannon which is streaming south from Hartley Bridge. The banks of both rivers are clotted with a forest of reeds. Behind them are the open fields, marshy and cattle-grooved. Sparse low hedges and random clumps of vegetation leave the confluence of the waters clear and exposed. Hills slope down to the reed thickets on the west bank. Tall brown rushes and waving grassheads gleam and sparkle in the sunshine beneath the decorative tendrils of the huge orb webs spun by the field spiders. A swan plays hide and seek in the concealing swaths of the reeds and a pair of exuberant mallards glide and dawdle in a linear water ballet through the confluence of the two rivers.

The Boyle River is wide and deep at this point. Despite this however, it is absorbed fully into the flood-plain of the northern waterway, the enlarged channel of which winds to the south-east in long sinuous curves, its current swirling just beneath the edge of the flat water-logged fields for about a mile and a half. Then it veers to the east for a short distance to reach its first river port at Carrick-on-Shannon.

Chapter Four

CARRICK-ON-SHANNON (CORA DROMA RUISC) THE COUNTY TOWN OF LEITRIM, has been a crossing place on the river, linking the provinces of Leinster and Connacht, from ancient times. Commercial activity began on the river in the 1750s when boats were drawn by horses and towpaths were essential. One hundred years later, between 1840/50 with the introduction of steam-driven craft, the bridges of the upper Shannon were repaired or reconstructed. The present bridge, built in the 1840s to replace an older one, is up to one hundred yards long with five arches and carries the main road from Dublin to Sligo. Carrick was busily engaged in river trading during the last century and the first half of the present one, when cargo boats plied their trade up and down the Shannon. Trading ceased in the 1950s due to competition from road and rail and commercial carriers were gradually replaced by pleasure craft.

To meet the challenge of this new and growing activity, Carrick, in the 1970s, removed an old jail complex and a swamp of reedy wild vegetation which had invaded the inflowing river, dredged and widened its channel, thus creating a spacious marina which now provides for a busy cruiser traffic in summer, and mooring facilities for scores of craft in winter. Close to the marina, two hire-boat companies, Emerald Star and Carrick Craft have their bases.

A small but busy town, Carrick has excellent shopping facilities, good hotels and guest houses, a range of water sports, and for most of the year is a lively angling centre.

As the Shannon flows away from the bridge, it rolls into a countryside shaped by drumlins which stretch from the stony foothills of Sliabh an Iarainn to give a distinct contour to the terrain of south Leitrim, making a wide expanse of pools, lakes, rivers and numerous streamlets. The drumlin, or 'droimin' from which the word is derived, means a small hillock between thirty and a hundred feet in height, a rounded heap of sand and gravel tightly welded together and covered by an overlay of grass, weeds and wild flowers. The hillocks occur in close belts and ridges, usually separated and fenced by ditches and hedgerows into a medley of small rush-strewn fields and twisting roadways. In the valleys and depressions between them, streams of water often converge and spread into large pools and lakes.

The drumlins were formed at the close of the Ice Age when melting slabs of ice, or glaciers, could no longer carry the rocky clay they had earlier engulfed in the frozen cracks and fissures. This gravel debris was dropped on the surface of the land in heavy compacted mounds upon which moisture settled and was slow to filter away, leaving a sodden and water-logged soil. Much of south Leitrim comes into this category. Its farmland is limited and infertile. Agriculture, apart from the raising of beef cattle, is an unprofitable occupation and is gradually being teamed with the more suitable growing of trees.

The bridge at Carrick-on-Shannon

Through this terrain, the Shannon flows on its course with a broad sweep, surging past a forest of reeds on its left bank, through which wooden walkways have been erected over stagnant pools for up to a mile, leading to various narrow wooden 'stands' cut through the reed forest to the edge of the streamy water at which fishing may be carried on. On the opposite bank, the Killucan River, on the upper reaches of which is a fine waterfall, joins the watercourse. Shortly afterwards, the private marina

Carrick-on-Shannon marina

Carrick-on-Shannon, west side

Loch Corry

Jamestown Bridge

Jamestown Village

The weir at Jamestown

Drumsna Bridge

Drumsna Village

The Jamestown Canal

Albert Lock

of Rosebank appears on the left bank. Operated by Flagline Ltd., it provides facilities for large craft. The river winds into a countryside of low hills, sparse hedges and small houses, a landscape dotted with lakes large and small, of which many are linked to each other and to it by numerous streamlets. In the course of its flow, the river inevitably occupies the lowest level of land, through which it carves a channel, so that it is in the depressions between the drumlins the Shannon steers its tortuous way, twisting and curving around their bases, seeping through the spongy limestone, eroding rocks and carrying away sediment.

Slow-moving and tranquil, lapping low stone-strewn banks, it merges into a patchwork of farmland, laced with uneven hedges and holding some stands of mature trees. There is an occasional belt of forestry visible beyond the right bank, as it expands into Loch Corry whose placid sheen beneath a dull autumnal sky hardly shows a ripple, a sheet of shadow-reflected water where margins flanked by reeds and small mounds of stone swell into inlets and bays on both sides. Yet there is movement as a pair of coots emerge from the reeds and make bubbling eddies in the shallows. A solitary moorhen flits furtively by the bank, while magpies, sleek and polished in black and white splendour, dart overhead to seek the shelter of the fields as a cruiser chugs downstream, slicing the placid surface into a wake of curling wavelets.

Loch Corry, known for trout and coarse fish has one small island, Inis Mucker, used in the past for farming purposes, but at present deserted. Swirling around the island, the lake expands into three large pools, joined together by narrow-waisted channels before casting its overflow into a smaller unnamed lake surrounded by reed beds.

From this modest stillwater the Shannon emerges, a fast-flowing river, and swings abruptly, in an eastward direction. It flows through woodland, its banks lined with trees, and having on its right shore the third waterway to be cut from its channel, namely the Jamestown Canal. A short distance farther on the reason for the existence of the canal becomes evident as Jamestown Bridge looms up. A five-arched stone structure, flanked by mooring quays, it marks the end of navigation on this stretch of the Shannon.

Here, the river undergoes a drastic transformation, passing from its role as a major waterway to being a shallow rapid stream, unnavigable for all boats larger than a dinghy. It veers through fields to round the small village of Jamestown, flowing by deeply wooded banks, gardens, short private piers, and a narrow graveyard which holds the ivied ruins of a Franciscan Friary, to reach a weir and sluice gates.

Below the weir a flush of mallards preen and play in the cascades sluicing into the shallow current which swirls speedily past the base of a promontory of massed trees to expand into a small unnamed lake. On the opposite bank, open fields roll to the water's edge where fishermen stand and obsessively cast their lines in the soft calm of the evening. Restless gulls soar and swoop. A flock of birds spiral in wild arcs with frantic abandon, as the purple and orange sunset gilds the water and contours the palisade of trees in deep shadow.

The river flows languidly out of the lake, narrows its channel to pass between two humped spits of land and streams behind an impenetrable screen of trees, where it winds along the margin of a wedge of heavily-wooded demesne. The wedge is roughly sculptured in the shape of a horse shoe and it is by this name it is known.

The 'horse shoe' is an area of great solitary charm where few sounds break the prevailing stillness but the whirring of flying insects over the watercourse and the occasional buzz of a chain-saw in the obscure regions of the woods. Nibbling at the low banks, making runnels and back lies, the river flows for the most part in an eerie silence. Rounding the angular corners of the 'horse shoe', it turns abruptly and flows southwards to the bridge at Drumsna.

An abandoned almost derelict look marks this old masonry bridge. Its seven arches stretch over a stream which has underscored its banks and widened its channel but continues to remain too shallow for navigation. It flows to the rere of the village of Drumsna where a small harbour with mooring quays, about fifty yards distant, indicates the end of navigation.

In this area is the ancient earthworks known as the 'Dún of Drumsna'. Constructed across the mouth of the Shannon's shallow loop, it is imposing in its dimensions and was, apparently intended to protect the narrow crossings at these river points and also to safeguard homesteads, the remains of six raths having been discovered in its vicinity. Its wooded hillocks and gravelled cairns may be observed on both sides of the Kilmore Road, a side turning from the main highway to Carrick-on-Shannon.

The Jamestown Canal which bypasses the shallow river section was built in the 1770s and upgraded in the 1840s. It is cut through the spongy right bank of the Shannon and runs across country for a mile, much of it gouged and blasted through boulder and stone. It passes beneath two small bridges, each with a single high arch, one at Ard an Aifrinn, the second at Corlara, and streams directly to Albert Lock which gives access to the main river. Flowing towards Dromod, six miles distant, the river passes through the small reed-girt Loch Tap, spanned at its narrow mouth by a bridge which carries the railway line from Dublin to Sligo. An adjustable arch enables large craft to pass beneath.

Emerging from the lake, the river streams directly into Loch Boderg. The first of a brilliant panorama of lakes, it is an unusual and complex sheet of water, which expands on its western margin to spill over the Roscommon shore, and spread into its hinterland in a myriad of narrow channels, inlets and small bays – a grand mosaic of grey, green and blue. From this enchanting maze, a narrow, fast-flowing river streams past the mooring quays and idling cruisers at Carnadoe Bridge which is sited on a minor road off the motorway from Carrick-on-Shannon. Downstream of the bridge, it expands into Carnadoe Loch where the watercourse, dwindling into a narrow channel, passes into the long slender Grange Loch and extends into Grange River. A cut in the channel called the Carrigeen Cut, joins it with the nearby Kilglass Loch and its tributary, the Mountain River.

Here one finds a labyrinth of watery avenues between tiny inlets and bays. There are numerous and diverse small channels, unexpected twists and turns, and quiet creeks to be explored and lingered over. The water spreads effortlessly, sometimes river, sometimes pool, but always navigable and without hazard. Great reed beds fringe this remote and beautiful backwater. Birds, plants and fish abound – a haven for the naturalist, the fisherman, and those who value peace and solitude.

There are mooring places by the banks and Kilglass Loch has a floating dock. Kilglass is a small village and at its back, the smooth low summits of a ridge of drumlin hills, break the monotony of the flat marshy fields.

Loch Boderg, the centre and pivot of this cluster of lakes, is unruffled and calm on a mild October day. It is wooded on the east side where the Derrycarne Forest Park comes to the water's edge. The lake is shallow at this point. A small amenity area has been laid out on its bank and the darkly shaded groves of oak, ash, yew and beech form a perfect foil to the shimmering brightness of its watercourse. It is almost four and a half miles long, its margins sharply contoured by inlets and small deep bays. To the west, low open fields recede from its verges, the land swampy and rush-strewn. It winds through a slender constricted channel called the Derrycarne Narrows and flowing around the margins of the Forest Park, enters Loch Bofin on its eastern border.

A narrow faintly-shimmering body of water, Loch Bofin is immensely peaceful, though squalls churn its surface from time to time. Deep woods line part of its shoreline behind a phalanx of gently waving reeds, two large thickets of which expand on to the surface of the lake, their brown and orange heads glinting in the sunshine. The water seeps and sucks about the low banks which are dotted with shallow pools, where spits are formed by small mounds of clay. A small island, called Rabbit Island lies halfway down its watercourse on the east side. It is marked by a black stake on its north-west margin and is hazardous to boats when the water level is low. The island stands at the tip of a long constricted inlet which fringes the third lake in this area, the short narrow-necked Loch Scannal. Opening off the eastern shore, Loch Scannal has no navigational channel. At its mouth a barrier of rock and boulder make perilous

Loch Bofin

Loch Scannal

Carnadoe Bridge

Dromod Harbour

A section of the 'Dún'

Loch Boderg

Dromod Village

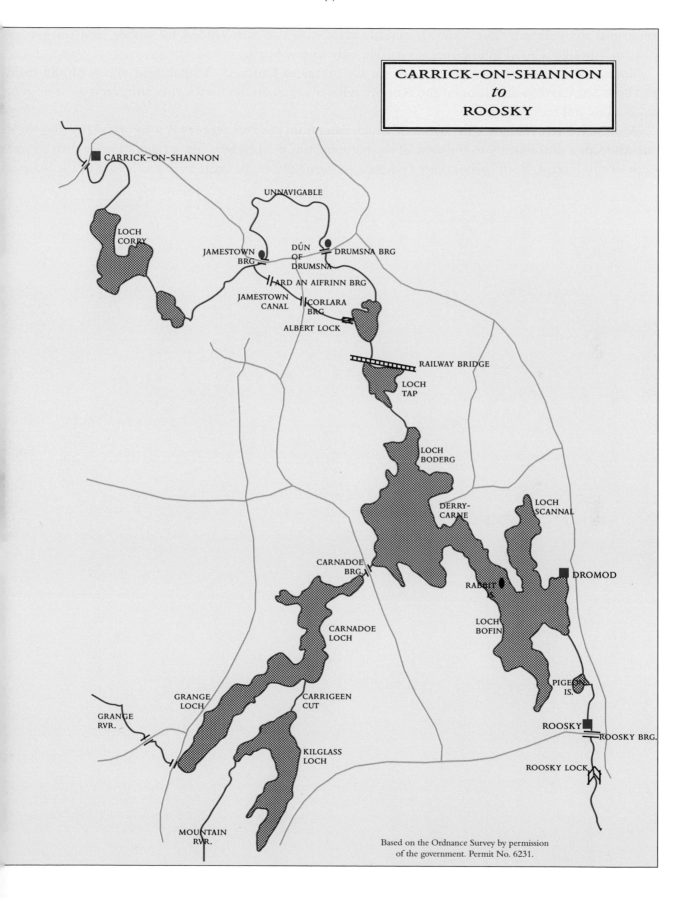

CARRICK-ON-SHANNON
to
ROOSKY

CARRICK-ON-SHANNON

UNNAVIGABLE

LOCH
CORRY

JAMESTOWN
BRG

DÚN
OF
DRUMSNA

DRUMSNA BRG

ARD AN AIFRINN BRG

JAMESTOWN
CANAL

CORLARA
BRG

ALBERT LOCK

RAILWAY BRIDGE

LOCH
TAP

LOCH
BODERG

DERRY-
CARNE

LOCH
SCANNAL

CARNADOE
BRG.

RABBIT

DROMOD

CARNADOE
LOCH

LOCH
BOFIN

GRANGE
LOCH

CARRIGEEN
CUT

PIGEON
IS.

GRANGE
RVR.

ROOSKY

ROOSKY BRG.

KILGLASS
LOCH

ROOSKY LOCK

MOUNTAIN
RVR.

Based on the Ordnance Survey by permission
of the government. Permit No. 6231.

conditions for sailing in low water. Scenically interesting,it is surrounded by woods, and thickets of reeds,and though a good fishing area is available only to row boats.

Close to the confluence of the two lakes is the village of Dromod. A small neat village on the main road between Carrick-on-Shannon and Roosky, it has many amenities for tourists, shops and guest houses, and is a bus and train venue.

Dromod has two harbours, the oldest of which dates from the 19th century A long and dangerous shoal extends from a promontory to the west of the harbour. It is marked by a black buoy to warn craft to pass south of this hazard. Both harbours are favourite mooring places for cruisers in the height of the season.

Chapter Five

THE SHANNON STREAMS OUT OF LOCH BOFIN, rounding the small Pigeon Island, and broadens its channel to flow directly towards the bridge at Roosky which is less than two hundred yards distant. On the east bank, it is fringed by a narrow green belt and is close to the motorway from Dublin to Carrick-on-Shannon. An avenue of trees marks its course on the west bank near which a cement pier, furnished with telephone facilities has been erected, so that cruisers may tie up here, call the bridgekeeper and alert him as to their special requirements before approaching the bridge. Built in the 1840s along with the weir and lock to replace an older bridge, it is constructed of masonry, has five arches and a lifting span. Over a hundred yards long, it carries the road from County Leitrim to County Roscommon.

Though a small village, divided in two parts by the Shannon, with its larger section on the Roscommon shore, Roosky, served by a main highway, is a growing hub of road and river traffic. Equipped with a dry dock and mooring facilities on the west shore, complemented by three jetties downstream of the bridge on the east bank, it provides safe berthage, fuelling and other amenities, so that a constant stream of craft moors here, while their crews avail of the services of cafés, shops and guest houses.

The river, fast-flowing and very wide, streams on to Roosky Lock, a short distance away. Buildings occupy the west bank while the east is pleasantly tree-lined and has a public pathway which stretches to the fields below the lock. Even on a dull misty day the area around the lock looks well-kept and pleasing. Flowers enliven the lawn close to the keeper's cottage. On the opposite bank, a level greensward is spaced with slender birch trees in short rows, their pink and cream trunks shining in the prevailing drizzle, their leaves turning to gold, a welcome contrast to the sombre brown of the wilting vegetation. The red contours of the lock gates, the mooring buoys, the rings and bollards, lend a sparkle of colour to the misty scene. Opposite the lock, on the west bank, a small weir, to which a footbridge leads, gushes and bubbles in the stillness.

Narrowing somewhat, the river flows south through pasture and meadow, but soon winds into a flat sodden hinterland, particularly on the Roscommon shore. The natural beauty of this county which borders the Shannon for seventy miles, the longest shoreline on its course, is in its northern sector, in the scenic Boyle River and its lakes and the lovely Carnadoe waters, all set off by a backdrop of mountain ranges, the Curlews and the Bricklieve. Towards the centre of the county there is an area of good farm land based on a limestone soil but, this soon fades as it approaches the river, to be replaced by a mosaic of rushy dismal fields, poorly drained, and often fenced by stone walls, making a familiar pattern of farmland,

The bridge at Roosky

swamp, marsh and eventually bog. There are low hedges and scrub, the thin soil dwarfing the growth of tall trees. Houses are few and villages far apart.

The river's course is largely straightforward with only minor twists and zigzags. Deep beds of reeds constrict its banks, as it winds sluggishly through the low-lying terrain. Behind the reed thickets crowding its watercourse, there is rough pasture in which cattle graze protected by barbed wire fences which prevent them from approaching the reed pools. On the east shore there are small fields with a scattering of houses and some sparse stands of trees. Out of the waving 'forest' a group of swans flutter and begin to dawdle in the stream, a calm monotonous stretch of water, dull in the darkening haze of the afternoon. Single trees look barren and desolate. Hedgerows are ragged and wind-beaten, with moss-covered stumps of wood and trailing creepers choking the shallow wet ditches.

The river's watercourse seems to be dormant. It is veiled with a solitary, silent charm, through which only a few sounds filter – the soft gurgle amongst the reed beds, as hidden birds, the grebes, goldcrests and water rails forage through the wilting stems, the rustling of frogs and mice in the tussocks of grass, and the light breeze playing with the drifting eddy pools, beside which, patches of wild iris, rush and fern have

Roosky Pier

Roosky Lock

The Shannon approaching Tarmonbarry

Loch Forbes

The River Rinn at Cloonart Bridge

Tarmonbarry Village

Tarmonbarry Bridge

rooted. In the distance woods begin to thicken on the east bank and against this dark leafy background, a red marking pole becomes visible in the navigational channel. The river passes through the Cloneen Cut and soon the heavily-wooded demesne surrounding Castle Forbes begins to appear – the only castle or large building on this stretch of the Shannon.

Three miles from Roosky, the river bulges eastwards, crosses the boundary between Leitrim and Longford and expands into Loch Forbes. A small narrow lake of quiet beauty, it is two and a half miles long and one and a half wide. Woods fringe its eastern shore, conifers, oak and beech; its other margins are shrouded with dense thickets of reeds and water-logged marsh, making access difficult. The lake is a fishing area. A mayfly hatch enhances its capacity and it can be fished for trout, and also pike and bream. A few small islands dot its course and there are spits of rock and boulder near the east bank.

Its tributary, the River Rinn flows in from the north-east. The Rinn rises near Mohill in County Leitrim in a lake of the same name and for part of its course forms the boundary between the counties of Leitrim and Longford. It passes beneath the Cloonart Bridge which is sited on the main road between Longford and Roosky. On its right, is a large open area, with buildings used as a hire-boat base and repair shop to which a marina is now being added. The Rinn is between twenty and thirty feet wide at this point, swollen by rain and tending to seep into the rushy mire of the fields. For its remaining half-mile to Loch Forbes, it is navigable, and has been since 1970, and cruisers are moored in its waters. Its banks are unconstricted for the most part, until adjacent to the lake, where the east shore is clotted with trees, scrub and vegetation, and the west bank becomes an impenetrable mass of reeds. As the Rinn enters the lake, there are rocky spits and shoals on its east side. The approach to its mouth is from the west which is narrow, with some unmarked boulders.

The lake's western shore continues to be reed lined and marshy, with some firm patches of farmland. In this area is the residue of the ancient religious settlement of Kilbarry. established in the 6th century by St. Berach. Known, historically, as the 'Seven Churches of Kilbarry', its influence in its heyday extended over many townlands. Now, a meagre group of ruins – church walls, doorways, and nearby, a Holy Well – it is overgrown by tall weeds and by wild vegetation.

It is also on the west side of the lake that the navigational channel moves towards the narrow tip from which the Shannon emerges. It flows in a south-westerly direction. Its channel has narrowed, its current is swift. It winds through slanting green fields for almost two miles. Trees appear on its open banks giving it a leafy pleasant aspect as it passes mooring jetties on the Roscommon shore and streams towards the bridge at Tarmonbarry. Constructed in the 1840s along with the lock and weir, it has seven arches and a lifting span, and is topped by a metal railing. The river spreads widely here and an island of trees, silt and vegetation close to the east bank divides it in two on both sides of the bridge. The narrower stream on the east shore winds sluggishly beneath three arches towards the weir, the main channel flows beneath the remaining four arches, partly towards the weir and partly towards the lock which is on the Roscommon shore. Normally, seven feet high, the bridge's lifting span needs to be raised for large cruisers.

Tarmonbarry, a small Roscommon village, redolent of fresh air and surrounded by a scenic countryside, is situated on both sides of the motorway which crosses the bridge. It is pleasant and welcoming with many amenities for the visitor. A roadway, bordered by trees, leads down the west bank towards the lock which is one of the largest on the river, being one hundred and twenty feet long and thirty feet wide. There are mooring areas in a shaded tree-lined stretch close by.

At the east bank are the weir and sluices towards which there can be a very strong flow. The weir at eight feet is the highest on the river excepting the one at the hydro-electric works at Parteen Villa which reaches one hundred feet. Water gushes from the weir in a cascade of eddies, rapids and whirlpools. Though hazardous to craft coming upstream, it is excellent for swimming, bathing and fishing. Seagulls glide overhead, shrieking in a frenzy of excitement. Farther on, swans tumble in the foamcapped streamy water and dabble their long necks beneath the wavelets in search of aquatic food.

A short distance downstream of the weir, an arm of the Camlin River flows into the Shannon on the Longford shore. Emerging from Loch Forbes side-by-side with the Shannon, a narrow slow-moving stream, the Camlin turns eastward, almost at right angles to the course of the larger river, and then veers south towards the village of Cloondara, two miles away. It passes beneath a metal bridge, sited on the main road between Tarmonbarry and Longford. Below the bridge it divides, one arm flowing on the left to Richmond Harbour, the terminus of the now unused Royal Canal, a commercial waterway of the last century linking the Shannon with Dublin. The canal was opened in 1817, and closed due to lack of trade in 1961. Since then the harbour has proved to be a popular mooring place for cruisers. The second arm of the Camlin flows to the right, joins the main river and passes beneath a road bridge in the village. Now, a narrow canal, rustling secretively between steep, treelined banks, it flows towards a small lock, which with the waterway, dates from the 18th century, and passes almost immediately into the Shannon. A pathway follows its course, and two quays, downstream of the lock, give mooring space for boats. The Camlin River and canal, fully navigable, provide an alternative sailing route to Loch Forbes and the Upper Shannon.

Streaming away from Tarmonbarry on its journey to Lanesboro, seven miles distant, the Shannon flows into a shallow stretch known as the Lodge Cut. Less than a mile long, it has unmarked boulders on each shore and deep water in midstream. A peat bank invades the channel lower down and boulders continue to make areas of hazard. The river turns south, creating a small expansion, and is entered by the Feorish, a narrow fishing stream. It flows into the Shannon on the west bank as the river continues to meander through a flat spongy terrain, relieved only by the hill of Sliabh Bán in the Roscommon hinterland. No more than eight hundred feet high, it dominates the flatlands around it, its lower slopes, a mixture of small field and morass, its summit crowned by a belt of trees. Between it and the river, marsh and swamp have, over the centuries, gradually changed into blanket bog.

The bog envelops both sides of the river, swelling out to occupy a massive acreage. In this area is located the first of the great bog farms established by Bord na Mona which, along with agriculture, forestry and the provision of electricity, constitute the four important industrial influences which affect the course of the river. The expanse of harvested turf sections rolls away from the Shannon in long, flat triangular swards, symmetrical and smooth, as they disappear into the far distance in unrelieved monotony. In the misty atmosphere the rich, chocolate-brown, peaty hues become indeterminate as do the soft pastel shades of the bog cotton, the purple heather, and the reddening sedge. It is a vast terrain of dark mahogany in which crooked black ridges streak across the landscape, speckled in part by the whitish blur of sheep grazing in the sparse roadside fields.

From the late 1940s this group of bogs, stretching away from the Shannon on both the Roscommon and Longford shores, and given the collective name of Cnoc Dioluin or Mount Dillon, has been in peat production. In the following decades, the acreage so harvested has been progressively increased until, at present, it occupies thirty square miles, backed by an incredible seventy-five miles of narrow-gauge railway line carried across the Shannon by a metal bridge erected in 1956, the Kilnacarrow Light Railway Bridge,

Tarmonbarry Lock

Tarmonbarry Weir

The Camlin River at Cloondara

The Royal Canal at Richmond Harbour

A lock on the Camlin River

Richmond Harbour at Cloondara

A section of the bog farm at Killashee

Heavy Machinery used on the bog farm

Wagons of milled peat at the powerhouse

Kilnacarrow Light Railway Bridge

Lanesboro Bridge

to expedite the delivery of its wagonloads of peat. In this period of growth, Bord na Mona was helped immensely by the building of a powerhouse at Lanesboro in 1958 by the Electricity Supply Board, a project that was mutually beneficial, since the powerhouse has trebled its capacity since then, and peat production has vastly increased. Nowadays, it is milled peat that is used exclusively in preference to sod turf, and it is delivered directly by train to the powerhouse.

All of this industrial activity initiated by Bord na Mona – the buildings of offices, workshops, large bays and yards, the massive units of cutting and milling machinery, stark yellow against the brown landscape, the chug and chatter of the little red and grey train as it bustles interminably to and fro, and the unceasing plumes from the powerhouse, – does not appreciably affect the environment, or the ecology of the river. The visible change is in the surface of the bog itself. Normally raised in hillocks above the level of the land, it has now become a flat anonymous region, waiting as it were, for a new development in its long and complex saga of change.

On its verges, wild growth is exuberant-giant orange-red ferns, thickets of alder and hawthorn scrub, tall clumps of rush and dark withering dock. Among this lush vegetation, scattered stumps and logs of oak and yew lie unearthed, fragments that have been preserved for centuries beneath the acidic blanket of bog.

In this stretch of countryside, the river is at its most sluggish and remote. Some peat silt has escaped into its waters. It is exposed and open. Rustling softly between the reeds, sending eddies and runnels into the swampy, rush-clotted banks, it shows little variation, lacking trees and houses, with some wooded areas on the east shore. Its depths vary and boulder-strewn shallows are clearly indicated by the navigational channel with its numerous red and black marking poles. The river continues to wind on its course in broad bends with few of the twists and meanders so characteristic of its earlier phases. Its tardy current is peaceful with a soft, cool and misty passivity. Moorhens sidle unalarmed by the low banks and the great-crested grebes forsake their niches in the reed beds to loiter in the sluggish pools.

As it approaches the steel and concrete bridge that spans its channel, the river becomes very wide. Used only for the transport of turf, the railway bridge contains a lifting span to facilitate the growing traffic in river craft. The speed of the current has increased as it seeps into the low stony fields of the Roscommon shore to form spits, islets, pools and runnels. Spatters of dandelion, thistle and foxglove appear in the thin covering of grass. The east bank is closely wooded with conifers, alder, willow, and forest-like vegetation. A short distance downstream, rounding a silting of peat on the eastern shore, the river makes a sharp turn to flow south-east and continues in a long gentle bend through open fields. The slope of the terrain becomes steeper and the current quickens its pace. It veers slightly west as it approaches the bridge at Lanesboro, then surges beneath with an unexpected access of speed to pour into the expanding watercourse leading to Loch Ree.

Lanesboro Bridge with six arches and a fixed span is a masonry structure topped by a metal railing. It was constructed in the 1840s to replace an older bridge and, up to the 1980s, had a lifting span which was then altered to a fixed section. The bridge provides a crossing between Leinster and Connacht, as does the small but growing town, well equipped as it is with shops, lounge bars, guest houses, and two hotels. It is divided by the river - Lanesboro, situated on the east bank in County Longford, and Ballyleague on the Roscommon shore.

Downstream of the bridge, an island has formed in the centre of the river, often submerged in flood but normally a long narrow sliver of mud, coarse grass and rush. Two adult swans tumble aggressively off its tip, where a rough wattle nest perches shakily on the mud, and turn to float beneath the shadow dimmed central arch just ahead. The island divides the river into two streams – the navigational channel being on the west shore beneath the fixed span. Immediately upstream of this section there are mooring quays, but the speed of the current rushing past makes it advisable for boats coming downstream to pass beneath the bridge, and turn below it before tying up. These quays were extended and improved in the 1980s. A cement pathway and landscaped area lead to the small harbour farther on, built in 1820 and also renovated in the 1980s, in which are additional mooring berths. Close to it, a nest of buildings and a boat restaurant are brilliantly illuminated and eye-catching at night.

Opposite the harbour, the ESB powerhouse, opened in 1958, the destination of the peat harvested on the bog farm, holds a commanding position on a low hill on the east bank of the river. Rows of tall evergreens form a leafy hedge in front of the building complex, while beneath it, a continuous outpouring of hot water swells the stream. This warmed stretch lures fish, particularly tench, into its eddy pools and bank fishing from cement pathways above and below the bridge is a popular pastime.

Downstream, a long railed section on the Roscommon shore provides mooring for boats, giving, in the height of the season, a marina-like quality to the busy scene. Landscaped and seating areas overlook the river's expansion into Loch Ree, complemented by a background of small, white-walled townhouses, and the vivid colours of hedgerows and gardens.

In the moist clear evening, a brilliant sunset transforms the merging of the Shannon with the wider pool that streams towards the lake into a kaleidoscope of red, purple and gold, with hints of pale green and blue in the darkening sky. The glowing reflections in the broad expanse of water on both sides of the bridge is mirrored in a thousand hues on buildings, trees, trafficways and cars. A sporadic evening breeze whips the surface into shallow ripples as the wavelets spread themselves widely, making tiny, stone-filled coves, eddy pools and small inlets along the deepening margins of the watercourse.

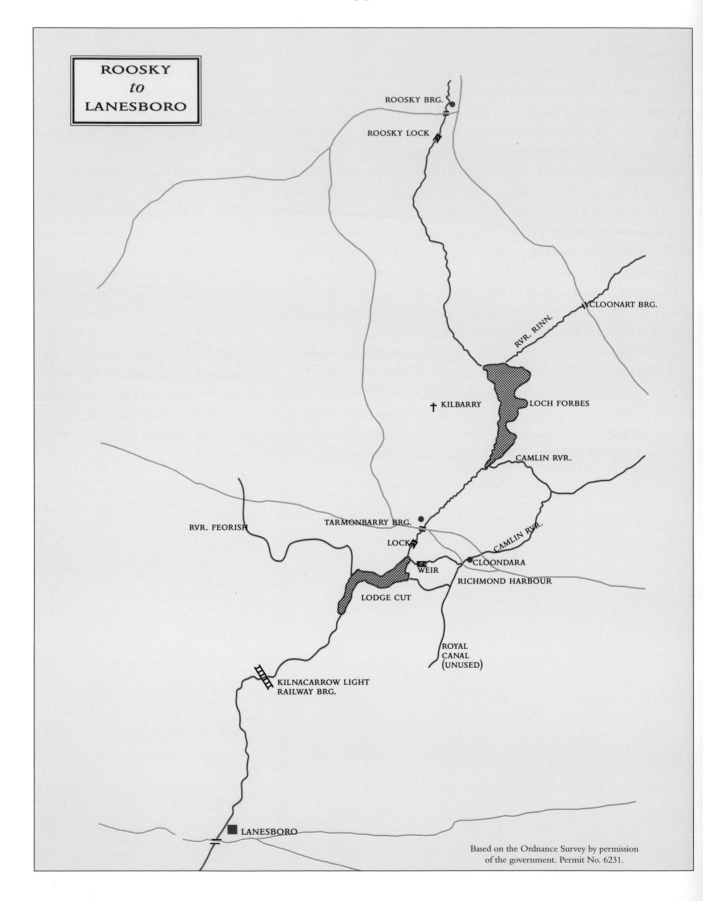

ROOSKY
to
LANESBORO

ROOSKY BRG.

ROOSKY LOCK

CLOONART BRG.

RVR. RINN.

KILBARRY

LOCH FORBES

CAMLIN RVR.

TARMONBARRY BRG.

RVR. FEORISH

LOCK

CAMLIN RVR.

CLOONDARA

WEIR

RICHMOND HARBOUR

LODGE CUT

ROYAL
CANAL
(UNUSED)

KILNACARROW LIGHT
RAILWAY BRG.

LANESBORO

Lanesboro

The ESB Powerhouse

Lanesboro Harbour

Chapter Six

THE SHANNON, SURGING FORWARD BETWEEN BANKS OF REEDS as it streams away from the bridge at Lanesboro, spreads at first into a wide lakelike pool, from which it narrows to flow through the dredged cut of Ballyclare. Passing Curreen Point, which is overlooked on the east side by the mournful ruins of Rathcline Castle, it then, unexpectedly, swells outward on both margins to pour into its second largest body of water – Loch Ree.

The Lake of the Kings stretches in an elongated shape, part wasp-waisted, part bulge, for eighteen miles south, into a countryside so flat, that the large hill of Sliabh Bán, three miles to the north-west has, by contrast, the towering and dominant aura of a mountain. Despite its low irregular margins, however, and the water-logged, insipid fields which flank them, especially in its northern section, it has all the wild, changeable and sombre grandeur of the peak-girdled Loch Allen rather than the scenic loveliness of Boderg, Carnadoe and Kilglass which, by comparison, appear like beautiful reed-girt pools.

The origin of its name, never fully explained, lies buried in antiquity, in the earliest periods of colonisation, the mythical times of the Fir Bolg, the Tuatha De Danann and the Milesians. The earliest historical records show that the lake was used from the first centuries A.D. by ancient Gaelic chieftains, notably the O'Connors, Kings of Connacht, as a means of transport. Many of its islands were chosen as sites for monasteries and churches, its inlets and peninsulas used for fords and defence works, its bays for shelter and anchorage. In the 8th and 9th centuries, the depredations of the Norse raiders ravaged its space, and after them, the iron grip of the Normans, from the 12th century onwards to the end of the medieval period, held its waters.

Today, it defies the imagination to picture this drifting sheet of water as an arena of gory carnage and bloody battle, while its streamy flow laves the quays and harbour of Lanesboro and its small foam-tipped wavelets suck at the soft mire of the low shorelines. Cruisers slip away from their moorings to traverse its many channels and explore its farthest corners despite wind and weather. Sporadic flurries of rain ruffle its surface and show up the tiny coloured lures of the bank anglers as they hunt for the secretive and elusive fish.

The lake forms the boundary between County Roscommon,occupying its entire west shore, and Counties Longford and Westmeath which share the eastern margin – a water barrier between Leinster and Connacht used, variously, throughout history, as a military challenge on the one hand, and a vast moat of defence on the other. It is the fifth largest lake in the country, its area being forty square miles. In its broadest section, which occurs about halfway down its course, and is measured from the mouth of the

River Inny on the Longford shore to Carnagh Bay on the Roscommon margin, it is seven miles wide. Its narrowest width, however, taken from Rindoon Point in the west to the Longford shore, is a little over a mile.

Though the lake is generally navigable, its depths vary a great deal. In this respect, it can be divided into thirds. The northern third from Lanesboro to Rinany is comparatively shallow, its depth scarcely above ten feet. However, depths lower than this may be encountered in the various fascinating waterways of this winding inland sea, in corners and coves, near islands and margins, by rocks and bays. The broad middle section averages a depth of twenty four feet, while the southern third is much deeper, its greatest depths being ninety feet close to Inis Ainghin, or Hare Island, and one hundred and twenty feet in the channel running north-west of Inis Mór, the largest island in the lake.

Based on the limestone strata of the Central Plain, Loch Ree is a solution lake. Its acidic waters, fuelled by its rivers and abundant rainfall, seep and ooze into the chalky clay of its bed and its margins, giving it a very long and indented shoreline. Its banks, layered with glacial drift, a residue of the Ice Age, are often stony, bearing weedy patches of grass and a mere sprinkling of wild flowers, and, for its length, even reed beds are infrequent. The west shore has nine large bays, the east shore thirteen. Numerous inlets, creeks and small harbours proliferate from the larger openings and many of these provide the soft muddy bottom which is a natural breeding place for shrimps, leeches, beetles and snails. The larvae and nymphs of the caddis and dragon flies find a habitat here also, and in the fishing season, lure trout from the niches and troughs in the depths of the lake to feed on this rich and abundant fare, which springs like a harvest from the shallows.

The Roscommon shore is low and stony. There are no banks for much of its length. Narrow inlets filter runnels and dykes into the drenched land. In the misty morning, broken by flurries of light rain, the lake is choppy with bustling wavelets sluicing the pebbled shore. Its broken and irregular margins curve inwards, as it rounds Clooneigh Bay which is entered by a small stream of the same name, and diverges into the narrow inlet of Rinany, which is then followed by the humped and shortened Cruit and Galey Bays, as they cut into the low-lying countryside. One of the few tributaries of Loch Ree, the River Hind, flows into Cruit Bay, just north of the harbour and amenity area of Portrunny. A scenic stream based on limestone and rich in trout and coarse fish, it winds through the Roscommon hinterland, its banks partly open, partly overshadowed by willow and hawthorn trees, as it passes under three road bridges before emptying itself into the lake.

Portrunny, a small pleasing backwater, is exposed and unsheltered in high east winds, but is otherwise a calm amenity and picnic area with a wide shoreline, a pier and harbour with moorings for boats that like to prowl in quiet corners. Further development is in progress here and the red and yellow rain gear of the workers glints and gleams in the relentless mist. Dark shapes of islands loom vaguely in the pale expanse of water like the spines of sleeping whales. In the background, stands of dripping trees rise above silent houses and gardens, as they look down on the idling cruisers and small boats shifting uneasily in the harbour.

Galey Bay, its nearest neighbour, is a pleasant boating and fishing area with a caravan and camping park. Hidden dangers lurk at the entrance to this bay in the shape of submerged rocks known as the 'Louisa Shoals', the feminine name being that of a luckless yacht, that fell foul of the hazards and went aground. Overlooking the bay are the ivy-warped ruins of Galey Castle, and a colony of small houses in the caravan park.

The low and sparsely wooded shoreline leads to Blackbrink Bay, a quiet peril-free area safe from the

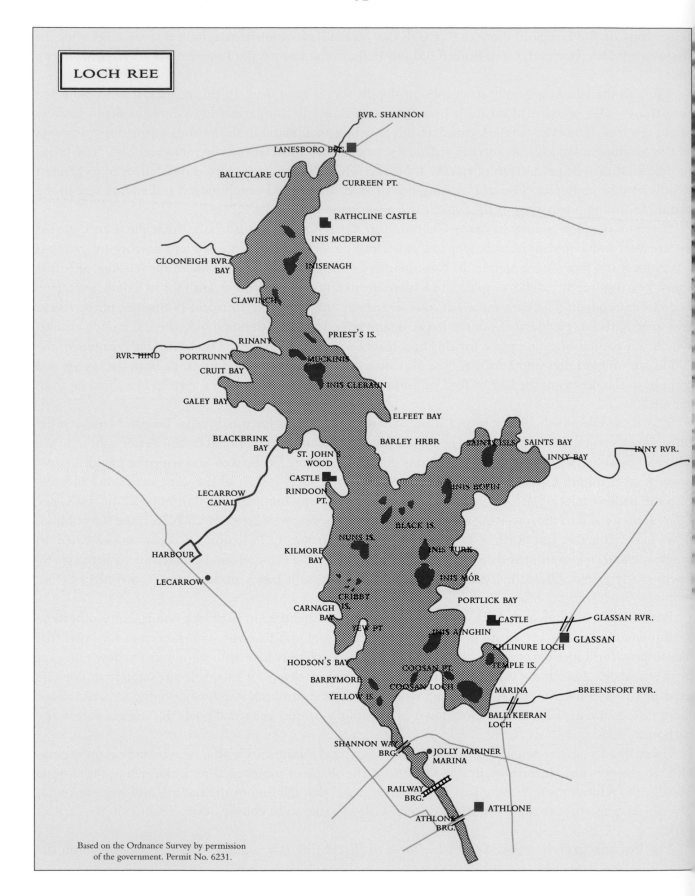

LOCH REE

RVR. SHANNON

LANESBORO BRG.

BALLYCLARE CUT

CURREEN PT.

RATHCLINE CASTLE

INIS MCDERMOT

CLOONEIGH RVR.
BAY

INISENAGH

CLAWINCH

PRIEST'S IS.

RINANY

RVR. HIND

PORTRUNNY

MUCKINIS

CRUIT BAY

INIS CLERAUN

GALEY BAY

ELFEET BAY

BLACKBRINK
BAY

BARLEY HRBR.

SAINTS ISL. SAINTS BAY

INNY BAY

INNY RVR.

ST. JOHN'S
WOOD

INIS BOFIN

CASTLE

LECARROW
CANAL

RINDOON
PT.

BLACK IS.

NUNS IS.

HARBOUR

KILMORE
BAY

INIS TURK

LECARROW

INIS MÓR

PORTLICK BAY

CRIBBY
IS.

CARNAGH
BAY

CASTLE

GLASSAN RVR.

YEW PT.

INIS AINGHIN

GLASSAN

KILLINURE LOCH

HODSON'S BAY

TEMPLE IS.

BARRYMORE

COOSAN PT.

MARINA

BREENSFORT RVR.

YELLOW IS.

COOSAN LOCH

BALLYKEERAN
LOCH

SHANNON WAY
BRG.

JOLLY MARINER
MARINA

RAILWAY
BRG.

ATHLONE

ATHLONE
BRG.

Based on the Ordnance Survey by permission
of the government. Permit No. 6231.

The Shannon Flows into Loch Ree

Ruined church on Inis Cleraun

onslaught of wind and gale and giving a measure of shelter to boats that wish to moor there. An additional point of interest is the presence of a short canal which enables them to reach the harbour and village of Lecarrow, a small scattered housing area with its centre on the main road from Roscommon to Athlone.

The Lecarrow canal, one and a half miles long, the only one of its kind on Loch Ree, was built originally in the 1840s for the purpose of transporting stone blocks from a local quarry to Athlone, where a new bridge and lock were being constructed.

Scenic calm on Loch Ree

When the primary purpose was accomplished and commercial activity on the Shannon gradually petered out, the short waterway suffered the fate of many of its larger kindred. It was abandoned and allowed to silt up, rendering it impassable for river traffic.

In 1966, however, a change of policy occurred, influenced no doubt, by the growing fleet of pleasure boats on the Shannon. The canal was re-opened, dredged, and cleaned of its weedy deposits, its banks shorn of arching willow scrub and wild vegetation. Today, a fine harbour, developed by the Board of Works, with wide walkways, rings and bollards, provides safe mooring for the cruisers idling at its piers, or tying up at the opposite bank. The canal, clear and uncluttered, streams through grazing land on its short journey from Blackbrink Bay to Lecarrow.

South of the bay on a receding inner shoreline is the tree-lined St. John's Wood with its faint references to the 13th century, when the Knights of St. John established a friary in the vicinity. Close by, on a hill above the lake, stands the Castle of Rindoon, built in the same period, its high roofless remains gazing sightlessly across the narrow stretch of water over which it once held strategic dominance. Its huddle of ruined buildings, partially covered with a woody scaffolding of vegetative growth, bear only the faintest echoes of ancient human power, and have become the haunt of myriads of insects, birds and tiny mammals – the not infrequent accompaniments of solitude and desolation. Beneath it, is the small scenic backwater of Safe Harbour, though no harbour as such exists. A secluded inlet, it is marked by a buoy and provides a sheltered anchorage.

The shoreline slips on to Kilmore Bay which has a small amenity area in a wide circlet of lake, remote and hidden. Flocks of birds spiral and glide above a nearby peninsula of mature trees, and a pair of swans dawdle in the watercourse. Wooded islets dot its expanse and fade from sight in the hazy distance beyond. A green strip of land juts into the bay and, close to its stony tip, a cruiser moves slowly into view.

Rocks abound on this shoreline, as it reaches out to Carnagh Bay, a sheltered arm of water which provides safe mooring and possesses a plantation of trees, known as the Wood of Muclagh, on its south side. Ballybay follows, leading to the narrow inlet of Yew Point, an area rich in trees, plants and flowers. A short distance farther on, is Hodson's Bay, undoubtedly the best developed anchorage on the Roscommon shore, having a harbour and parking area, a caravan and camping section, a hotel and golf course. South of Hodson's Bay is the small natural marina of Barrymore with tiny jetties and a shingle beach. Its waters, broken by the reflections of nearby trees and houses, are dotted with light cruisers and tilting rowboats in the season. Close to the centre of the watercourse are the wooded Yellow Islands, gay with autumnal colours, and beyond their leafy contours is the narrow mouth of the Shannon, as it approaches its exit from the lake.

· · · · ·

Although a number of access ways lead to Loch Ree, they are largely winding side roads, often not signposted and usually ending in rutted grassy pathways, or weedy tracks across fields. The views obtained of the lake in these circumstances are seldom satisfactory, cut off as they are by high ridges of ground, stands of old trees, or the irregular thrust of the shoreline. This is particularly evident on the northeast shore, where the wooded Longford margin runs into Elfeet Bay. Reached by a minor road, which passes through the pleasing, flower-decorated village of Newtowncashel and which dwindles into the inevitable laneway as it approaches the lake, a small park runs along the shoreline, with willow and hawthorn trees and sharp choppy wavelets babbling at the water's edge. A few miles south, Barley Harbour, similarly isolated by copse and spinney, opens its narrow inlet to cruisers and rowboats which are tied to the bollards on the broad stone pier. Rocky channels, on both sides of the harbour, cut into the land and shoals close to its entrance can make it hazardous for boats. Adjoining it, is a grassy amenity area with trees and parking facilities.

Winding directly south, the shoreline, spattered with rock and shoal and punctuated at intervals with reed beds, reaches the widest section of the lake. An out-flung convoluted arm, which encompasses Pollagh Bay and its near neighbour, Portanure Bay, lying in the shelter of a coniferous forest, and Saint's Island, part water girt, part mainland, stretches out from Derry Bay to the most easterly part of Loch Ree, the estuary of the River Inny. Despite the long twisted straggle of its shoreline, its many bays and peninsulas, the lake has few tributaries, whether rivers, canals or cuttings, leading to supporting waterways. With the exception of the Shannon, the Inny which forms the boundary between the counties of Longford and Westmeath for part of its course, is the only other river of note.

Having its source near Oldcastle in County Meath, the Inny makes a scenic waterway for fifty-five miles, passing through four lakes on its course – Sheelin, Kinale, Derravaragh and Iron and streaming under a number of bridges before reaching Ballymahon in County Longford. It is a fast-flowing river but shallow and unnavigable except to row boats. Continuing to the bridge at Shrule, a metal-barred construction with the sightless eyes of an old mill gaping down from the Leinster bank, it passes into the hinterland of Loch Ree and a short distance farther on, streams beneath a wide barred footbridge, the Red Bridge, a noted fishing venue. In this area it is joined by the narrow, weed-ridden River Tang. For the next mile or so, it flows through flat fields with rush and low vegetation. Its banks are clear of trees as it meanders around bends and corners, uncluttered by weeds and debris. Wild flowers lend it colour – buttercup and dandelion, purple thistle and blue scabious. Brown mushrooms lurk in the grass between clusters of red berries and the green flags of the iris. As the river approaches its confluence with the lake, it spreads into inlets, overflowing the low sodden fields. Thickets of reeds jut into the watercourse. Wildfowl loiter in the reeds and prowl in the shallows. Moorhens, coots and swans make sorties into the swirling eddy pools, only to disappear swiftly into their shadowy fastnesses. Two poles, red and black, mark the channel, where it empties itself into Loch Ree.

A receding shoreline succeeds the eastward spread of the Inny Bay. Contoured in small arcs and inlets with some reed beds, it leads to the Bay of Portlick, a smooth tranquil expanse of water, drifting in shallow wavelets into the low reedy margins. There is an amenity walking area here and forest paths to be explored. Meadowsweet, blue scabious and marguerite sparkle in the grassy verges and beneath the trees. Some distance away on a slight hill, the aged stonework of Portlick Castle, a privately owned mansion, appears from within the shelter of a belt of trees.

Though rocks and shoals restrict the northern and southern entrances to Portlick Bay, it provides a relatively safe anchorage for craft. From it, a tree-girt shoreline links Rinardo Bay with Killinure Point on the southern margin of the lake. This part of Loch Ree is very beautiful. There is a wide expanse of water and a number of islands, large and small, spacing its rippling channels. Houses, chalets and clustering trees rim its margins until it reaches Killinure Point, from which the largest harbour on the lake opens out. Many cruisers are moored here, a private complex, and a number shift at anchor in the narrow channel of water which stretches from Killinure Point to Coosan Point, a hillside landmark on the opposite margin. The channel between, divided at the centre by a strip of wooded islet, forms the opening to the small and lovely complex of island, wood, reed and water, known as the Inner Lakes. There are three of these – Killinure, Coosan and Ballykeeran.

Loch Ree the fifth largest lake

The River Hind

Portrunny Harbour at Cruit Bay

Galey Bay

The ruins of Galey Castle

Lecarrow Harbour and canal

The ruins of Rindoon Castle

Hodson's Bay and Harbour

Barrymore Marina

Barley Harbour

The River Inny passing the Bridge at Shrule

The estuary of the Inny

Killinure, the largest of the lakes, stretches east for up to two miles. Its islands are, Garnagh, close to the centre, and Temple Island farther east, a wooded and swampy area which has become a winter habitat for migratory birds. Rocks, snags and islets appear on this margin where a small river, the Glassan, enters an inlet in the lake. Flowing beneath a road bridge at Glassan village, it is very narrow, its banks concealed by weedy vegetation and unkempt hedges. It winds across country for a short distance before emptying itself into Killinure Loch. In this area, also, on the edge of the lake, a golf course is being prepared within a landscape of low-lying fields and wooded hills. Killinure Loch is linked by a narrow channel to Coosan Loch which spreads south-east of Coosan Point.

Three miles north of Athlone, the approach road to Coosan Point leads to a housing complex and a hotel. From the hillside, a panoramic view meets the eye. On the left is the beautiful Inis Ainghin, or Hare Island, so close that its masses of trees are clearly discernible, as is the tiny pier on its south side and the small, grey stone building jutting out from the woods of beech, fir and hazel. In front is Killinure Point with its colourful flotillas of boats and cruisers. In the east, is the tranquil island-studded swell of the Inner Lakes.

At Coosan Point, pathways lead to the water's edge where a copse of willow, alder, ash and hawthorn, and a myriad of creepers and weeds jostle for space on the brink of the lake. There is a short broad pier, a wooden jetty and a shingle beach stretching along the shoreline and providing space for row boats. Mallards sun themselves on the stones and the wooden jetty, unalarmed by passersby. Seagulls skim the wavelets and scan the shallows, while a group of swans zigzag slowly across the streamy watercourse.

The channel connecting Coosan Loch to Killinure Loch is constricted and runs between two islands, the small Cnocanamuck in the west and Friar's Island in the east, a large, thickly-wooded area where nothing now remains of the friars' occupancy but a delapidated ruin, concealed under layers of bush and vegetation. Coosan Loch, the most elusive and secretive of lakes to which access by land is difficult, has two small islands, Thatch and Gibraltar. It has no harbour, though sheltered as it is by woods and reeds it forms a safe anchorage. From its southern bank it looks like a vast garden pool of tall waving reeds. A few houses can be vaguely discerned on the opposite margin but belts of trees tend to obscure the distance. The grassy shoreline is sprinkled with light tussocks of rush and dock. Blue scabious and red-berried shrubs dot a protective woodland of holly, hazel and willow.

On its east shore another channel makes its appearance. It is wide and deep and leads to Ballykeeran Loch, the smallest of the three lakes. The approach to this lake is by a short pathway from the tiny village of Ballykeeran. A small ancient stone bridge in the village passes over the narrow but fast-flowing Breensfort River which streams a further short distance to join the lake in its south-east corner. A camping and caravan park is sited on its shores. Though this part of the lake has no pier or jetties, trees, reed beds and scattered islets provide sheltered mooring places, while on its northern margin a narrow channel leads into Killinure Loch, thus completing the round trip through the lakes. However, the proximity of the lake to the Athlone/Ballymahon Road has brought about the welcome development of a spacious harbour, a marina, an amenity area and an hotel on a wooded shoreline of beech, hazel and fir, close to the village of Ballykeeran. Nearby, are the private marina of Portaneena and the Wineport sailing centre.

Peaceful and largely undisturbed, this cluster of lakes and islands is one of the richest habitats of bird and animal life on Loch Ree. A refuge for wild life in general, it has a large winter inflow of birds, and shelters, among others, ducks, coots, great-crested grebes, pheasants, moorhens, and reed buntings, which use the bracken, the reed thickets and the heavy swaths of rush for nesting, food and safety. Small mammals also abound – rabbits, badgers, squirrels, otters and occasionally, hares and foxes.

All of these tranquil and reed lined waterways with their connecting cuts and channels are navigable and have markers, stakes, buoys and mooring places in each section. Above all, they are free from rocks and shoals, whether visible or submerged, which form the most usual and deadly menace to sailing craft.

· · · · ·

One of the distinctive features of Loch Ree's watercourse is the prevalence of shoals, rocks, spits and crags, making whole sections, coves and bays, particularly, in the centre, by the eastern shoreline, and in the south, dangerous to traverse. Many of these bear familiar names and are clearly marked. Others unnamed and usually submerged, become visible only at low water. Perhaps the most hazardous occur in the narrow stretch from Barley Harbour in the east to St. John's Wood on the opposite shore, where, close to the centre, the Iskeraulin Shoal, a heap of jagged boulder and stone, often submerged in floods, and the Wood Shoal some distance to the west, sandwich the navigational channel. Lying across the entrance to Galey Bay are the Louisa Shoals, while farther south, on the east side, are the Long Shoal and the Hexagon Shoals, with the smaller Godiva Shoal close to Coosan Point.

Rocks protrude from the surface of the lake in many places. Snags proliferate around the edges and in the shallow parts of bays. Slate and Pinnacle rocks are landmarks in the south-west, the Napper and Welch rocks in the south-east, along with Adelaide rock towards the centre. Some areas are infested with crags and boulders, such as those between Rinany, on the Roscommon shoreline and Muckinish Island, in the north-west, and between Inis Mór, and the Napper rocks in the south-east.

Beacons, buoys, red and black markers, indicating the navigational channel, abound in Loch Ree. However, a second factor and often the over-riding one in exploring the spacious expanse of inlets, coves and bays and avoiding the surface hazards, is the changeability of the weather which can, and does, veer through most climatic variations – storm, heavy rain, fog, frost, and occasionally, snow. Backed by the dark turmoil of louring clouds, or the massed strata of a purple-black sky, visibility is rendered difficult and markers indistinct even to the point of obliteration. Because of its largely unprotected shoreline and the wide empty spaces on its margins due to lack of reed beds, woods and forestry belts, the lake becomes a mass of churning wavelets even in fair weather. Strong winds cause tempestuous waves, submerging rocks and shoals, and giving them an additional eerie quality of menace. Occasionally, the watercourse freezes over and slabs of ice disrupt its surface.

Yet the weather conditions, though important, are but one of the many facets which characterise Loch Ree. Perhaps its most striking feature is its extraordinary wealth of islands of which over fifty are named and countless others unnamed. The tremendous loads of sediment, of rocks, boulders, clay and stone, swept down from the northern hills by the Shannon and its tributaries, are in large measure responsible for the size and variety of this unique archipelago. Some of the islands, like Inis Mór and Inis Ainghin are large and well wooded, some lie in groups like the small Black and Cribby chains, while others are little more than stony spits or crags like the Welch Rocks, perching stations for birds. Shoals and boulders surround many of them, making mooring and anchorage difficult, if not impossible.

But though the physical and geological formation of the islands is deeply interesting, it is the evidence they provide of human habitation, endeavour and creativity, from the earliest centuries A.D. to well into the medieval period, that mark their very real importance as part of our cultural heritage. Early historical records show that the islands of Loch Ree were a frequent choice of monks and nuns for the establishment of religious communities. There were sound reasons for this. Because of the narrowness of parts of the

lake and their positions close to the margins, many
of them were readily reached from the mainland and
transport in small boats available. An abundant
supply of food and fuel, fish, game, wood and water,

Killinure Loch

Glassan River

was ready to hand in unlimited quantities. Above all,

the empty solitudes of this great undisturbed
expanse, seemingly invulnerable, and broken only by
the shrill symphonies of bird life and the rustles and

Coosan Point

Coosan Loch

squeaks of small mammals in the undergrowth

backed by the rhythmic gurgle of the wavelets on the
shore, seemed ideal for that deep mystical silence and
contemplation which are so essential a part of
monastic life.

In these centuries were created the first
developments in art and architecture – the building
of houses, churches and stone crosses, manuscript
illumination, writings and book shrines, inscribed

Ballykeeran Loch with the Breensfort River

Ballykeeran Harbour and Marina

Inis Mór, the largest island (a section)

grave slabs, and later on, High Crosses and Round Towers. With the coming of the medieval period, from the 12th century onwards, and the influx of religious orders from the continent of Europe, the Augustinians and the Franciscans, the Dominicans and the Cistercians, armed with new disciplines and new skills, there gradually emerged the construction of friaries, abbeys and cathedral type churches. A group of the islands have residual remembrances of ecclesiastical life and five are named directly because of their religious associations – Priest's, Nun's, Friar's, Saint's and Bethlehem Point.

The first island to be chosen for a monastic settlement is said to be Inisbofin which lies in Derry Bay near the entrance to the estuary of the River Inny. It was established by St. Rioch in the 6th century. The ruins of two churches with nave, chancel, transept and grave slabs remain and contain features that were added at later dates – a

Ruined church on Inis Cleraun

Ruined church on Saint's Island

A section of Inis Ainghin

Romanesque window and two 15th century windows, and a sacristy which indicates that a community may have been in occupation in medieval times. Legend has it that St. Liobhán established a monastery on Inis Mór in this period and an ancient ruin still exists in a corner of the island.

Inis Cleraun, the best known of the ecclesiastical sites, is said to be named after Clothrann, a sister of the renowned Queen Maeve of Connacht. The queen is reputed to have met her death here while bathing, killed by a stone from a sling, fired from the Longford mainland, less than a mile away, in revenge for her capture of the famous bull of Cuailgne from the King of Ulster.

This island, chosen in the 6th century by St. Diarmaid for his foundation, contains the remains of seven churches and a group of early Christian grave slabs. The largest of the churches, Teampall Mór, was built at a later date, probably between the 13th and 15th centuries. The Belfry Church, or Clogas, is sited on the highest point of the island, and to the south is the Women's Church. The ruins stand stark and weatherbeaten. Weeds fill the ancient niches of prayer. In past ages, choirs of human voices sanctified these once holy edifices now reduced to remnants of moss covered stone. Today, the high shriek of seagulls, and the sharp whistling of the north-west wind slice incessantly through these gaunt apertures of decay.

Inis Ainghin, also called Hare Island, because of the number of hares and rabbits that once roamed its woods, became the site of St. Ciarán's first church, established in 541 A.D. Shortly afterwards, he appointed a successor, and leaving the small settlement to his disciples, travelled farther south to build beside the Shannon, what became in later ages, his greatest foundation, the monastery of Clonmacnois.

Inis Ainghin contains the ruins of a small church of the Romanesque type, dating from the 12th century, and the remains of a friary of the Order of St. Augustine.

In the 12th century also, it is probable that the Priory of All Saints was founded on Saint's Island. A ruined church and cloister, and some traces of domestic buildings are all that remain. The Priory was well-maintained, had a number of scholars and valuable manuscripts and there is evidence that it lasted until the 15th century.

Unfortunately, the visions of peace and mystical contemplation so desired by the religious communities of Loch Ree did not materialise except for short periods. Their fame, modest prosperity and apparent defencelessness, led to harassment by Connacht and Munster tribes. This was vastly augmented by the ravages of the Viking hordes who swept up the Shannon estuary in continuous waves from the 8th to the 10th centuries, and whose attacks fell most heavily on the monastic settlements. The Norse grip was shattered by the death of Turgesius, their leader, killed by the King of Meath in 844. Over a century later, in 980, Brian Boru, King of Munster, having defeated the Norse of Limerick, contested the growing power and presence on Loch Ree of the then King of Meath, Mael Sechnaill II, and established a large fleet on the lake. During this period of struggle, the plundering of the monasteries continued intermittently until, in 997, the two kings agreed to make peace.

With the 12th century came the vicious and persistent attacks of the Normans. A relic of this period is the gaunt sombre ruin of Rindoon Castle on the Roscommon shore and its adjoining group of decayed buildings which formed a small town at its inception, but is now a shapeless mass of creeper-ridden stone. Constructed on a height above a peninsula in the narrowest section of the lake, probably replacing an old fortress, it occupied a commanding and strategic position for attack and defence. It was begun in 1227 by the Norman, Geoffrey de Marisco, and was surrounded by a defensive moat and wall. It had a number of square towers and was approached by a causeway fortified against attack from the Roscommon mainland. Outside the wall are a graveyard and the remains of a church founded by the Knights Hospitaller of St. John. Other castles were built in the following centuries and their ruins are visible on both sides of the lake. Galey in the west, Rathcline and Elfeet in the east and farther inland, Ballynacliffy, Kilfaughny and Kilkenny West.

The continual conflicts on the lake and the merciless and savage raids on the island monasteries led to their destruction and eventual abandonment. They had remained in existence for up to a thousand years, and their religious significance was still felt in the 17th and 18th centuries, when people furtively attended the outlawed Mass on the forbidding and deserted Priest's Island, hidden behind rocks on the Longford shore, and friars made stealthy journeys from Friar's Island in the Inner Lakes to say Mass on the mainland. One of the final acts in this long and tortuous saga of survival was the destruction of the convent of the Poor Clares at Bethlehem Point on the east shore, by soldiers of the Athlone garrison in 1641, when the escaping nuns, it is said, fled to an island in the centre of the lake now known as Nun's Island, in which a ruined church and two graves are still visible.

Some of the islands have small piers, jetties and landing places and over the centuries became inhabited by farming and fishing communities. Inis Mór, the largest island, Inis Cleraun and Inis Ainghin and some of the chain of Black Islands had small colonies who lived a plain and simple life, travelled to and from the mainland by boat, reared cattle and caught fish. Since the 1950s the islands have been unlived in and are now largely habitats for flora and fauna except for the cattle that are transported from the mainland to cull the fertile fields and the rich grassy stretches. Some of them are privately owned, are wooded and cultivated. Saint's Island is one of these, having a causeway to the Longford shore. Farming families reside here and it has facilities for summer homes, a development which is spreading to other islands.

Unlike the margins of the lake which are stony and meagre in flora, the islands, in many cases, have rich meadows, stands of mature trees and hedgerows, like Carberry Island and Inis Aingin. From spring to autumn, they are bright with wildflowers – buttercup, foxglove, iris, marsh marigold, meadowsweet, dog rose and a host of others. Small mammals prowl in the undergrowth – badgers, squirrels, rabbits and hares. At nightfall, the nocturnal predators – the otter, stoat and owl – forage incessantly in their various ways. Birds flit and spiral as they use these quiet havens for feeding and nesting-blackbirds, wrens and thrushes, magpies, wood pigeons and rooks. The larger birds, the heron, the cormorant and the black-headed gulls range the entire watercourse in their voracious quest for food.

In the winter months parts of Loch Ree become a 'wetland' for migratory geese and ducks. Widgeon and tufted duck arrive in large numbers with lesser groups of wild swans and white-fronted geese and make habitats chiefly at Blackbrink Bay, the swampy Loch Ross on Inis Mór, and Temple Island in the Inner Lakes. Waders that are habitually on the water and circling the islands are the mallards, coots and moorhens, while mute swans and grebes nest in the reed thickets along with reed buntings and sedge warblers.

All of the larger birds feed on fish and the lake is a rich fishery, with an abundance of brown trout, and a large variety of coarse fish – tench, bream, pike, perch and eels. The mayfly hatch, occurring in early May, and later, the sedge hatch, lure trout from their hidden lairs in the depths of the lake to the shallows around the shoreline and the islands, and to the mouths of rivers, where clouds of insects rise above the surface of the watercourse and are devoured in unlimited quantities by them and by the screaming waves of black-headed gulls streaking from the nearby shores where they nest. The lake is heavily fished, in season, from the banks and from row boats as anglers expectantly cast their lines into the deluge of trout. Coarse fish is plentiful in every part of Loch Ree, especially in the Inner Lakes and, on the opposite shore, at the small Robin Island and the inlet of Ballybay, noted for its angling of the predatory and wily pike.

In general, there are not enough access roads and amenity areas around this large and interesting body

Waders

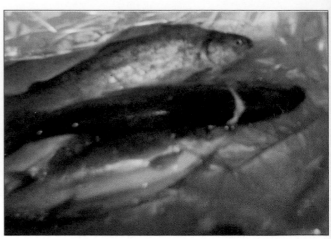

Trout

Foxglove

of water, nor are there sufficient quays, jetties and sheltered mooring places for the growing fleet of pleasure boats that like to cruise in its winding channels, to fish, to explore, to visit the islands, or simply to linger in quiet coves and bays.

The Shannon traverses the entire lake and with it, the red and black poles of the navigational channel which runs almost directly down the centre, with diversions to Blackbrink Bay and the Lecarrow canal on the west shore, to Derry Bay and the estuary of the Inny on the east shore, to Inis Ainghin and the Inner Lakes in the south-east and to Hodson's Bay in the south-west. From this point, all navigational lines come together, passing the Yellow Islands in the neck of the lake as the Shannon makes its exit, flanked on the east shore by Ballyglass Hill, dominated by a cross, erected to mark the Marian Year in 1953, and by the Loch Ree Yacht Club, its jetties and mooring bays, and on the west by the small marina of Barrymore and a stand of mature trees known as the Hill of Berries. It flows for a further mile and a half to Athlone, the central town of the Midlands.

Iris

The Shannon leaving Loch Ree

Chapter Seven

THE SHANNON, A BROAD FAST-FLOWING WATERWAY as it emerges from Loch Ree, widens its channel as it streams past woodland, houses and gardens to Athlone. There are three bridges on its short course of a mile and a half. The first of these, the Shannon Way, is also the most recent. It was opened in 1991 and carries the motorway from Dublin to Galway, bypassing the town of Athlone in an effort to relieve its traffic congestion. It is a concrete bridge with a high central archway and two side arches. Immediately downstream, is the Jolly Mariner Marina, the hire base of Athlone Cruisers, and many boats normally tie up here. In midstream, to the right of the marina, is the small Charlie's Island, named after a previous owner.

A short distance farther south is the railway bridge, built in the 1850s. Painted white, its long, decorative arched railings designed in metal, and the great circular piers that support it make it highly visible on the river's course. It has two navigational channels and up to the 1930s there was an opening span which has since been altered to a fixed section.

The third bridge is the town bridge with three arches and a navigational span on the Roscommon shore. A masonry construction erected in 1844 – part of its stone parapets have now been inset with metal railings – it replaced a narrow older bridge which was the historic bridge of Athlone, renowned for the part it played in the life of the town during the Cromwellian wars of 1641-1651, and the Jacobite struggle of 1691. During the Napoleonic era, from 1795 onward, it was fortified and equipped with artillery, the first of a line of fortifications so prepared, stretching along the Shannon from Athlone to Portumna, to defend the river crossings in the event of a French invasion.

Athlone, the Ford of Luan, has been the principal crossing on the Shannon between Leinster and Connacht from pre-historic times. Originally, it was known as Ath Mór, the Great Ford. With the passage of years, however, the word 'Luan' replaced the former ending and became an indivisible part of the name. Legend speculates about the identity of Luan and many tales are woven about him. Was he a chieftain, a lover, a soldier or an innkeeper? The mists of the past give no answer. They do not readily yield up their secrets and the identity of Luan remains an enigma, a name solidified in story and stone.

Sited on the Eiscir Riada, the broad impacted ridge of gravel which skirts the huge morass of the Bog of Allen and stretches from Dublin to Galway, making a natural travel route from east to west, the crossing became a ford, aided by the fact that the Shannon at this section was very narrow. The existence of ring forts in the surrounding districts suggest that people lived here from pre-historic times, and from the 6th century A.D. religious settlements in Loch Ree and at Clonmacnois, eight miles downstream, indicate continuous human activity on the river.

It wasn't until the 12th century, however, that the importance of the ford as a military base began to be considered. The then King of Connacht, Turlough O'Connor, built a wooden bridge at the ford to expedite the passage of troops into the province of Leinster in his forays against the kingdom of Meath. The bridge, made of wood, was easily damaged and had to be replaced a number of times. In 1129 he erected a castle by the ford, probably a wooden building which was later destroyed.

The approach of the 13th century saw the rapid progress of the Norman Invasion, and its penetration to the boundaries of Connacht and the Shannon. In 1210, John de Grey, deputy of the English King John, had a bridge built at the ford and began the construction of the stone castle on the west bank of the river. But it was not until the 16th century, with a resurgence of English activity, that the castle had a permanent garrison.

In 1567, a stone bridge was built across the Shannon, the forerunner of the present town bridge. It was very narrow, the river was fast-flowing beneath it but was unnavigable. Two centuries later, the task of making the Shannon navigable at Athlone was tackled and overcome by the building of a canal on the west shore, exiting from the river a short distance downstream of the bridge, bypassing the narrow watercourse, and re-entering the Shannon about half a mile upstream of the bridge. This arrangement lasted until the 1840s when the coming of steam-driven boats which made the use of towpaths and horses redundant, materially altered the navigation of the river. The present bridge, incorporating the previous one, was built in 1844 as part of a general reconstruction programme, carried out on the bridges of the Upper Shannon between 1840 and 1850, with the exception of that of Drumsna, which is sited on the unnavigable section of the river near Jamestown. At the same time, the narrow section of the river above and below the bridge was dredged, widened, and made navigable. This led to the abandonment of the canal which is now partly derelict and partly filled in. It also led to an expanded traffic on the river, with freight-laden barges, turf boats, and steamers, plying their trade and creating a busy river port. However, with the growing use of railway and road for the transport of goods in this century, river trading slowed down, became unprofitable, and, in 1961, ceased altogether.

· · · · ·

On its approach to the town bridge, the Shannon attains the widest span of its seventy eight mile journey from its source in County Cavan. It is about three hundred feet in width and six to seven feet deep. A calm rippling sheet of water, chequered by sunlight, it bears a majestic appearance as it laps its low banks with force and speed, and surges irresistibly southwards past a line of buildings and jetties on its east bank, and a leafy pathway beside quays and mooring places on the Connacht shore. This impressive effect of largeness, light and space is heightened by the presence of the most dominant buildings in the town, sited close to each other on the west bank of the river – the Catholic Church of SS. Peter and Paul, built in 1937, and across the road by the waterside, Athlone Castle, that bleak circular bastion of military might which originated in the 13th century.

The castle has the distinction of being not only the oldest piece of architecture in the town, but also one of the oldest on the entire course of the Shannon, a building which is still a solid edifice, functional and useful. Erected in the first instance to protect the river crossing and later, the town bridge, which was of prime strategic importance because of its location as the central gateway to Connacht, it has been altered and added to over the centuries. Its long turbulent history ended finally in 1922 with the establishment of the Irish Free State and the end of British rule. Up to 1970, it was held by the Irish Army and was then

The Shannon Way Bridge

The Jolly Mariner Marina

The Railway Bridge

The Bridge of Athlone

A section of the derelict canal

The Shannon Approaching Athlone

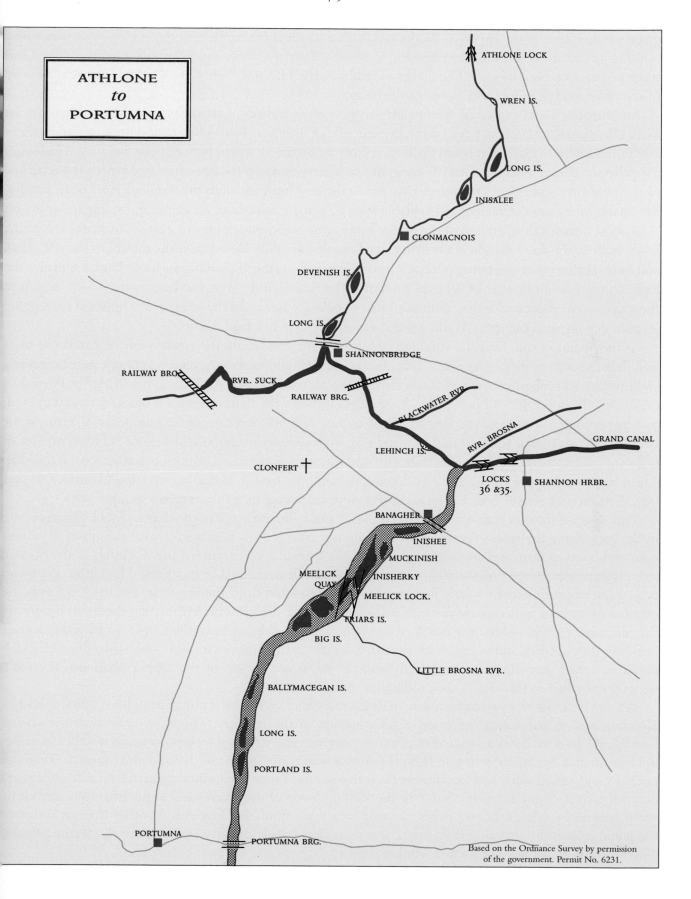

ATHLONE
to
PORTUMNA

ATHLONE LOCK

WREN IS.

LONG IS.

INISALEE

CLONMACNOIS

DEVENISH IS.

LONG IS.

SHANNONBRIDGE

RAILWAY BRG.

RVR. SUCK

RAILWAY BRG.

BLACKWATER RVR.

RVR. BROSNA

GRAND CANAL

LEHINCH IS.

CLONFERT †

LOCKS
36 &35.

SHANNON HRBR.

BANAGHER

INISHEE

MUCKINISH

MEELICK
QUAY

INISHERKY

MEELICK LOCK.

FRIARS IS.

BIG IS.

LITTLE BROSNA RVR.

BALLYMACEGAN IS.

LONG IS.

PORTLAND IS.

PORTUMNA

PORTUMNA BRG.

Based on the Ordnance Survey by permission
of the government. Permit No. 6231.

given to the Office of the Board of Works and made a national monument. Today it is open to the public, housing an historical and folklore museum, a café and Tourist Office, and a Visitors' Centre which hosts three permanent exhibitions – The Sieges of Athlone, the Life and Times of John McCormack, a native of the town, and the Flora and Fauna of the Shannon.

Athlone, the county town of Westmeath, has now a population of almost twenty thousand people. Its main urban development has been on the Leinster side of the river. With a fine road system, and the railway line from Dublin to Galway, it is still the busiest crossing on the Shannon between east and west. No longer the prisoner of its dramatic military history - it was a garrison town for three hundred years - it has turned to light industry and textiles for prosperity, and to the development of its position as a river port, making the Shannon, its most attractive and valuable feature, a major waterway for cruising, fishing and tourism.

A short distance downstream of the bridge is the commodious lock on the west shore. Forty feet wide, it was built in the same decade as the bridge, and opened in 1849. Below it, is the mouth of the old canal, and beyond this point the narrow River Cross flows in from the Roscommon hinterland. Opposite the lock, on the east shore, a set of eel traps is followed by an expansive weir also built in the 1840s, which to the spacious river scene adds the continuous roar of falling water amid the screams of a horde of scavenging seagulls delving into the spray. Buildings and mooring quays line both banks.

As the Shannon rolls over the weir and begins to wind slowly into the countryside, it enters the most significant stretch in its long course – a significance which embraces agriculture, ecology, peat harvesting and military and religious artifacts. In its thirty five mile stretch from Athlone to the bridge at Portumna on the northern border of Loch Derg, it meanders through the flattest terrain it has so far encountered, passing through a section of the Bog of Allen, an area of 6,500 acres occupying the Central Plain of the country. Swards of bog fringe it on both banks for up to twenty miles downstream of Athlone, an area of eight square kilometres. It has fallen only fifty one feet since it streamed out of Loch Allen and is less than a hundred feet above sea level. It is not flowing through the land so much as traversing its surface. It cuts no valley, carves no river bed, but seems as if it were supported by giant stratified sponges.

This sluggish meandering waterway has proven a grave disadvantage to the development of agriculture in the area, since the river's floodplain is enormously enlarged on both banks with the onset of winter rains,and tracts of farmland are submerged and made unavailable for general use. Farming in the normal sense is impossible,since the waterlogged soil will not admit of manual or mechanical handling. Plans and projects to stop this massive yearly flooding have been mooted from time to time, but the huge expense entailed in such an undertaking prevents it from getting off the ground. Meanwhile the fields bordering the Shannon remain sodden for much of the year. Termed callows from the Gaelic word 'cala', a river meadow, they are old, undrained, uncultivated, but yield in the summer months when they dry out, a rich nutritious grass, providing food for farm animals. As in the region of the Upper Shannon, the main agricultural effort in this area is the production of beef cattle.

Yet, the flooding river, so unfortunate in its general effect on the local population, has made the Middle Shannon and its tributaries the finest wildlife habitat in the country. This may be seen in the winter months, when it becomes a wetland of prime importance and is visited by an enormous number of geese, wild swans and ducks, crowding in from the frozen wastes of Greenland, Iceland and Siberia. Widgeon, pochard and tufted duck can be numbered in thousands. There are constant flurries of motion up and down the river. Sometimes this is due to the shifting levels of the river water as the Shannon, driven by sharp breezes or gales, rolls and swirls, creating new eddy pools and lagoons. At other times it is due to the panic aroused by shooting from boats, as wildfowlers invade the area and frighten the feeding flocks. The Shannon is not yet a protected wildlife habitat.

After the bird migration at the end of March and the callows begin to dry out with the approach of summer, grass grows freely and clusters of wild flowers show riotous colour. Grassy tussocks and hummocks provide havens for the native breeding birds, the lapwing, snipe and corncrake among others. The waders, coot, teal, mallard and moorhen frequent the reed beds, while overhead, the seagull, heron and cormorant patrol the watercourse.

The river continues to wind sluggishly over its spongy underlay. Its banks are fringed with reeds and beyond their quaking fronds, frequented by reed buntings and water rails, the moist marshy fields are full of a myriad of insects and small mammals. It curves in large arcs and the navigational channel is well marked. Yet this stretch of water has a remote and dismal look, not seen since the emergence of the hillside river from the fields of Golath. Houses are few and widely separated. Access from the distant roads is difficult and possible only to the hiker. Nature has remained unchanged in these ancient river meadows for centuries, and water, soil and insect, bird and mammal life, have formed a sympathetic and immutable bond of their own.

The river continues to curve in long slow bends and the navigational markers increase in number to offset the hazards of boats drifting into sodden fields during flooding and becoming grounded. There are few trees. Sections of the river margins are deeply reed-fringed, and mooring places are almost non-existent. The channel forks to form the small Wren Island and some distance farther on winds around a larger spit of land called Long Island, a popular fishing venue. This island was man-made when a navigational channel was cut on the west shore to bypass the deep easterly curve in the river. At a later period the canal was abandoned and the river reverted to its natural role as the navigational channel. The island affords some mooring space at its tip and, close to the point at which the canal joins it on the southern side is a rocky protuberance, a mound of heaped stone and clay, abutting the east bank, called the Three Counties Pile. As the name implies, it is regarded as the meeting-point of three counties – Roscommon, Westmeath and Offaly.

From this point the Shannon flows in a south-westerly direction, curving around the small island of Inisalee, passing through soggy fields with low hedges and some houses built well back from the assaults of the river floods, near which a sprinkling of cattle graze. For a short distance it flows rapidly on a straight course, passing a stretch of boulders on its eastern shore. It then takes a sharp curve westwards and meanders south in a rough semi-circle. Skirting river meadows and spreading into lakelike pools, it winds around its most distinctive and ancient monastic settlement - that of Clonmacnois.

Here, on a bleak and desolate hill on the Leinster shore, a religious foundation was established by St. Ciarán in the middle of the 6th century, about 548 A.D. He had already built a small abbey on Inis Ainghin in Loch Ree, but forsaking his austere cell and giving the building into the care of his disciples, he travelled down the Shannon with a few companions and eventually chose this remote and bare height for what turned out to be the centre of his life's work.

He died very shortly afterwards but his zealous band of followers developed the monastic site, attracting a large student population in the following centuries, enlarging and enriching its work and its group of buildings.

Yet the history of the foundation which lasted for a thousand years has not, on the whole, been a peaceful or contemplative one. On the contrary, calamity, both natural and man-made, threatened its existence from the 7th century onwards. Its houses, made of wood, had to be constantly rebuilt because of the devastation caused by fire and storm. Disease took its toll of the inhabitants. Its very size and particularly, the artistic and scholarly work for which its fame became widespread, - statuary, monumental

Athlone Castle

Church Street, Athlone

Athlone Lock

Athlone Weir

The Flooded Shannon

Teampall Doulin, Clonmacnois

St. Finian's Church and McCarthy's Tower

King John's Castle

The jetty at Clonmacnois

Wildfowl

and inscribed grave slabs, altar crosses and high crosses, altar vessels in gold and silver, shrines, manuscripts and books, notably Leabhar na hUidhri (The Book of the Dun Cow), and the Annals of Clonmacnois – attracted raiders, brigands and thieves. The harassment of the Connacht and Munster tribes, the savage assaults of the Norsemen, and the continual plundering of the Normans, eventually brought about the decline of the monastic foundation. Damaged by storm, it was finally ransacked in 1553 by a troop of English soldiers from the garrison at Athlone.

Abandoned totally for a period, it is now a national monument. Its seven churches and the remains of a cathedral, built in stone from the 10th century onwards, its High Crosses and Round Towers, and a series of sepulchral slabs covering many centuries of its existence, draw thousands of visitors. Amenities such as, a Tourist Information Office, a book and souvenir centre, a museum of statuary and murals, and a car park, have been added.

The Shannon ripples beneath the hill where a jetty provides mooring for boats. It is wide and flooding and its callows are waterlogged and sodden. Above it, to the left of the monastic ruins, a second hill bears the gaunt incongruous hulk of a Norman castle. It is known as King John's Castle and was named after the English King John. Erected in the beginning of the 13th century, when the building of castles became the symbol of Norman occupation, it survived until the 1640s, when it was destroyed during the Cromwellian campaign.

Though the choice of site for the ancient and sacred city may seem odd today, as it stands bare and derelict on its windswept hill in the complex of bog, river and marshland that surrounds the Shannon, at the time it was selected, it must have seemed an apt choice for it occupies part of the most solid ground in the area. It is here that the eiscir riada meets the river. One of the chief residues of the Ice Age, it is a long curved sequence of wide and solid ridges which form,with the Bog of Allen, the most distinctive features of the landscape of the Midlands. The ridges are composed of impacted gravel and sand that mark the courses of rivers formed beneath the glaciers. When the covering mounds and slabs of ice melted away, the sandy river gorges became exposed to erosion. Denuded of their glacial blanket, they were stranded above the level of the surrounding countryside.

As a raised plateau, the eiscir riada was used as the main travel artery, or Sli Mór, between the kingdom of Meath and that of Connacht. Traversed by pilgrims, traders, soldiers and monks, it formed a natural boundary line in ancient and Christian Ireland, dividing the country into halves – Leath Cuinn, the northern half, and Leath Mogha, the southern half, both of these names being rooted in the titles, Connacht and Munster. It was here, at its junction with the Shannon, that Ciarán laid the foundation of the great religious city of Clonmacnois, giving it an approach by land and water.

As if to offset the silent isolation of the monastic ruins, a stark silhouette against the vault of sky, giving the onlooker a sense of awe, tinctured with loneliness and even fear, the callows in the bends of the river give sanctuary to birds in the winter months – wild swans, white-fronted geese, teal, widgeon and tufted duck. The constant movement of the flocks, their flutters and quacks, the aerial spirals and the skeins of sudden flight, lend sound and motion to the cold grey skyline. In the summer, the river meadows, drying out, sprout lush grass dotted with a myriad of wildflowers, and give the bare landscape bands of soft, breeze-fanned colour over which meadow pipits, skylarks and corncrakes flit and feed and voice their alarm notes.

Flowing away from Clonmacnois and its small mooring jetty sited below the ruins of the Norman castle, the Shannon continues to wind through very flat terrain, seeping into the margins and spreading out in lakelike pools. Its banks are largely free of trees and vegetation particularly on the Roscommon shore. Curving deeply to the west, it forks its channel to form Devenish Island which has a wooded shore, repeated on the Leinster bank by stands of trees. It then streams directly south to Shannonbridge where it divides again to form the grassy wooded Long Island just upstream of the bridge. A short distance downstream of the bridge, it reaches the end of the long seventy-mile Roscommon shore and passes into County Galway.

Shannonbridge, six miles from Clonmacnois, is the longest bridge on the river. It has sixteen arches and dates from 1757. Almost a century later in 1845, an opening span was installed as an aid to navigation during a period of busy commercial trading. In 1961, trading ceased, giving way to pleasure boats and holiday cruising. The opening section of the bridge was reconstructed in 1984 and turned into a fixed span, an arrangement sponsored by the Offaly and Roscommon County Councils. Like Athlone, the bridge and village are built on a solid ridge of the eiscir riada and provide a crossing into the province of Connacht.

This factor led to the erection of a grim, three-storey blockhouse on the west bank of the river, overlooking the bridge. It is a remnant of the line of fortifications built in the Napoleonic era from 1800 onwards, in preparation for an expected French invasion. Equipped with batteries, it was supported by a gun emplacement, sited on Long Island upstream of the bridge.

The harbour master's house, erected in the last century, a preserved building like the blockhouse, is beside the bridge on the east bank, facing the long street of the village. Its previous occupants stamped and registered the barges and cargo boats which were then so much a feature of the river scene. Today, they have been replaced by cruisers which tie up at the long quays stretching north and south of the bridge on the Offaly shore.

There are amenity areas throughout, picnic and seating areas and a car park. An interesting addition is the metal exhibit downstream of the bridge, standing alone in a designed plot. It consists of two large pieces of mechanism taken from the redundant opening span of the bridge, painted a light grey and placed on broad cubes of concrete to form a distinctive piece of modern sculpture.

Downstream of the bridge, the Shannon streams sharply east and, in the bend, receives its most important western tributary, the River Suck. A significant river system in itself, draining large areas of Roscommon and Galway, it rises in Loch O'Flynn, north of Castlerea in County Roscommon, and flows for sixty-seven miles in a south-easterly direction passing into County Galway in the first section of its course. It streams through five small towns and has over ten named tributaries and attendant rivulets. In its early stretches, it is broad and fast flowing, it becomes sluggish, narrow and deep later, with bogland and callows on both banks. From its confluence with the Shannon, the Suck is navigable for only two miles of its course. Its water levels vary. It is muddy and constricted by shallows, shoals and small islands. A Bord na Mona railway bridge, built for the transport of peat, crosses its channel through the surrounding bog. In the last century the Ballinasloe Canal was constructed in this area of bog for the purposes of trade with the Grand Canal at Shannon Harbour. No longer in use, much of it has been filled in. With Ballinasloe, the nearest town to the Shannon only four miles away, a project to widen and dredge the fords on this short stretch of the Suck has begun in order to make it navigable for river cruisers. Running largely over a limestone terrain, the Suck with its network of tributaries makes a wide and valuable angling area for trout and coarse fish. To complement this abundant wild fishery, part of which may be damaged by the dredging of the river, the Office of the Board of Works proposes to build a salmon fishery downstream of Ballinasloe.

A second natural role occupied by the Suck and its environment is that of a 'wetland'. Its isolation and

Shannonbridge

Rachra, the adjoining village

The blockhouse at Shannonbridge

Long Island, Shannonbridge

The flooding Suck

Blackwater Bog, west of the Shannon

The ruins of Clonfert Cathedral

Blackwater Bog, east of the Shannon

ESB powerhouse, Shannonbridge

Bord na Mona railway bridge

The Blackwater River

The River Brosna (left) joins the Grand Canal

bleakness, its waters and food supply make it an important winter haven for birds. Vast flocks of widgeon, Whooper and Berwick swans, the lapwing and the golden plover, frequent its muddy banks, feeding on the sluggish and fertile stream and on the adjoining callows.

A short distance inland on the boggy west shore are the ruins of an ancient piece of architecture, the Cathedral of Clonfert. A monastic settlement, it was founded by Brendan the Navigator in 563 A.D. The doorway, finely designed, and the well-preserved door, subtly carved in a variety of natural objects - human and animal heads,leaves and foliage – is an example of the Irish Romanesque style of the 12th century onwards. Behind the cathedral is a graveyard with a walk of ancient yew trees and nearby is the derelict bishop's palace which dates from the 17th century.

In this wilderness of peatland on both sides of the Shannon, lies the second of the great bog farms surrounding the river. Blackwater Bog, or Uisce Dubh, centred on both the Offaly and Galway shores, is the largest in the country. The terrain in this section of the Shannon reaches the lowest level of its course. The only heights to be seen are the long spiny ridges of the eiscir riada which run like a sinuous backbone through the landscape, the only solid ground in this waterlogged expanse of peat, pools, sphagnum moss and dark fossils of oak and yew.

Flowing swiftly from Shannonbridge, the river streams into a south-easterly bend, passing, on the east shore,the ESB powerhouse to which the harvested peat is delivered. The outflow of hot water from the powerhouse makes this stretch a popular fishing venue. Downstream,and quite close to it, is the Bord na Mona railway bridge, the second in the area, the other being on the River Suck. A long concrete construction, it crosses the river's very wide watercourse at this point,as it streams between open and exposed banks, from which flat fields roll away to distant woods on the west shore.

Downstream, the Blackwater River, narrow and slow moving, flows through the bog from the east. Thickening beds of reeds bend and quiver in the breeze. Rush, bramble and sedge suck and drag at the water as it passes through a stretch once shallow and rocky, but which is now dredged clean of impediment. The hoarse gurgle of a snipe erupts from a tussock of heather as it flees into the shelter of the bog. In the upper air the cry of a kestrel rakes the wind while it scans the low banks for small vulnerable mammals or unprotected nests.

The river divides to round Lehinch Island where there is an unmarked shoal close to the fringe of reeds on the Offaly shore, and a smaller island just south of it, before reaching the mouth of the tree-lined waterway leading to Shannon Harbour, a quarter of a mile inland. This waterway, over a hundred yards long, is a merging of the River Brosna and the Grand Canal, both of which, flowing through the boggy terrain of Offaly arrive in the vicinity of the Shannon side by side. The Brosna rises in Loch Ennell in County Westmeath and has a run of over fifteen miles to Shannon Harbour. It flows southwest through the vast harvesting area of the Blackwater bog which gives it a residue of peat mould and sediment. Draining a wide area of morass and swamp, it flows sluggishly over the second half of its journey to the Shannon, entering the same area as the Grand Canal which streams through the Central Plain from Dublin. Water meadows line the river's banks in this area and flooding occurs in winter, providing a haven for a large number of wildfowl. A fine fishing river, it yields trout, coarse fish and a small run of salmon. As it reaches its junction with the Grand Canal, it is wide and slow-flowing with scenic tree-lined banks. Close to the mouth of the canal, it deposits a large mound of peat silt.

The Grand Canal, an ambitious project designed to promote trade between Dublin and the Shannon region, was begun in 1765 and opened in 1805. Its terminus close to the Shannon was called Shannon Harbour where a spacious basin, warehouses and a hotel were built. It has thirty-six locks on its course, the 36th and last opens just above its confluence with the River Brosna which adds a hazard to the merging in the form of a bar of peat silt. In order to bypass this obstruction, it is necessary for craft to remain close to the canal's east bank. On its approach to the Shannon, the canal passes beneath a narrow, humpbacked stone bridge with one high arch and flows directly into the large harbour in which the 35th lock is sited. When trade flourished here in past decades, barges, cargo boats, eel boats, turf boats and passenger steamers plied up and down the canal, to and from the river. Since trading ceased, however, the canal port has lost its initiative. The hotel and warehouses are empty and unused, seeming to resign themselves to inevitable decay with swaths of ivy foraging around their windows and birds wheeling in to roost. Instead of the previous bustle, noise and excitement, and sense of continuous activity, there is an air of drab monotony in which the small quiet village at the rear seems to sleep.

The harbour, busy in the summer months, is full of craft of all shapes and sizes, from colourful large cruisers to rowboats, including an old derelict barge, symbol of the past. Otherwise, it is a boatyard, silent and motionless, with all craft tied up, and the only visible movements coming from a sprinkling of fishermen passing along the towpaths on both banks.

At the junction of the Shannon and the combined stream of the Grand Canal and the Brosna, the river becomes wide and open. It was at this section the Ballinasloe Canal originated, and remnants of its existence still remain. A lock called Fanning's Lock was installed at the east bank, and a wooden bridge was constructed across the river to the Galway shore to enable the towpath horses to cross. With the coming of steam boats the bridge was removed, but a segment of it remains connected to the small Bullock Island.

Streaming away from Shannon Harbour, the river continues its journey past a long tract of callows, notably on the Galway shore, where lush grass grows in summer, and flocks of river birds flit and skim over the watercourse. In winter, expansive flooding invades the fields providing a feeding ground for wildfowl. Up to three miles downstream, the river reaches the climax of a great south-easterly bend which began at Shannonbridge, and turns westward to pass beneath the bridge at Banagher.

Originally a six-arch bridge with a lifting span, it was erected in 1843 to replace an earlier stone bridge which figured prominently in the Jacobite War of 1691. In 1971 it was altered and widened. Stone parapets were replaced by metal railings and the lifting span gave way to a fixed section. The bridge provides a crossing between Offaly and Galway, and one, that like Athlone and Shannonbridge, was considered important enough to merit special fortifications which are still in evidence around it. The circular stone bulwark of Cromwell's Castle, so named because it was built on the site of an old foundation of the Cromwellian period of 1649–1651, gazes grimly from the Galway shore at the west end of the bridge. Nearby, also on the Connacht side, is a Martello tower, built in 1812. Both buildings were furnished with artillery during the years of possible invasion.

The old castle stands upon the Canal Bank, so named because a canal was built here in the early 19th century to bypass the shoals at Banagher ford. When, however, a general reconstruction of the Shannon's bridges was undertaken in the 1840s, the canal fell into disuse and was eventually filled in.

On the Leinster side of the river, a military battery called Fort Eliza, is sited downstream. Closer to the bridge, also on the east side, are the ruins of the Old Barracks which housed soldiers and artillery up to the 1860s. Behind it, is the old Waller malthouse, leading to Waller Quay downstream of the bridge, the historic stopping-place for the commercial traffic of bygone decades.

Banagher, or Beannchar, meaning 'pointed rocks', is a quiet uncluttered small town with a long curving main street which includes cafés, pubs, hotels and guesthouses. Noted in the past for busy market days and a great yearly fair, it now relies on light industry and its potential as a river port for progress and prosperity.

Shannon harbour on the Grand Canal

Banagher Marina

Banagher Bridge and Harbour

The 36th Lock on the Grand Canal

Cromwell's Castle

The Martello Tower

Banagher

Meelick Lock

The Little Brosna River

Meelick Weir

Meelick Quay with Martello Tower in the background

Connacht Harbour

To this end it has developed a spacious marina and a recently built harbour with mooring quays, walkways and seating accommodation, backed by an amenity area and a car park. A number of wooden jetties add to the facilities and rows of pleasure craft tie up here. All are sited upstream of the bridge, close to the pier. Close to the marina are the buildings, offices, and boat bays of two hire-boat companies, Silver Line and Carrick Craft whose boats and facilities have contributed much to the popularity of the venue. Another contributory factor was the regulation of the water levels by the building of the marina which was designed for this purpose so as to offset the hazards of the seasonal flooding of the Shannon in this area.

From Banagher the river flows due west. Its current becomes faster, the slope of the terrain deeper as it enters a new and tortuous phase of its course. Forking continually, it streams into constricted channels, creates islands and forms shallows before merging its waters again. It passes the reed girt island of Inishee at which Shamrock Cruisers have a hire-boat base and marina. Streaming on towards Shannon Grove and Muchinish, it curves southwards with a fast and hazardous current. As it approaches Meelick, the watercourse spreads widely in flooding periods. There is no bridge at Meelick and no crossing although a section upstream of the small quay on the west bank, known as the Keelogue shallows could have been used in this way when the river was low. Downstream of the quay a stile and towpath lead to the Meelick weir and sluices.

In this area the river has become a lake, divided by two islands into three channels. The central channel is also the navigational channel, a canal leading to the large Meelick or Victoria lock, sited between the two islands. Both canal and lock were constructed n 1843. Upstream of the lock are long, wooden mooring jetties on the east side. From the lock, a towpath leads on the west side to the tip of the central island from which Meelick quay and weir are visible. It is even possible to cross to the weir from this vantage point by using a narrow boardwalk supported by metal bars just two feet above the watercourse, if one is intrepid enough. This broad channel lapping the Galway shore is not navigable to cruisers because of its shallowness, its shoals, and the number of islets which dot its course, as it streams south of the hill upon which Meelick church and graveyard are sited. The third channel on the Offaly shore is crossed by a long footbridge which connects it with the central island. Though wide and with a brisk current, this channel is also unnavigable, except to rowboats. In the last century there was a canal and lock, known as Hamilton's Lock, in this section, but both were replaced by the existing arrangement.

A short distance down from the footbridge the Little Brosna river flows into the Shannon on the Offaly shore. Important from the point of view of ecology and fishing, the Little Brosna rises in County Tipperary. Flowing through Offaly, it passes the town of Birr and, from this area to the Shannon, is encircled by callows on both banks. This circumstance makes its floodplain one of the most extensive along the Shannon, and also one of its finest 'wetlands', together with the two islands facing it on the opposite bank at Meelick, Big Island and Friar's Island. A wildlife sanctuary in which shooting is forbidden, it provides a winter home for huge flocks of wildfowl and swarms of smaller birds. It is also a fine fishing river with trout, coarse fish and a run of salmon, as is the entire stretch of the Meelick watercourse.

Meelick is the fourth site on the Shannon in which fortifications were erected to guard against a French invasion from 1796 onwards. Some of these stoneworks are still in place. A Martello Tower, still in good condition with a gun platform on the roof, stands on the summit of the island across the channel from the quay at Meelick. On Inisherky Island, north of the lock, a battery and blockhouse were built for the purpose of defending the ford of Keelogue, then the most shallow crossing point on the river.

Both sides of the river may be reached from Banagher - Meelick, by a turning off the road to Eyrecourt, and the Offaly shore by a sideroad from the village of Lusmagh. Downstream of Meelick Church, an embankment approached by a mile-long towpath has been constructed. It has pumping stations, is backed by a short canal, and runs close to the Galway shoreline towards Portumna, in an effort to control flooding in this area.

All three channels of the river merge downstream of Meelick Lock where there is a mound of stone and clay topped by a small tree close to the east bank. This landmark is regarded as the point at which three provinces meet – Connacht, Leinster and Munster, as the Offaly shore gives way to that of Tipperary.

The river narrows as it curves to the west and bends southward, its banks thickly fenced with reeds. It winds past Ballymacegan Island at which there are mooring facilities, then veers widely again between thickets of reeds on both banks, with woodland and trees farther inland. It swirls around the sinuous wooded Long Island and immediately downstream of it, Portland Island. Close to Long Island is White's Ford where, in 1602, O'Sullivan Beare, the Kerry chieftain and his followers crossed the river on their ill-fated journey to O'Rourke's castle in County Leitrim.

The river winds onward, passing Herring Island and Munster Harbour on the east shore, and on the west, Connacht Harbour, sited on a short canal, with the Emerald Star hire-boat marina just below it. The canal streams into the river just north of the bridge. Moorings are available in this complex and at the quay nearby.

The bridge at Portumna has four spans, one of which is a lifting span, sited on the west bank, which must be raised for all craft. The bridge was built in 1911 as a replacement for a former wooden bridge. It is of modern design, made of concrete, topped by metal parapets and resting on cement columns.

A quarter of a mile inland is the small market town of Portumna in south Galway, from which the bridge takes its name. Situated in a triangle formed by the Shannon and the northern margin of Loch Derg, it has become a centre for tourism and angling in this area. Its most distinctive feature, however, is the splendid Forest Park which has been established on the former Harewood estate by the Forestry Commission. The park, a protected area for birds and small mammals, is five hundred acres in extent, with woods of beech, oak and alder, a rich variety of plants and wild flowers and a number of scenic streams. Its wildlife includes fallow deer, badgers, pine martens, foxes and other species. Beyond the park, on its western shoreline, a section of Loch Derg has been set aside and developed as a wildfowl sanctuary. A group of small islands which dot the northern part of the lake, provide essential nesting sites for mallard, coot and shelduck, and for smaller birds, plover and lapwing. Close to the islands, a large area is flooded each year to provide feeding grounds for waders, gulls and terns. For the bird watcher and the naturalist, an observation tower, sited in the park and overlooking the lake, adds an endless source of interest.

Here also are vestiges of history. Portumna Castle, a Jacobean mansion, built in 1605 and destroyed by fire in 1826, is still an imposing edifice. Constructed for defence purposes, it is approached by three gardens, the two inner ones surrounded by stone walls which include deep oval gateways and small blockhouses. The castle is presently undergoing restoration by the Office of the Board of Works. Also within the park are the preserved remains of a Dominican Priory established in 1426 and destroyed during the Cromwellian campaign of 1641, standing bare and austere against its dark background of trees.

In the south-east corner of the park, a harbour has been recently constructed which provides ample space and mooring facilities for craft. Beside it, are an amenity area and a car park. Jutting out from the harbour, wedges of reeds wade into the wide watercourse, and splendid scenic views of the northern section of Loch Derg may be obtained. East of the harbour area, the Shannon curves away from Portumna Bridge, swirling around the small island in its channel on both sides of the bridge. Its watercourse is broad as it seeps into the soft verges, its current remains brisk. Its banks are thickly reed-strewn, as it flows through low-lying fields cluttered with brushwood and dense vegetation to reach the northern margin of Loch

Portumna

Derg. On its left, on the brow of a hill, are the ruins of Ballynasheera Castle.

The Shannon approaches the lake through a deep basin-like depression. Portumna Harbour is on the west side, on the verge of the Forest Park, while the Bay of Terryglass stretches to the east. Between them the Shannon passes Derry Point and streams into Loch Derg.

Portumna Bridge

Emerald Star Hire Base

The bird sanctuary at Loch Derg

Portumna Castle

The ruins of Ballynasheera Castle

Portumna Harbour

Chapter Eight

IN LOCH DERG (LOCH DERG-DHEIRC) THE SHANNON REACHES THE LARGEST EXPANSION of its protracted course to the sea. As the river merges with the lake at Derry Point, the latter spreads widely on both shorelines – to the narrow angular Bay of Terryglass in the east and in the west, the smooth, spacious marina-like breadth of Cloondavaun Bay, making the northern boundary one of the widest sections of the lake – a distance of eight miles. From Cregg Point at the southern margin of Cloondavaun Bay, to Hare Island at Church Bay, both on the western shoreline, it stretches for most of its length in a sinuous twisting arc with few peninsulas, and is not more than two to three miles wide at any point. South of Hare Island, it reaches its widest span, measured from Scarriff Bay in the west to Dromineer on the eastern coastline, and is reckoned at thirteen miles.

Twenty four miles long, Loch Derg has an area of fifty square miles as it stretches between the Tipperary margin in the east and in the west, dividing its shoreline, so that the northern section is in County Galway, up to but excluding the village of Whitegate, and the southern section is in County Clare.

Its colourful and dramatic name, the Lake of the Red Eye, appears to have no relevance to this scenic and beautiful watercourse. According to legend, it stems from ancient pre-Christian days, and the tense relationships that often existed between kings and bards. The story describes a macabre episode in which Eochy MacLuchta, a warrior king who had lost an eye in battle, welcomed Ahirny, a well-known poet and musician whose sharp tongue and scathing comments often inspired fear in his hosts. As he was about to depart, Eochy promised him a gift and in a misguided and grandiose gesture, offered anything the bard chose to name. Ahirny, contemptuous of the boastful old man, asked malevolently for his remaining eye. Bound by his promise, Eochy removed the eye and gave it to his callous tormentor. Led by his attendants to the lake, he began to bathe the bleeding cavity and the water ran red with his blood. And so the lake was christened – Loch Derg-Dheirc, the Lake of the Red Eye. Today, it mirrors a more peaceful harmony of colours, the brown, blue and green, of mountain, sky and field.

A solution lake like Loch Ree, it rests for three-quarters of its length on a bed of carboniferous limestone, and in its final quarter, its southern extremity, on the residues of Silurian and Devonian rocks, where the Shannon has carved its way through non-soluble shale to reach the sill at Killaloe. Its depths vary enormously, influenced as they are by three major factors. The first of these is the annual flooding from the Upper Shannon, from Athlone to Portumna, and especially from Shannon Harbour and the Meelick watercourse, including the floodplains of the two rivers, the Brosna and the Little Brosna. Flowing through the bog farms of Offaly in their diverse courses, they carry with them a constant run of turf mould and clay. Peaty brown in colour, this copious torrent of water affects the levels of the lake. In depositing its silt in the shallows and on waterside plants such as Phragmites, however, it tends to increase the natural food supply for the crustaceans of plankton so necessary for fish life.

A second consideration is the effect of heavy continuous rainfall which results in an immediate and enormous raising of water levels, estimated as reaching up to 30 cm. in particularly strong downfalls. And a third factor, the most important one since it is a permanent arrangement, is the lake's role as a major storage reservoir for the hydro-electric station at Ardnacrusha, where large volumes of water are essential and are drawn continuously from the lake, thereby causing variations in its levels, although the navigational minimum of a depth of five feet is always maintained. Generally speaking, the deeper parts of the lake run through the central section and in the south where a depth of up to 30 metres is common, particularly close to Parker Point in the south-east and the Scilly Island close by. A shallower area spreads from Mount Shannon on the Clare shoreline to Dromineer on the east margin. Close to the verges of the lake, the water is, for the most part, very shallow.

Loch Derg's shorelines are not only very long, they are also convoluted and very irregular. Stratas of limestone are more abundant here than by Loch Ree. Layers of glacial debris are thinner, while areas of boulder clay become less frequent, resulting in a more fertile soil and better plant growth, especially in the centre and the south. Flat arable fields, mixed with patches of bogland, and interspersed with low hills, surround the north-western margin, rising in graded heights as they follow the shoreline to the peaks of Sliabh Aughty and Sliabh Bernagh on the Clare shore and matched on the opposite side by the slopes and summits of the Arra mountains, the Silvermines and Sliabh Kimalta in the Tipperary hinterland. Much of the shoreline is pleasantly wooded, with yew, arbutus and white beam as well as the familiar oak, hazel and alder, particularly in the east, where green and brown copses hug the inlets at Slevoir and Gortmore in the north, Brookfield, Urra and Hazel Points in the centre, and the tree-lined Youghal Bay and Parker Point in the south. In the west, the woods of the Forest Park, Bonaveen and Rossmore Bay, make a scenic break in the monotonous sequence of cove and creek.

The dramatic beauty of Loch Derg, as it streams onwards and narrows beneath the green terraced hills on both sides into a deep, canyon–like declivity. is as unexpected as it is breath-taking. Nothing in the long journey the Shannon has already traversed, from the bare slopes of the Cuilceagh mountains to the flat, peaty water-meadows of the Central Plain, gives an inkling of the panoramic beauty that invests the southern half of the lake. Large bays add to the feeling of grandeur, light and space evoked by the rising slopes of the surrounding hills - from the smooth, semi-circular expanse of Cloondavaun Bay flowing away from the Portumna shore, and the sweep of Scarriff Bay to Youghal Bay in the south.

The bay at Cloondavaun, almost a small lake in itself, as it spreads from the massed tree line of the Forest Park into the Galway hinterland, is a calm and scenic watercourse with a number of islets of which the Silver group is the best known. A bird sanctuary, its solitude is broken only by the shifting movements of birds, nesting in the tussocks, hummocks and clumped water-weeds, such as the great-crested grebes, reed buntings, terns and swans, or wading in the streamy currents, the coots, and mallards, moorhens and tufted duck. The grey heron, brooding solemnly on its craggy, stick-like legs, patrols in a ceaseless hunt for unwary fish, while seagulls skim and spiral and cast freakish images on the water surface.

Into the north-west corner of the bay, a shoreline beset with rocks, shoals and thickets of reeds, flows one of the few tributaries of Loch Derg, the Kilcrow/Killimor River which winds south from central

The Shannon flows into Loch Derg

Galway, and is joined by two smaller streams, the Lisduff and the Cappagh, as it meanders to the lake. Based on limestone soil, these rivers have good stocks of fish but tend to become choked with weeds in the summer.

Rounding the southern margin of the bay, passing the semi-ruined castle of Clondagough, the

A scenic view of Loch Derg

Parker Point – deep water

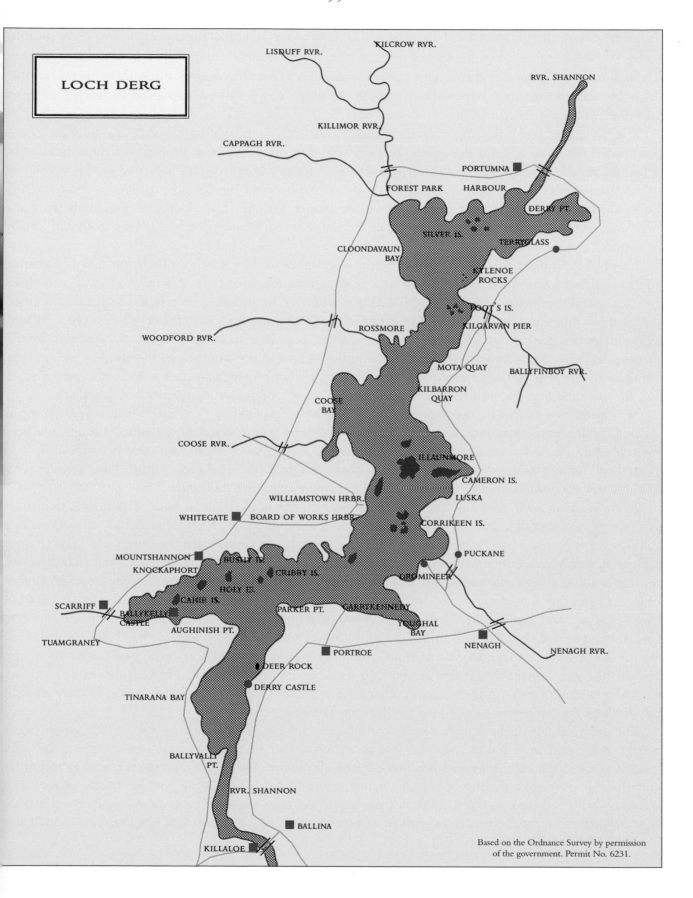

LOCH DERG

KILCROW RVR.

LISDUFF RVR.

RVR. SHANNON

KILLIMOR RVR.

CAPPAGH RVR.

PORTUMNA

FOREST PARK   HARBOUR

DERRY PT.

SILVER IS.

TERRYGLASS

CLOONDAVAUN
BAY

KYLENOE
ROCKS

WOODFORD RVR.

ROSSMORE

FOOT'S IS.

KILGARVAN PIER

MOTA QUAY

BALLYFINBOY RVR.

KILBARRON
QUAY

COOSE
BAY

COOSE RVR.

ILLAUNMORE

CAMERON IS.

LUSKA

WILLIAMSTOWN HRBR.

WHITEGATE   BOARD OF WORKS HRBR

CORRIKEEN IS.

MOUNTSHANNON

BUSHY IS.

PUCKANE

KNOCKAPHORT

CRIBBY IS.

DROMINEER

HOLY IS.

SCARRIFF

CAHIR IS.

PARKER PT.

CARRYKENNEDY

BALLYKEELLY
CASTLE

YOUGHAL
BAY

AUGHINISH PT.

TUAMGRANEY

PORTROE

NENAGH

NENAGH RVR.

DEER ROCK

DERRY CASTLE

TINARANA BAY

BALLYVALLY
PT.

RVR. SHANNON

BALLINA

KILLALOE

Based on the Ordnance Survey by permission
of the government. Permit No. 6231.

shoreline curves sharply into the narrow central section of the lake, making a deep arched recess of inlet and cove which is marked by a grove of trees, as it leads southward to the small Rossmore Bay and quay. Though it is a wide tree-lined area with a broad pier, and is a favourite fishing venue, there are no facilities for boats, and no amenities. Exposed to the south and south-east winds, mooring and anchorage are risky, and shelter non-existent.

The Woodford River flowing from the village of Woodford, four and a half miles to the west, enters the bay a short distance from the quay. The river which forms a marina at Woodford Bridge and can be fished for trout, is narrow, shallow in parts, and in the summer very weedy. Boats have used it in the past to bring supplies to the Woodford mills but, though a channel has been dredged to allow access to it from Loch Derg, no attempt has yet been made to develop it farther. The river is clotted with trees and vegetation in many places and is difficult of access, but in its back lies, pools and ledges, trout can usually be found.

South of Rossmore Bay the shoreline recedes once more, until it reaches the rocky, heavily indented and reed-fringed Coose Bay which bulges irregularly into the landscape. A small waterway, called the Coose River, empties itself into the bay. Close to its southern boundary, a stretch of trees breaks the stony reed-strewn margins, as the shoreline approaches Williamstown. Neither a town nor a village, Williamstown is denoted by a cluster of buildings, a hire-boat base and a harbour set in the rugged terrain by the lake shore. The original harbour dates from the 1820s and was built to cater for anglers and tourists, attracted to the area by the fine salmon fishing for which Loch Derg was then noted. Steamers plied to and fro for some decades, and when this trade ceased, the harbour declined and fell into neglect.

At present, it is owned by the Shannon Castle Line who have set it up as a hire-boat base with repair shops. The harbour is spacious with wooden walkways and scenic views of the lake. Though in a very sheltered position, it has a narrow entrance and may be subject to swells and breakers in east winds.

A short distance to the south off the same roadway, the Board of Works has built another harbour with a long entry channel, cement walkways, berths and ample space for anchorage.

From Williamstown, at which there are no amenities, the nearest village being Whitegate, two miles to the west, the shoreline curves to make a number of rocky bays of which Church Bay with access to a fishing area is best known. Beyond these, fertile undulating farmlands form the hinterland. The thinner soil of the northern section, with its patches of bog and swamp, has given way to grass and rich meadow, to houses and grazing cattle and sheep. Mountshannon, an attractive village, sheltered by a background of hills, with pleasing houses and a tree-lined street, is sited close to the lake. A very popular venue for trout fishing, its pier and harbour were built in 1845 and used for commercial purposes, until the 1960s when such trading ceased. Boating and fishing began to increase in popularity and, in the 1970s, the Board of Works developed and extended the harbour, providing slipways, and adding to the facilities for moorings and anchorages. Since then, it has grown into a successful fishing, sailing, and racing venue, and is a favourite halting place for hire-boats and other craft, especially in the trout fishing season in early May. In the 1990s additional berths were added by Shannon Development.

The enlargement of the harbour gives commodious and secure shelter to craft, except when heavy storms break and high waves roll over the outer and newer sections. In gale-type weather, the safer moorings are in the inner part which is in the lee of a protective wall. Landscaped, with seating and other amenities, it overlooks clusters of islands, including the Cribby, the Young and the Bushy groups. Inis Cealtra, or Holy Island, is but a short distance away and boat trips to it are available. Two miles from Mountshannon, along the western shoreline of Scarriff Bay, is the small quay at Knockaphort, which also has sailings to Inis Cealtra.

The shoreline, as it continues onward, stretches boldly into the Clare hinterland to reach its most westerly point in the small town of Scarriff, situated on a hilltop about one mile from the bay. Scarriff, or Scairb, a 'stony shallow spot', referring to a fording place on the Scarriff river, is and was a market town of some note and, until recent times, retained an old weighbridge in the main street. It is a well-known, coarse fishing centre. The river gushes rapidly beneath a bridge on the south side of the town, and, at one time, was navigable only when the water levels of the lake were high. Dredged in the 1840s, when a harbour was constructed, its entrance is on the south side of the river to which it is connected by a short canal. It is fully navigable to this point. Pleasantly landscaped, the harbour provides moorings for cruisers and other craft. A second facility is the Tuamgraney quay, a short distance south of the harbour, and formed on a curve of the Graney river which flows into the bay.

The village of Tuamgraney, less than half a mile from the quay, is a tranquil secluded place with historical associations. St. Crónan is said to have built a monastery here in the 7th century. The church, which is still in use, is one of the oldest in the country. Part of its structure is said to belong to the 12th century. Close to the church is a ruined castle of the O'Grady clan and a short distance away is Raheen Wood with stands of ancient oak trees, one of which is named after Brian Boro. Legend says it is one thousand years old. In the small village there is a memorial park dedicated to those who fought in the War of Independence, 1916 to 1922.

At the tip of Scarriff Bay, the shoreline makes a circular bend, swings inward and winds directly east for up to four miles, forming the Ogonnelloe peninsula from which, the lake reverts to the narrow, central type waterway, typical of most of its length. The lake margins are wooded in many places and reed beds follow their irregular course, making access difficult.

Though a number of houses have been built near the lake, pathways to its margins are relatively few. An air of remoteness clings to the area, heightened by the ruins of Ballykelly Castle which stand desolately on a rock-girt spit of island in forgotten isolation. Near it is the larger Cahir Island. Close to the junction of the shoreline with the narrow central channel of the lake, one of the most dangerous obstacles to navigation exists – the Lushing Rocks – and all craft are advised to stand clear of them. Deep water occurs here, especially in the centre of the channel around the Scilly Island and on the east shoreline directly opposite, at Parker Point.

At the narrow tip of the peninsula is Aughinish Point which, with Parker Point, form two of the most distinctive landmarks in the southern section of the lake. Aughinish, though not easily accessible, is noted for its beautiful woods, its nature trails and leafy walks.

The shoreline, rounding the peninsula, passes south, skirting the small Crow Island and then bulging outward in twists and curves to form the narrow Tinerana Bay, in which shallows occur and spits of rock are visible. From this point, the road runs close to the lake shore. Here, the Shannonside and Water Sports Centre provides all amenities for outdoor enthusiasts. Close by, is the Ballycuggeran public park and activity area, leading to Ballyvally Point, two miles farther on, where the Shannon streams out of the lake.

• • • • •

The eastern shoreline of Loch Derg like that of its western counterpart is based on limestone covered by a thin gravelly soil composed of glacial drift. As it approaches the centre and south, the glacial debris decreases, leaving a high content of limestone which makes a fertile soil. Patches of bog occur in the

Trees of the Forest Park

Castlelough Woods

The Kilcrow River

The Cappagh River

Rossmore Quay

Woodford River

Williamstown Harbour

Board of Works Harbour, Williamstown

Mountshannon

Mountshannon Harbour

Scarriff

Scarriff Harbour

northern area but the terrain, in general, consists of grassland, pasture and parkland.

The northern shoreline is carried inland into County Tipperary by the Bay of Terryglass which stretches to the north-east, making this boundary the second widest in the lake. Trees grow in the inlet opposite Derry Point, where the Shannon enters Loch Derg. A white triangular cairn marks the navigational turn for Portumna Harbour, close to the Forest Park which lies due west of the river's mouth. Rocks encompass the bay as it stretches to the north-east. At its tip, the shoreline curves sharply and sweeps towards the south-west, making a deep recession, as it reaches the wooded Slevoir Point, and a short distance farther on, the village and harbour of Terryglass.

A small neat village, a winner of the Tidy Towns competition, Terryglass is sited in a sheltered fold of the bay and possesses the amenities of guest houses, cottages for rent, cafés and shops, and an art and pottery centre established in a converted old church. Close by, is the commodious harbour and slipway, a landscaped seating and picnic area and a car park. Birds frequent the small pools beneath the tree-lined shore, and a panoramic view of the lake reveals itself as it rolls dreamily to Cloondavaun Bay in the west.

Beside the harbour, lie the ruins of Oldcourt, an ancient Norman castle. Dating from the 13th century, it is sited on a hill above the lake, and is now being preserved by the Board of Works.

On the hillside, towering above the harbour, is the distinctive, Roman Catholic Church which is said to possess a relic of the True Cross, an artistic set of Stations of the Cross and some unusual plaques. The religious history of Terryglass dates from the 6th century, when St. Colum founded a monastery on the site now occupied by the church. Famous for its learning in the 9th and 10th centuries, it survived until the 12th century. The Book of Leinster, it is said, was begun here. Raided many times by the Norse and by native tribes, it eventually succumbed to a disastrous fire.

South of Terryglass, the shoreline, marked by reed beds, stands of trees at Gortmore Point, and outcrops of rock at Kylenoe, receives the Ballyfinboy River, on which the nearby village of Ballinderry is sited. It winds past the shoal-girt group of the Foot Islands and on to Kilgarvan Pier. The pier is approached from the south side of the shoals, the channel to the harbour being marked by red and black buoys. A secluded place, it is pleasantly wooded with a cluster of boats tied up in the harbour. It has a car park, a picnic area and other amenities. The harbour is small with, at times, shallow levels of water, and the end wall of the jetty is unsafe in high winds. Fishing and boating are popular activities at this venue.

A tree-lined and scenically beautiful area fringes the shoreline as it leads to Mota Quay, where there is a spacious, wooded amenity area not yet developed. A short distance farther south is Kilbarron Quay, with a small slipway. The shoreline is close to the road and swans dapple in the shimmering watercourse. Woods continue to hug the margins to Belleview Point, south of which is the Goat's Road, a jagged line of rocks, often submerged, which stretches westward into the narrowest width of the lake. The twisting shoreline protrudes east, passing Castletown Bay and on to Luska Quay. A fine viewing point, giving wide vistas of the lake, its wooded inlets and small islands, Luska is reputed to have the earliest of the mayfly hatches which herald the opening of the trout-fishing season in early May.

Continuing to the rocky Urra Point, the wooded shoreline rounds Dromineer Bay and reaches the village and harbour of Dromineer. The largest harbour on the lake with excellent access, Dromineer has been a sailing centre for well over a hundred years. The Yacht Club dates from 1837 and is one of the pioneer sailing clubs in the world. Regattas and boat rallies have convened here for many years. The first harbour was built in 1829 and the quay dates from the 1880s. In 1929, the pier was erected and afterwards given navigational lights and incorporated into a large modernised harbour which, however, is difficult to enter in strong north-westerly winds.

Nowadays, the attractions of Dromineer have widened considerably. There are facilities for children, boating tours, water skiing, and wind surfing. Fishing is popular at this venue, and slipways and car parking facilities are available. Other amenities are the Shannon Sailing Hire-boat base, and a hotel, guest house and shops in the small village which has religious and historical relics of the past. The ruins of a 12th century church stand in the old graveyard, and close to the harbour wall is the ivied shell of a medieval castle, built in the 12th century and destroyed in the 17th, during the Williamite Wars.

The Nenagh River flows into Loch Derg at Dromineer, the only tributary of any note on the eastern shoreline. Rising in the Silvermine mountains, it winds north-east for twenty-eight miles, passing the town of Nenagh. In its upper reaches, it is a fine fishing stream for trout and a small stock of salmon, but as it approaches Loch Derg, its final stretch becomes deep, weedy and sluggish and is largely void of fish.

From Dromineer, the shoreline runs south past the wooded Hazel Point and bites sharply into the lake's margin at Ryan's Point, emerging to drift eastward to form Youghal Bay and the widest section of Loch Derg. Turning sharply at the tip of the bay it swings westward to the harbour of Garrykennedy. A very small village with not more than a dozen houses, it was one of the stations of the Shannon Steamship Company who constructed the harbour in 1829. It is a sheltered harbour with facilities for cruisers and small boats. A narrow entrance, however, makes it difficult to enter or leave in strong north-westerly winds. There is an amenity area and a slipway, and further mooring places have developed in recent years. Garrykennedy Harbour gives access to Youghal Bay which is shallow in parts, with short wooded inlets and narrow creeks. The small Youghal River runs into the bay.

Garrykennedy is the only harbour on this section of the lake, between Youghal Bay and Parker Point. The water is generally deep along this part of the shoreline, as it winds south-west to Parker Point where the greatest depths in the lake are to be found. Here the shoreline joins the constricted central channel, which breaks away from the widely flung bay of Scarriff in the west, and the outward bulge of Youghal Bay in the east, almost at right angles. Its rocky base is composed largely of Silurian strata ringed by red sandstone, giving a type of acid soil which is not conducive to plant life. Flowing through a beautiful scenic gorge, not more than a mile wide, except at the rounded swell of Tinerana Bay, its greatest depth is in the centre. It is fringed by the cliff-like slopes of Sliabh Bernagh, rising to 1,766 feet on the Clare shore and, on the Tipperary side, the Arra mountains of which Tountinna, the highest peak, is 1,500 feet.

The shoreline sweeps directly south, past the foothills of the Arra slopes. From the Look-Out, a landscaped viewing area on a hill-top above Parker Point, a panoramic vista of the lake meets the eye. Just beneath, the bulge of the Point juts into the watercourse, the Scilly Island lies towards the centre, and Aughinish Point, hidden in its woods, dominates the Clare shore. The margin of the lake has become a residential area, and houses, arable fields, and grazing animals, are visible along its course. Two landmarks show themselves in the channel, the Deer Rock, accompanied by a black marker which denotes a shallow area, and farther south, the gaunt ruins of Derry Castle, surrounded by brushwood, saplings and vegetation, on a small island off the east shore. The castle was once linked with the shore by a causeway, and the remnants of a disused old harbour still exist from which, in the past, cargoes of slates, quarried on the slopes of Tountinna were shipped to various destinations.

South of Derry Castle, the lake gradually contracts to a narrow waterway, from which the Shannon emerges at the wooded Ballyvally Point.

Tuamgraney Village

The Nenagh River

Tuamgraney Church

Aughinish Point and Woods

The ruins of Oldcourt Castle

Dromineer Harbour

The ruined church

Youghal Bay

Tuamgraney Quay

Terryglass Harbour

The Ballyfinboy River

Kilgarvan Pier

Kilbarron Quay

Luska Quay

Garrykennedy Harbour

Chapter Nine

WHEN ONE LOOKS OVER THE SCENIC EXPANSE OF LOCH DERG FROM ANY VIEWPOINT, two spectacular features, at once beautiful and hazardous, take the eye. The first is its numerous islands, stony, wooded or flower sprinkled, that are visible in every section of the watercourse, and the second, often side by side with the first, is the looming presence of residual rock, frequently protruding above the surface with jagged attendant shoals, largely submerged. The islands of Loch Derg, with the exception of Inis Cealtra, lack the religious and historical significance of many of those in Loch Ree. They make continuous patterns throughout the lake, an ecological rather than a human development, though some of them were inhabited in the past. Rocky spits and tiny hummocky islands are seen in the bird sanctuary at Cloondavaun, clusters like the Silver Islands at the entrance to the bay, Foot's Islands close to Kilgarvan Pier, the Cormorant and Corrikeen groups in the east channel and the Cribby Islands in the west near Mountshannon. There are single islands, increasing in size, from the small Hare, Horse and Bushy Islands off the western shoreline, Cameron and Buggane in the east, with Cahir Island and Scilly Island in the south. Finally, the two largest and best-known are Illaunmore and Inis Cealtra, or Holy Island.

Illaunmore, the largest island, is circular in shape and is sited about half-way down the lake near Castletown Bay on the Tipperary shore. It has a large area of grassy fertile land, some dwelling houses, and a number of small quays. At one time occupied, it has been uninhabited since the early 1960s, but still provides grazing for animals, brought by boat from the mainland. The waters on the north and east sides of the island are deep, have many submerged rocks, and are dangerous to craft.

Inis Cealtra is the second largest island on the lake. It is close to the western shoreline and is reached from Mountshannon and the small pier and slipway at Knockaphort, a short distance farther south. In its long history of religious endeavour, and in the scope of its ecclesiastical remains, it is comparable to the foundation at Clonmacnois. Its first monastic settlement was established by St. Colum about 520 A.D. A century or so later, St. Cáimin built or restored a monastery at this site. The settlement grew and prospered. During the following centuries, a round tower, churches and burial places, crosses and incised grave slabs were added to the original foundation despite plundering by the Norse and by native tribes. It continued in existence until the 16th century when the continual depredations brought about by the Normans led to its eventual demise.

Today it is a national monument, having a round tower, eighty feet high, though without its belfry and circular top. With it are the ruins of five chapels. St. Cáimin's Church, begun in the 10th century, contains a Romanesque doorway, and was partly restored in 1978 by the Board of Works, when a chancel and a section of the west wall were re-built. The largest church, St. Mary's, was erected in the 13th century. Following it, are St. Michael's, or the Baptism Church, the Oratory, and smaller artifacts like the Confessional, the Saints' Graveyard, and the Ladies' Well. Annual pilgrimages used to take place to the island in the past and the Pilgrims' Path, giving a processional tour of the holy places, attracted a large group of people. At present, many visitors make the short trip to Inis Cealtra, and it is still being availed of as a burial place by some local families who transport their coffins by boat to the quay at the island.

The shoreline of the lake, particularly in the centre and the south is especially favourable to flora. This is also an interesting and delightful feature of the chains and skeins of islands, where colourful plants and flowers emerge from spring to autumn even on the smallest spit. Among the familiar wild vegetation - the grasses, docks and ferns, the primrose, daisy and buttercup, is the flowering buddleja whose massed purple blossoms make a glowing contrast with the olive shades of the juniper, the light pink of the wild rose and the vivid blue of the gentian.

Crowding the water's edge are marsh marigolds, water lilies and the flags and flowers of the yellow iris. In the sandy pebbles the water germander spreads and mats its roots, while on the gravelled spits, tansy, celery and hemlock bind themselves tightly in the soft mire. Water crowfoot climbs to the surface, showing flowers wrapped in their leaves, while cara tormentosa grows beneath it, rooting in the bottom mud.

On the margins, brilliant yellow gorse and white hawthorn, blossom with the coming of spring, coupled with vinca, celandine, primrose and violet. Bluebells toss and flourish in the wooded stretches and parklands, while meadow sweet, marsh pea, scarlet ribes and buttercups bloom in the adjacent hedges and pastures, as the summer approaches. In the peaty patches off the north-west shore, moss, fern and sedges, the bog bean and bog cotton, flower unobtrusively, and in the bird sanctuary close by, purple moorgrass makes sheltered tussocks for nesting birds. The pink spirals of the foxglove, loosestrife, the long-stemmed marguerite and the glowing poppy, flower in summer in clusters and random clumps. Autumn brings the purple thistle and the blue scabious, while the red berries of bryony make brilliant spots of colour in the other wilting vegetation.

Some rare plants grow on, or close to the shoreline at Loch Derg. One of these is Blueeyed Grass, a plant with leaves like blades of grass and a blue flower, which blooms freely in the damp callows on the banks of the Woodford River, and close to the Scarriff River, as well as on the Tipperary shore. Growing on the northern margin and stretching eastwards as far as Dromineer, is the Inula, a willow-type leafy plant with a flower head shaped like a dwarf sunflower. It is unique in this area since it does not occur elsewhere in Ireland, but grows freely in Europe.

On the low margins of the shoreline are the small plants sprouting from niches of clay and stone - figwort, water-hemlock and angelica, surrounded by the ever present nettles, docks and marsh bedstraw. Near them are the weaving grassheads, clumps of flowering rush and tussocks of moss, and in the shallows, bur-reed, willowherb, horsetails and bulrushes cast crooked shadows on the eddying wavelets lapping about their stems.

Haunting the flowers and plants are the inevitable hordes of flying insects engaged in their age-old double role of propagating the species on the one hand and feeding themselves and their numerous progeny on the other. Bees, wasps, moths and long-tongued flies busily extract nectar and pollen, rivalled by the flitting, fragile butterflies – Orange Tip, Yellow Brimstone, and the various types of Brown and

Foot's Islands

Bushy Island

Cattle being ferried to the Island

Blue amongst others for whom nectar is the only food. Around and beneath them are the armies of ants, beetles, caterpillars and snails, and an uncountable multitude of lesser scale feeding on leaves, seed, stems and roots.

Gorse

Marsh Marigold

Vinca

Inis Cealtra

The fish ladder at Parteen

The Mayfly

Scarlet Ribes

The surface of the watercourse itself is the playground of droves of insects, especially in summer and early autumn. It dimples and puckers to the movements of the water boatmen, the diving beetles, the pond skaters, the dragonflies, stoneflies

Rocks at low tide

Celandine

and mayflies. Perhaps the richest source of natural life is within the depths of the lake which has an abundance of plankton, of Daphnia, Bosmina and Cladocera, food for fish fry and for the fly larvae and nymphs. Hidden also in the bottom mud are additional sources of food – shrimps, leeches, snails and water-mites.

This plenitude of natural food and the unbroken process of the food chain gives Loch Derg a high trophic quality and makes it one of the great freshwater fisheries in the country though of lesser status than it enjoyed in the beginning of the century when its salmon stocks were famous. The rich salmon fishery was one of the regrettable losses sustained when the waters of the lake were deployed to serve the hydro-electric works in Ardnacrusha in the 1920s. The ecology and shape of the Shannon was so disturbed that salmon could no longer make their way to their native rivers to spawn. The introduction of a fish ladder at Parteen Weir was but a partial success and the number of salmon entering Loch Derg dwindled away.

A similar type of deterioration has, at the present time, begun to affect the stocks of trout, pollan and coarse fish which make the lake such a major attraction for anglers. But the cause is different; it is rooted in pollution of various kinds. Over the past thirty years a great increase has occurred in the number of pleasure craft using the lake and in the consequent provision of shoreline amenities, particularly in the southern sector – harbours, slipways, carparks, hotels, picnic and sporting areas, buildings and residential areas. In their wake pollutants have followed from the boats, oil spillages and wastes of various kinds, and from the buildings, domestic pollutants, stemming from wastes, the use of detergents, and inefficient sewage systems. Added to these is the volume of peat and silt swept in by floods from the upper Shannon which deposits itself largely in the shallows. The most lethal of all, however, is the chemical effluent draining from the slurry pits and the silage heaps of the surrounding farms, which by the media of rain, stream and rivulet, empties itself into the lake. The combined action of these pollutants has a disastrous effect on fish life and on the quality of the lake water, once known for its purity and clearness. Because of them, algal growth mushrooms on part of the watercourse, absorbing the supply of oxygen and literally wiping out large numbers of shell-fish, fish fry and mature fish.

The seriousness of the problem has not yet been fully recognised and methods to deal with it are tardy and incomplete. A project, supervised by a working group, has been set up for the very necessary task of monitoring water quality in the lake, and pin pointing the sources of pollution prior to treating them. A floating laboratory has been installed on the lake to be used permanently for this purpose. Its efforts are being complemented by those of the three local authorities involved, the County Councils of Clare, Galway and Tipperary, and by the Research Unit of the Department of the Environment.

Yet despite these unfortunate and avoidable occurrences, Loch Derg, with the possible exception of the northern sector where fish stocks tend to be meagre, has a great and resilient fishery which springs to abundant life with the mayfly hatch in early May. This begins in Luska Bay on the east shoreline, when a vast drove of fly nymphs drift up from the muddy bottom of the lake on the stems of water plants and float to the surface. They shed their skins and emerge as winged insects, purple and shining with moisture, and attempt to reach the nearby shore. Should they succeed, they hide behind stones, grasses and weeds, relying on their protective colouring for concealment. In the evening, in the short period of dusk, they rise into the air in a throbbing mating ritual which culminates in the falling of the drakes to die on the shoreline, while the duck flies reel back over the watercourse to drop their eggs which drift beneath the surface, to be buried in the soft slime of the bottom mud. After which, they too die, and find a new name, that of 'spent gnat', which also describes a fishing routine. Though the mayfly hatch is enormous, it is by no means the only one. Other hatches, more localized, are those of the caddis and stoneflies, olives and chironomoids, and later in the season, the sedge hatch. This unchanging natural process turns out to be a fascinating 'snare' for the trout, the most sought-after fish in the lake. With instinctive awareness of the impending hatch, they surge up from their caverns, ledges and back lies in the water's depths and invade the shallows where the flies are rising in cloudlike motion. Behind the trout come the fishermen. They use flies as bait, searching for them as they lie hidden behind stones, or clinging to wilting fronds and tiny twigs on the shoreline. The harvest of trout, as well as of flies, is bountiful, especially in the shallow waters between Mountshannon and Dromineer, and north of the Corrikeen Islands nearby. Other areas are also prolific – the stretch from Mountshannon to Scarriff, the waters near Garrykennedy, from Youghal Bay to Parker Point and farther west to the Scilly Island and the shallows near the rocky Middle Ground.

Along with trout and pollan, there are sizable stocks of coarse fish in Loch Derg, mainly pike, perch and bream. Coose Bay on the Galway shoreline is fished for pike as far as Illaunmore. North of the Scilly Island and at the deepest part of the lake near Parker Point, bream and pike are plentiful. From the Corrikeen group to Cameron Island on the eastern shoreline, there is fishing for pike and perch.

Fishermen, however, are not the only predators of the vast clouds of insects and their attendant trout as they ooze from the surface of the watercourse. Numerous birds flock to the scene. The most spectacular and noisy are the black-headed gulls which nest on islands and small pools off the shoreline, who dive in frantic greed to gorge on the tiny winged insects seeking shelter on the shore. Swifts, swallows, grey wagtails and kingfishers take their toll of the erupting harvest on water and on the shoreline. Herons, too ungainly, too large, to take part in this macabre aerial feast, stalk in the shallows, spearing small fish drawn to the scene. For the cormorant, which dives and swallows its 'catch', there is an ample harvest. Otters, nocturnal hunters, though rarely seen, feed lavishly on the lake fish. In the autumn, other food supplies present themselves to the smaller birds. Meadow pipits, starlings, finches and blackbirds eat the red berries on the islands' flowers and shrubs, and devour the ground insects.

Loch Derg is not a winter 'wetland' in the sense that Loch Ree is. Apart from its bird sanctuary in Cloondavaun Bay, where waterbirds and waders normally nest and feed, only a small number of white-fronted geese frequent a corner of Terryglass Bay, while some flocks of mute swans and minor groups of diving duck occupy sectors in the centre and in the south.

In the woods along the shoreline, pheasants, owls and wild pigeons nest. Crows roost in the tree-tops and croak their alarm signals at every disturbance. Magpies strut through the grassy shadows beneath the trees, while thrushes, wrens and robins rustle and flit as they continue their incessant pursuit of insects. In the wet hollows and ditches, frogs leap and croak, and from the boggy swamps beyond the Woodford River, snipe and curlew make their rasping calls. The tussocks, the low twigs and tall grass, exude the scents of fox, stoat and badger, squirrel and rabbit, while their lesser brethren, the hedgehog, fieldmouse and shrew, hide in holes and crevices in every copse and spinney. In the wedges of reeds by the lake are the great-crested grebes, the sedge warblers and reed buntings, concealed and protected by the tall waving pennants.

Loch Derg's shoreline and hinterland have proved, not surprisingly, to be a favourite choice for the building of castles and tower houses over the centuries. Changes in architectural style from the type of castle met with on the shores of the Shannon in earlier periods are evident. The first Norman castles were of the motte and bailey design – the motte being a high earthen mound surrounded by a deep fosse or ditch, the bailey a large enclosure adjoining it also surrounded by a fosse. Athlone Castle was originally a motte type. In the next century, stone castles were built with strong central keeps and high defensive walls, of which Rindoon on Loch Ree is typical. As the centuries slipped by the defensive wall was

Luska Bay

Fishing for trout

Medieval ruins at Dromineer

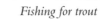

Black-headed gulls

Clondagough Castle

Kingfisher

Fishing area between Mountshannon and Dromineer   *Rocks at Garrykennedy*

Derry Castle   *Marina at Killaloe*

Ballyvally Point

eliminated, the strong keep retained and towers added at each corner. Such buildings are often called 'tower houses' and Oldcourt, adjacent to Terryglass village and to Loch Derg, though in a state of ruin, is clearly an example of this style.

Between the 15th and 17th centuries a number of such houses were erected on or near the shores of Loch Derg. Four families were chiefly engaged in maintaining status and prestige by the erection of these castles. Two were Irish, the O'Kennedys and the O'Briens; two were of Norman extraction, the Dillons and the Butlers. Many of these houses are now in ruins and only their parklands, avenues and ornamental gateways remain to indicate past elegance. Some, however, have been redesigned as private residences and hotels, such as, Slevoir House, Drominagh, Gortalough and Waterloo, all on the eastern shoreline. The ruins of Annagh Castle and Castletown House are also in the east, with Ballykelly and Clondagough Castles on the west shore, and Derry Castle in the south-east.

Perhaps the only unattractive natural feature of Loch Derg is the prevalence of residual rock and jagged underwater shoals in all sections of the lake. Many of the rocks are named, and almost all are indicated by black and red markers as they sub-divide the watercourse between them. In the north-west section, are the Hagen, Split, Stick and Benjamin Rocks. In the south-west, are the hazardous Middle Ground area and the dangerous Lushing group. On the east shore, are the Kylenoe Rocks and farther south, the Mountaineer and Deer Rocks. Shoals are even more prevalent than single rocks. On the western shore they penetrate deeply into Cloondavaun Bay from the Silver Islands. They appear at Horse Island, Middle Ground and the Scilly Island to the south. A continuous chain of shoals fences the eastern shore from Terryglass Bay to Foot's Islands near Kilgarvan Pier. The Goat Island and Cormorant Island shoals stretch westwards into the narrow lake channel. Others are at Buggane Island, the Corrikeen group and Urra Point, while at Garrykennedy, shoals line both sides of the harbour. All of them are indicated by red and black markers.

With navigation goes that inescapable feature of our climate - the weather. All climatic changes from sultry heat to rain, wind, fog, frost and snow may occur on the lake the shoreline of which has, for the most part, little protection from extremes of weather. The winds, often rising to gale force, are perhaps the most hazardous. Sailing in fresh winds can be awkward, in strong winds it may be perilous and difficult. A storm can whip the lake into high rolling waves and masses of broken water. The most troublesome area is at Parker's Point on the south shore. Rising wind which tends to roar north from Killaloe and to come in conflict with the south-westerly winds from Scarriff Bay causes a wild surging whirlpool of water. Stormy conditions bring turbulent and darkened clouds, which often make it impossible to see buoys and beacons clearly, adding to the perilous situations in which boats may find themselves. In winter, days of heavy frost may cause a thick sheet of ice to form on the lake. Only a narrow central channel remains open and swans and waders can be observed seeking food as they turn and twist on the icy spits. Slabs of ice may break away, forming additional hazards.

Because of the great increase in boating on Loch Derg, Shannon Development, in 1991, undertook to add to the existing facilities by providing more accommodation at the various ports and piers. An increase of 320 berths is in process of being implemented and a number has already been put in place at the well-known venues of Dromineer and Mountshannon.

The Shannon leaves Loch Derg at Ballyvally Point, less than a quarter of a mile from the bridge at Killaloe. It curves towards the west and flows in a broad smooth stream. Approaching the bridge, the river's watercourse expands into a spacious marina, flanked on both banks by houses, moorings and anchorages, as the long bridge links two villages – Ballina on the Tipperary shoreline and Killaloe on that of Clare.

Chapter Ten

THE BRIDGE AT KILLALOE, A LONG NARROW BRIDGE WITH THIRTEEN ARCHES was built between 1825 and 1840. It has pedestrian recesses and a plaque affixed in commemoraion of the four Clare men, McMahon, Egan, Gildea and Rogers – who lost their lives in the War of Independence. It links the Tipperary shore with that of Clare, the village of Ballina with that of Killaloe. In the east sector is the navigational span at which a strong and rapid current is often encountered, while at its western entrance the recently built Tourist Office has been located. Here, too, is a segment of an old canal now used as a mooring place.

Ballina, a small village, tucked beneath the Arra mountains, extends along the Tipperary shore above and below the bridge. It has an extensive marina, a hotel, waterside park and swimming pool. There are river walks, seating accommodation and restaurants. Along its shoreline are the buildings and jetties of the Killaloe Yacht Club. From it, roads lead to Nenagh and Limerick.

Opposite it, on the west bank, is the larger village of Killaloe in County Clare. Between them, spreads the smooth and spacious watercourse, one of the finest on the river. Craft often abound in this stretch which marks the limit of sailing for hire-boats. Amenities flourish on both banks, providing facilities for swimming, boating, and a variety of water sports, so that it has become the most popular venue on the river. The Derg Line provides cruisers for extended trips, while a river-bus, the Derg Princess, makes daily trips to Dromineer. Shannon Activity Centre at Ballycuggeran, a short distance north of Killaloe, offers a wide variety of boating and water sports as does Loch Derg Caravan and Camping Park.

Killaloe, now a Heritage Centre, steeped in the history of the past, both in its monastic and political aspects, wanders peacefully up a hillside on the slopes of Sliabh Bernagh. St. Lua, after whom the small town is named, founded a church here in the 6th century. He was followed, a century later, by St. Flannan, to whom the Cathedral and Oratory nearby are dedicated.

Built in the 13th century of pale sandstone, the Cathedral has a chancel and nave, transepts and a central tower. The chancel is distinguished by a tall, finely designed window dominating the east wall. It has three sections and is intended to symbolize the Trinity. Decorative stained glass enshrining the theme of Christ and the Apostles was installed in 1865. There is a richly carved Irish Romanesque doorway in the south wall, which was salvaged from an older church built by Donal Mor O'Brien, King of Munster, in the previous century, and devastated by fire in 1185. In front of the doorway stands a Thorgrim stone, which is part of the shaft of a cross and is named in memory of a Viking convert. Rare inscriptions still exist on each side of the stone, one in the Irish ogham, the other in the Scandanavian runic, both asking for prayers

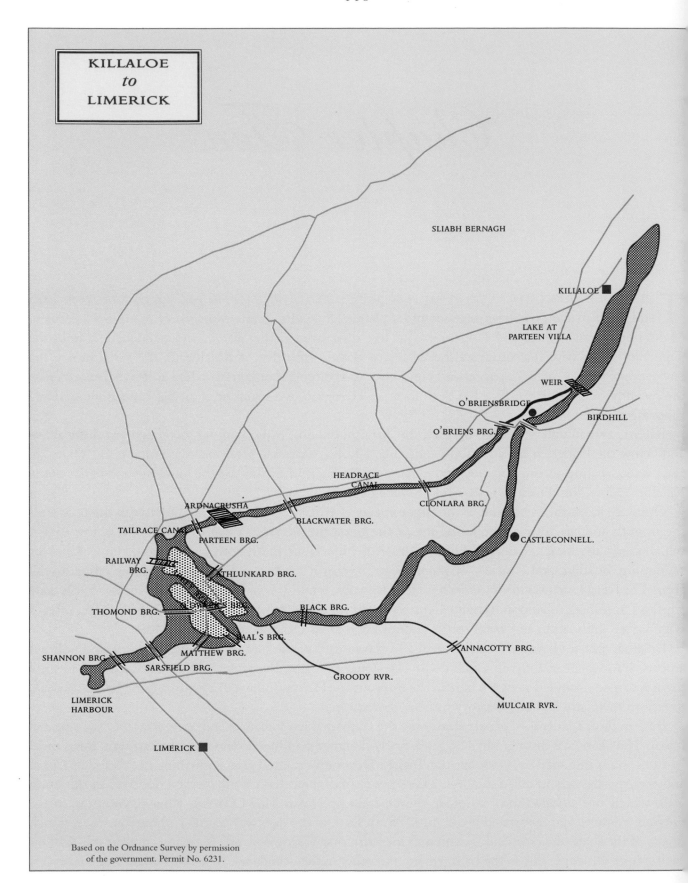

KILLALOE
to
LIMERICK

SLIABH BERNAGH

KILLALOE

LAKE AT
PARTEEN VILLA

WEIR

O'BRIENSBRIDGE

BIRDHILL

O'BRIENS BRG.

HEADRACE
CANAL

CLONLARA BRG.

ARDNACRUSHA

BLACKWATER BRG.

CASTLECONNELL.

TAILRACE CANAL

PARTEEN BRG.

RAILWAY
BRG.

ATHLUNKARD BRG.

BLACK BRG.

THOMOND BRG.

BAAL'S BRG.

ANNACOTTY BRG.

SHANNON BRG

MATTHEW BRG.

SARSFIELD BRG.

GROODY RVR.

LIMERICK
HARBOUR

MULCAIR RVR.

LIMERICK

Based on the Ordnance Survey by permission
of the government. Permit No. 6231.

The bridge at Killaloe

The village of Ballina

Killaloe

The Oratory of St. Lua

St. Flannan's Cathedral

St. Flannan's Oratory

Section of old Canal

The Lake at Parteen Weir

for Thorgrim. In the grounds of the Cathedral is St. Flannan's Oratory, a small stone building with a high pitched roof also made of stone and dating from the 12th century. Its chancel has disappeared. Only the nave remains and a small chamber beneath the roof, which may have been used to store church property. Its most significant feature, apart from the high roof, is the west door, constructed in three arches with jamb shafts, all simply designed. A Sunday service is still held in the Cathedral.

On the summit of the hill above the town is the Roman Catholic Church. In its grounds is the small Oratory of St. Lua. Built originally on Inis Lua, an island in the Shannon, downstream of Killaloe Bridge, it was in danger of being submerged in the changes planned for the river's channel in the 1920s. Removed, stone by stone, the tiny building was re-sited in its present position. The church, of which little remains, consists of a nave and chancel, a narrow window in the east wall, the inner sill of which is approached by a number of steps. The stone roof is high pitched and contains a small cavity beneath. Built mainly of yellow sandstone, it is very old, and dates possibly from the 10th century. Close by, is the modern Catholic Church, built in 1933, noted for its Romanesque arches and distinctive, stained glass windows.

Killaloe became a centre of political importance from the 10th to the 13th centuries due to the emergence of the O'Brien family, and particularly to its most famous member and the most renowned of Irish High Kings, Brian Boru. The palace of Kincora, built and inhabited by his family for some time before his birth, is said to have occupied the top of the hill, the site upon which the Catholic Church now stands. The second part of his name is believed to derive from that of a large fort named Béal Borumha (Mouth of the Tributes), meaning a place at which cattle were counted and including a levy or tribute. Sited close to Ballyvally Point, it dominated the northern approach to the palace of Kincora, barely a mile to the south. There is some evidence that it was used for defensive purposes prior to the reign of Brian. It became derelict in the 12th century and little of it remains today apart from a large circular ridge surrounding a deep fosse or quarry, ringed by trees and undergrowth. It is a preserved area.

Brian died in 1014 A.D., in which year he defeated the invading forces of the Norse at Clontarf, a coastal area near Dublin, a victory which ranks as the greatest in Irish history. His breaking of the Viking power, however, brought about his own death. His family and followers came under heavy attacks from rival factions, and their military power gradually decreased. The palace of Kincora lasted for a further century and was then destroyed so completely that no traces of it remain. Killaloe's period of political prestige soon evaporated in the continuous conflicts of the times, when, in 1276, it was occupied by the Normans, though it remained the major highway between Dublin and Limerick for a further period.

The next important change in the town's progress came with a development in the Shannon. The difficulties encountered in navigation on the river in its upper and middle stretches applied with equal force in its final run of eighteen miles from Killaloe to Limerick, and it was solved in similar fashion, that is, by the building of canals – three in all. They were constructed by the Limerick Steamship Company in the last century. Their function was to bypass the rapids in the river, particularly those at Doonass, seven miles downstream, which formed a huge natural obstruction. The canals were linked to navigable parts of the Shannon which, in turn, linked them to each other to form an efficient navigational system. Along with the canal at Killaloe were locks, a weir and sluices. The weir was built in 1842, and the sluices added in 1880, both designed to regulate the levels of water in Loch Derg. In the 1920s, in the reconstruction on the river at this point, they were removed with the greater part of the canal. The section that remains may be used by boats, not only for mooring, but also to sail past the bridge and join the river downstream.

The newly established canal navigational system linking the town with Limerick gave Killaloe an era of river trading. It became a Shannon port, the venue of passenger steamers, cargo boats, turf boats and barges, sailing to and fro from the upper Shannon and connecting with the Grand Canal at Shannon Harbour. In 1961, commercial trading ceased on the Shannon and has been replaced by pleasure cruising and attendant activities, all of which has given Killaloe a new kind of prestige. It is the centre of tourism, of boating and angling in the area. A splendid venue for water sports, its scenic surroundings offer hill walks, nature trails, historic places of interest, churches and old buildings.

Between 1925 and 1929, Killaloe witnessed the beginning and completion of the most ambitious industrial project ever to be undertaken in Ireland up to that time – the harnessing of the Shannon's waterpower to provide electricity on a countrywide basis. The Shannon Scheme, as it was then known, had been mooted for some time, arousing caustic opposition from many quarters. Derided by some as a 'white elephant', it was deplored by others as a threat to the flora and fauna of the river, and suspect by the general public as an alarming waste of public money. However, the government of the day decided in favour of the project, allotted a sum of six million pounds to finance it, employed the German firm of Siemens-Schuckert to plan and construct the work and appointed Dr. T. J. McLoughlin, an engineer, and the chief promotor of the scheme, as general supervisor.

The section of the Shannon chosen for development was its final stretch, that between Killaloe and Limerick City, a distance of eighteen miles. The reason for this choice was abundantly clear - a sudden and steep fall in the river's gradient in the first half of this short range due to the configuration of the terrain, and its abrupt transformation from upland, hill and peak, to valleys and lowlands. The river had reversed motion as it were. Having meandered through the midlands from Battlebridge to Killaloe, a distance of over a hundred miles, sometimes desolate, often beautiful, with its flattest stretch on the approach to Loch Derg, it then carved its way through hard shale and sandstone at the base of the surrounding mountains, poured over the rocky sill at Killaloe and raced unimpeded into the low-lying fields of east Clare. Seven miles from Killaloe, the torrent reached the Rapids of Doonass, an area formed of heaped slabs of rock and stone, up to half a mile in length, over which the huge volume of water plunged, a vast continuous cataract which, above the Falls, was up to forty feet deep and three hundred yards wide, forming a spectacular watercourse which bore witness to the power and force of the rushing river.

The Rapids of Doonass, one of the natural wonders of the countryside, a source of admiration and delight to spectators, was, also, a total block to navigation on this stretch of the river, a natural obstacle to boating and commerce. Hence the canal system of three short waterways linked to the navigable parts of the river and to each other, the Errina Canal, the middle section, by-passing the Rapids completely. When in 1925, the hydro-electric scheme got underway, the inevitable first casualties were the canal system and the celebrated Falls.

The re-designing of the face and flow of the Shannon at Killaloe necessitated many basic changes. The normal furnishings of a river port over almost a century were swept away - the greater part of the navigation canal, the weir and sluices, a lock downstream and changes in the rocky dam of the bridge itself. Excavation in the bed of the river downstream of the bridge resulted in higher levels of water, submerging sections of land, fields, houses and islands, and creating a large lake which stretched from Killaloe to Parteen, five miles to the south.

At Parteen a vast weir was constructed across the Shannon to hold the continuous flow of water from Loch Derg, and to raise its levels to that of the newly-created lake. In doing this, it regulates the flow of the current, and diverts the build-up of water into a man-made canal, named the Headrace, which emerges from a unit called the Intake Building, sited on the west side of the river and interlinked with the weir.

Parteen Weir

The Headrace Canal

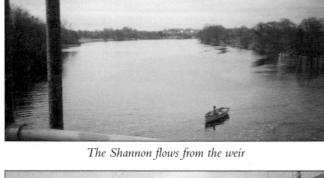

The Shannon flows from the weir

The Tailrace Canal

The Kilmastulla River

O'Briensbridge

O'Brien's Bridge

Castleconnell

The ruined de Burgo Castle

Fish 'beats' and rock fragments

Doonass

The Mulcair River joins the Shannon

Trees and brushwood clot the channel

Athlunkard Bridge

O'Dwyer's Bridge

The Abbey River flows out of the Shannon

This building controls the flow of water into the Headrace. It has four openings, one of which, the Ship's Pass, enables boats to enter the canal.

Streaming south at the base of a chain of low hills on the Clare side of the Shannon, the canal is approximately thirty five feet deep with high wide embankments, constructed to prevent flooding. The speed of its current is controlled to facilitate navigation. A number of rivers had to be diverted and discharged into the Shannon, during the building of the weir and canal, two at the weir itself, the Black River from the Clare side and, on the opposite bank, the Kilmastulla River from Tipperary. Up to nine others, of which the Blackwater is the largest, were directed under the Headrace canal to empty into the Shannon downstream. Three concrete bridges were constructed to span the Headrace where it encountered local roads – O'Brien's Bridge, Clonlara and Blackwater Bridges. The canal has a run of seven and a half miles to the powerhouse at Ardnacrusha, where extensive units of machinery convert the huge volumes of water flowing in, to electricity.

A large mass of water is released from the powerhouse and directed by an Intake Building to a second canal, known as the Tailrace. Two locks were installed to facilitate the movement of boats from the Headrace to the Tailrace. A mile and a half long, the canal passes beneath the fourth of the specially constructed bridges, Parteen Bridge, close to a village of the same name, and streams south to merge with the Shannon a short distance downstream.

Meanwhile, the Shannon, slow and shallow, continues to flow in its natural bed as it emerges from the weir. Denuded of its normal strong currents, it receives through the weir's sluice gates, the necessary minimum of water to protect fish and fishing. Joined at this point by the Kilmastulla River which had to be diverted from above the weir, the Shannon meanders south to O'Briensbridge, a small neat village, the last on the Clare shoreline, with an extension on the east side of the river called Montpelier. There is an attractive amenity area and park here. Boating and coarse angling, walks and nature trails are popular, while the smooth wide channel of the river, no longer subject to torrent or rapids, is a venue for water sports.

Named after the family of Brian Boru, its old masonry bridge has twelve arches. Destroyed in the 16th century, and later rebuilt, it provided a crossing over the river for the Cromwellian army in 1650.

Pursuing its course the Shannon enters the County Limerick and streams on to the village of Castleconnell. Originally, Caisleán O gConaing, part of the lands owned by the O gConaing clan, it was eventually occupied by the Norman family of de Burgo, later to become Burke, who erected a castle on the bank of the river beside the village. Now an ivy covered ruin, it was destroyed by the Williamite army in 1691.

A pleasing village, Castleconnell was noted before the 1920s for salmon fishing and rod making, and was also, for a time, a fashionable spa. The salmon fishery, however, suffered heavily because of the construction of Parteen Weir. To compensate for the loss sustained, the Electricity Supply Board built a salmon fishery, adding streams and pools known as 'beats' and numbered for the purpose of rotation, providing a run of fish in season, often complemented by salmon from the estuary. Bank and boat fishing are available. This stretch of the river, once so turbulent, is now calm and smooth-flowing and coarse angling is popular. Pleasantly scenic, riverside walks and nature trails invite exploration, and water sports form an attractive alternative.

A short distance south of Castleconnell is the once famous 'Falls' of Doonass which can be reached by a river footbridge which has salmon 'beats' above and below, or by road. A wooded, insect-haunted area, it is now deprived of the mighty volumes of water which once made it such a spectacular and awe-inspiring sight. Reputed to be forty feet deep, and three hundred yards wide, the massive flow tumbled down a course half a mile long, clogged with immense slabs of rock, boulders and loose stone. The Shannon had battered these unwieldy crags in a continuous explosion of sound. Now a deep peace prevails as the residue of shelved and jagged spits and ridges jut silently and nakedly from the shallow trickles of water and the slanting eddy-pools, which dribble out of the niches to the stream below.

The river is wide, full of stone and broken rock, islets, streams, backwaters and tiny waterfalls. Trees grow on the islets which provide stepping stones from bank to bank. Bird song, the buzz and whirr of insects, and the murmurous splash of the stream, are the only sounds that break the silence. Walks and nature trails appear up and down the river side. There is a pub lounge here, and with it, an amenity area with wide lawns and picnic tables. It is named The Angler's Rest.

The Shannon continues to meander southwards into the suburb of Castletroy, its banks on both sides lightly wooded with barriers of reeds, flags of iris, hogweed and rush, mixed with small clumps of young trees and brushwood. Here, it is joined by the Mulcair River, a stream rich in trout and salmon, flowing from County Tipperary on a 16 mile run. It passes beneath a road bridge at the village of Annacotty, four miles east of Limerick City, where it forms a fine waterfall. A high metal footbridge, now disused, crosses its channel, close to the confluence.

Small islands continue to proliferate in the Shannon, where willows, alders, sycamore and sally, grow profusely and the giant hogweed, eight feet tall, distinctive with its spreading caps of white florets, its huge, spiky green leaves and thick woody stems, takes on the appearance of a young tree. The current is slow but busy, its flow seeping into the soft banks, forming coves, backwaters, creeks and tiny beaches. Clumps of vegetation root in the bottom ooze, sprinkling the shallow verges with weaving grassheads and wild flowers.

It curves around the grounds of the University of Limerick and the National Technological Park at Plassey. A towpath skirts its left bank, as it winds beneath the Black Bridge, a footbridge much used by fishermen. Turning northward, it is joined by the Blackwater River on the Clare side, and the narrow Groody stream on the Limerick side, and a short distance later, by a disused arm of the old canal, a segment of the previous navigational system.

Meanwhile, the Shannon, still on its northward course, flows beneath the 5-arched Athlunkard Bridge, built in 1830. It has entered the Corbally district and is here at its most serene. Very wide, divided by a number of small wooded islets into streaming channels in which swans and mallards float idly, it has a sheltered creek, which houses rowboats and punts. Close by, are the Corbally Falls, a low but bustling outflow of water when the tide is high. On the right bank, a distinctive group of residential houses send their smooth lawns down to the river. Downstream, the Tailrace Canal, flowing south from Ardnacrusha and Parteen Bridge, joins the main channel.

The Shannon, now a complete river once more, turns directly south. It is broad, weedy, slow and shallow, its watercourse studded with spits, ridges and islets, as it erodes its banks, making inlets and strips of sandy mud and stone. Trees, saplings and wild vegetation grow in every niche and crevice. Soon a disused railway bridge looms up and just below it, on the Limerick bank, spreads the mouth of the Abbey River, the shortest of the Shannon's tributaries. The main channel winds leisurely onwards, passing Thomond Weir to Thomond Bridge, one of the oldest structures on the river. It dates from 1210 and was rebuilt in 1844. Beside it, is the ancient and custodial castle of King John, also dating from the 13th century.

The Abbey River, less than a mile long, flows around the ancient Inis Sibhtonn, now known as King's Island, a heavily built-up area. It cuts a wide swath, its current quietly busy, its surface gleaming dully in the mist-laden atmosphere. Possessing the kind of rural charm, though somewhat desolate, of much of the

Baal's Bridge

Matthew Bridge

The Abbey River flows into the Shannon

The Black Bridge – a fishing venue

St Mary's Cathedral

O'Connell Street, Limerick

Thomond Bridge

Thomond Weir

Upper Shannon, it winds sluggishly through green fields. Its banks are low-lying, the water seeping and gouging into the soft mire, making pools, gullies and tiny canals. Clumps of reeds have waded into the channel, carrying litter and silt, making spits and bars for rooting grass, twig and rush. On the verges, the soiled, wheat-coloured stems of last year's reed harvest lie tattered and bent in the mud. Withered brown dock waves dismally in the slight breeze. There are few birds to be seen, dipping and skimming over the surface of the water, yet a thin skein of sound betrays their unseen presence, as they flit furtively among the cloudy brown thickets of bush that crowd the banks. Wagtails, and reed buntings, meadow pipits and finches - their shrill pipings pierce the dull air.

Abruptly, the river begins to curve and turn inland beneath low hills. Here it passes beneath the first of its three bridges, O'Dwyer's Bridge, a concrete structure with four spans, built in 1930. Its speed increases, as it rolls towards the one-arched Baal's Bridge, the second oldest in the city. Erected about the year 1340, it, originally, had four arches but no battlements. It was called the Bald Bridge, a name that lasted for some time, until it was altered to its present version. In 1830, the bridge was re-designed and given one wide arch. Surging beneath this bridge with abrupt violence, as it falls under the influence of the tidal waves racing from the estuary, the river takes on the wild aspect and uncontrolled force of a flood. It sweeps towards Matthew Bridge, an old masonry structure with three arches, built in 1761, and re-structured in 1844. It streams between Georges Quay and Charlotte Quay, passes beneath a blue metal footbridge and empties itself into the Shannon below the Custom House.

The great changes made in the Shannon from Killaloe to Limerick destroyed the old canal system, leaving remnants at Killaloe, O'Brien's Bridge and Limerick, but provided for navigation by making the Abbey River the final navigational arm. From Killaloe, boats are conducted downstream along the artificial lake to Parteen Weir, and to the Headrace Canal on its western shoreline. Here, they are directed through the Ship's Pass, which is part of the Intake Building, and continue to sail down the canal to the powerhouse at Ardnacrusha, where they enter the largest locks on the river. These carry them to the low-level, exit canal, the short Tailrace. This small canal leads directly to the main river flowing from Castleconnell, to the Abbey River, and to the Shannon at Limerick City.

The splendid salmon fisheries for which Loch Derg and Castleconnell were famous before the 1920s were not so fortunate. The natural breeding cycle of the salmon, as they swam up the estuary from the Atlantic Ocean to reach their spawning grounds in the small freshwater streams and rivers, was severely disrupted by the hydro-electric scheme, which changed the physical appearance of the river, altered its water levels and made it almost impossible for these large and powerful fish to follow their instinctive routines.

Hatcheries for the rearing of salmon fry have been established at Parteen Weir, and smolts are regularly placed in rivers and streams. The Mulcair River and its tributaries are some of these, and have a plentiful stock of salmon and grilse in season. Fine runs of salmon, both sea and freshwater, occur at the Plassey and Black Bridge stretches of the river, at the Long Strand, at the mouth of the Abbey River, and at Thomond Weir, all of which are on the approach to Limerick.

· · · · ·

A city with a population of over sixty thousand people, Limerick, or Luimneach, the name means 'a bare, barren place' and derives from the Norse word, Hlymreker, began its existence on the small island of Inis Sibhtonn, huddled between the Shannon and the Abbey River, at the lowest fordable place in the area now called, the Curragour Falls. It was a place scarred by wind and weather, and that is how it must have presented itself to the Norse invaders who established a settlement and base of operations upon it in the 9th century. Sailing up the 60-mile estuary from the Atlantic Ocean, they found it a convenient place, from which to attack and ravage the religious institutions along the shorelines, the churches and monasteries of the 'Golden Age', and carry away their 'wealth' of ornaments and vessels in gold, silver and bronze.

Continuous waves of Vikings arrived at the settlement, where they set up formidable raiding parties, not only in the estuary, but also in the Upper Shannon. They became so powerful that they succeeded in making repeated military sorties to Loch Ree, attacking and being attacked by native tribes, resulting in loot, carnage and destruction. Towards the end of the 10th century, their dominance was brought to an end by two brothers of the Dalcassian clan, Mahon who inflicted a crushing defeat on them at Sulcoit in County Tipperary, and Brian, later to become famous as Brian Boru, who destroyed their military supremacy in Limerick and on the estuary.

The O'Brien dynasty eventually made Limerick their centre of power and maintained their hold for over a hundred years. During this time, the Norse gradually abandoned their warlike ways, developed their island home as a small town and settled down to become craftsmen and traders. In 1172, Donal Mor O'Brien, King of Munster, built St. Mary's Cathedral within the limits of the Viking town, a Romanesque-type church of great architectural interest with transepts, aisles and chancel. It underwent much renovation in the following centuries and fine carvings were added to it. From its tower, a panoramic view of the city and countryside may be obtained.

With the death of Donal Mor O'Brien towards the end of the century, the family power and influence began to decline. The Norman invasion, begun in 1169, engulfed Limerick by the beginning of the 13th century. The Viking town was overrun and taken possession of. Determined to retain and protect it, the Normans built Thomond Bridge in 1210, and later, King John's Castle, adjoining it. In time, a small settlement know as 'Irishtown' began to grow on the south bank of the Abbey River, and, as its name implies was inhabited by the native Irish. In 1340, Baal's Bridge was erected across the Abbey River to link the two sections into one township. Watch towers and defensive walls were added later.

King John's Castle was a fortified unit commanding Thomond Bridge from its inception. A notable example of Norman architecture, it has now undergone restoration and is being put to contemporary uses as an international heritage and tourist centre with historical exhibits, audio-visual shows, and an Interpretive Centre, forming an interesting focus for many visitors.

In the 17th century, the Castle and the walls of Limerick became famous in history as they withstood three sieges. The first occurred in 1650, when, after a year-long siege, the Cromwellian forces captured the city. The second was in 1690, during which the Williamite army was temporarily beaten off, and the third in 1691 when the Williamites, attacking again, breached the walls, a disaster which compelled the Irish army to capitulate, and resulted in the ill-fated Treaty of Limerick.

By the middle of the 18th century, in 1760, the walls were being demolished, and only a few traces of them now remain - fragments behind Lelia Street and also near St. John's Hospital. With these obstacles removed, the developing town began to spread west and south into County Limerick. Its future shape was formally planned to occupy the district of Newtown Pery, in a series of parallel streets, wide and long, small pleasing squares and terraced houses. This basic plan has not been altered by modern additions — railways and highways, public buildings and apartment blocks, institutes of education and shopping centres. Historic sites, pleasant walks and fishing venues are numerous, while Shannon International Airport is just

The Curragour Falls

King John's Castle

Sarsfield Bridge

fifteen miles distant on the Clare shoreline.

On the west side of Thomond Bridge, in Clancy Strand, is the Treaty Stone, a memorial to the Treaty of Limerick, 1691. It overlooks a magnificent watercourse, as the Shannon flows rapidly westward, streaming between high, walled banks, solid and steep. It has achieved an urban identity for the first time in its long meander from the hills of Cavan. A short distance downstream, it is crossed by the Curragour Falls, a series of wide spiky slabs of rock strewn across the river's channel close to the mouth of the Abbey River, and seen clearly only when the tide is low.

On its west bank are the Clancy and O'Callaghan Strands, behind which are residential areas, and on the opposite side, a succession of quays, from Merchants Quay, close to the Custom House, to Arthurs Quay just above Sarsfield Bridge. The best-known of the city's bridges, it was built between 1824 and 1835, has five arches and a navigation span and carries the main trafficway to North Clare and the Midlands. It has been named after Patrick Sarsfield who led the defence of the city in the sieges of 1690 and 1691. The line of quays continues on the city side below the bridge, Harveys and Howleys Quays, the Bishops Quay and Russell Quay, reaching the most modern crossing on the river, the Shannon Bridge, built in 1989. Downstream of the bridge, is Steamship Quay, from which a hovercraft service operates, offering tours on the river and on the estuary. A short distance onward are the docks and Limerick Harbour.

The Treaty Stone

Shannon Bridge

Limerick Harbour

The small but expanding harbour is situated on the outskirts of the city in the district of Newtown Pery. It is the successor of an ancient harbour built beside the Viking town in the 13th century. Enlarged by reclamation work, by deepening, dredging, rebuilding and extending the dock area, work begun in 1946, it has become progressively modernised, with floating and graving docks, up-to-date handling equipment and warehousing. An industrial estate, that of Corcanree, is located close to it, on the Limerick shoreline.

Sited at the head of the estuary, it is at the shallowest part of that long expanse, its depth being from 16 to 18 feet, capable of accommodating vessels of 4, 000 tonnes deadweight. It imports commodities such as, animal feedstuffs, fertilisers, coal, cement and petroleum, and exports barytes and ore concentrates. With road and rail connections, freight lorries and tankers, it is in a favourable position for wide inland distribution. The Limerick Harbour Commissioners provide the management for the port and the estuary.

Chapter Eleven

A S THE SHANNON PASSES INTO THE ESTUARY the river's urgent compulsion to reach the sea has come to an end. Its pattern of rapids, meanders and lake formations, its curves and zigzags into field and bog, dictated by the changing face of the terrain and the inescapable pull of the gradient, is at last over. It now responds to a new enforced momentum, generated by an unbreakable natural rhythm, the ebb and flow of the tides, twice in twenty-four hours.

The river has not come empty-handed. In its current, its streams and its pools, it brings with it, from mountain slope, craggy hill and marshy valley, an incredible amount of sediment – rocks, clay, loam, mud, gravel, mineral salts, plant and animal residues – a liquid conveyor-belt of nutritious abundance flowing continuously and so enriching the waters of the estuary, that it becomes the most fertile of all natural feeding grounds.

The Shannon estuary stretches directly west from Limerick Harbour for sixty miles. Here, between Loop Head in County Clare and Kerry Head in County Kerry, it makes its final and dramatic exit to join the Atlantic Ocean. Basically a submerged river valley of varying widths and depths, its narrowest section is in the area of Foynes, twenty miles from Limerick Harbour and the only seaport the county possesses, and is one mile across to the Clare shoreline. Its largest width is at its mouth, the panoramic stretch between Kerry Head and the Loop peninsula. Similarly, its depths vary widely. The deepest section, from sixty to one hundred feet, stretches from its mouth to the Fergus estuary, forty miles upstream. Above this line the depth begins to lessen and diminishes to about sixteen feet at Limerick Harbour.

The shorelines, curving smoothly for the most part, fringe on three counties. The northern bank is in County Clare for its entire length. The southern is divided between County Limerick, up to but excluding the village of Tarbert, a distance of forty-eight miles, while the remaining twelve miles are in County Kerry. A long calm expanse of water, turbulent only under the stress of tides and storm, the shorelines are flanked by low green fields in which animals graze, reaching frequently to the water's edge, sometimes wooded but mostly open.

The soil, however, shows wide variation. Though limestone is to be found at all parts of the shorelines, it is only in the area east of the River Deel that it is present in such abundance as to create the most fertile land in the country, known as the 'Golden Vale'. West of the Deel, the limestone becomes progressively adulterated with shale, old red sandstone and boulder clay, making for barren hills, boggy tracts and rushy marshland. Boulder clay creates a deficient soil, holding water to such an extent that it forms pools and

The Shannon flows past Limerick Harbour

muddy ooze in crevices and hollows, causing land to remain soggy and waterlogged, a breeding ground
for clumps of rush.

This pattern is more evident on the Clare shoreline where less limestone and more boulder clay is
apparent. Parkland, interspersed with drumlins, hills lined with boulder clay, old red sandstone and grits,

A wooded section of the upper estuary

Béal Strand

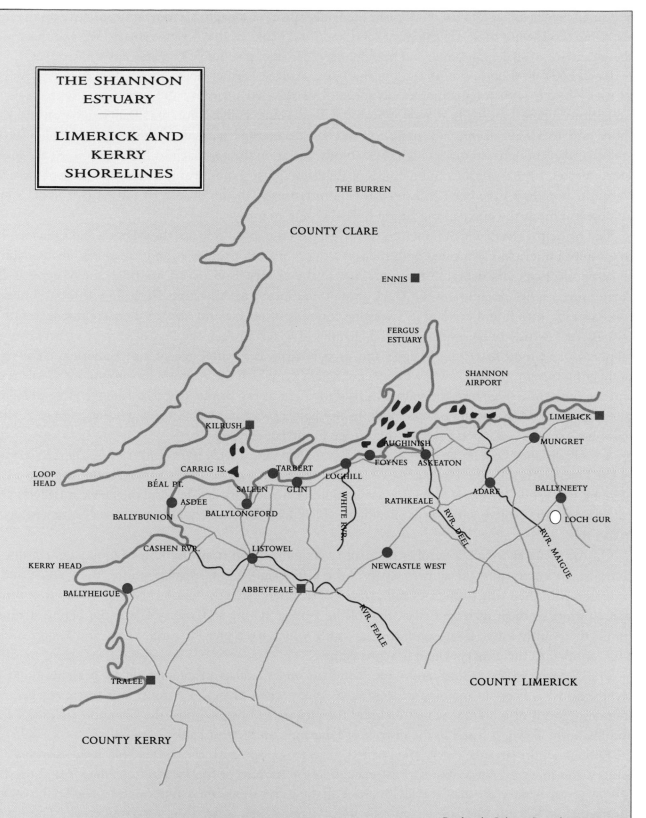

THE SHANNON
ESTUARY
———
LIMERICK AND
KERRY
SHORELINES

THE BURREN

COUNTY CLARE

ENNIS

FERGUS
ESTUARY

SHANNON
AIRPORT

LIMERICK

KILRUSH

AUGHINISH

MUNGRET

LOOP
HEAD

CARRIG IS.

TARBERT

FOYNES

ASKEATON

BÉAL PT.

LOGHILL

ADARE

BALLYNEETY

SALEEN

GLIN

RATHKEALE

RVR. DEEL

LOCH GUR

ASDEE

BALLYLONGFORD

WHITE RVR.

RVR. MAIGUE

BALLYBUNION

CASHEN RVR.

LISTOWEL

KERRY HEAD

NEWCASTLE WEST

BALLYHEIGUE

ABBEYFEALE

RVR. FEALE

COUNTY LIMERICK

TRALEE

COUNTY KERRY

Based on the Ordnance Survey by permission
of the government. Permit No. 6231.

and small creeks full of alluvial mud, form the landscape of Coonagh, Cratloe and Bunratty on the upper shoreline. Following these are the great sand and mud banks of the Fergus estuary. West of this estuary, the incidence of shale, sandstone and boulder clay increases, patches of bog and fen are frequent.

Reed beds are found on both sides of the upper estuary. Farther downstream, however, narrow strips of rocky beach with rough shingle and mounds of seaweed surround the perimeters with a few rare exceptions where long wide strands appear – at Béal Point, Ballybunion and Ballyheigue on the Kerry shore, and, to a lesser degree, at Carrigaholt and Kilbaha on the Clare side. Cliffs are generally low, broken and irregular, though a stretch of high rocky bluffs appear on the approach to Ballybunion. At the mouths of tributaries, large sandbanks and mounds of alluvial mud are exposed at low tide, and parts of these areas on both shorelines have been reclaimed for industrial uses. In the mouth of the estuary itself, a broad sandbank inhibits the entry of the largest bulk shipping of today.

The principal rivers which flow into the estuary on the south side are the Maigue and the Deel, both in County Limerick. Connected with them is a maze of small tributaries and streamlets, all contributing to carry silt, loam and debris to the shorelines of the estuary. Both rivers are tidal, the Maigue as far as Adare, seven miles distant, and the Deel, three miles inland to Askeaton. Both flow through limestone soil, gouging into it and eroding it, sweeping mounds of pebble and clay to their confluences with the estuary. At low tide only a narrow central channel of water flows in the bed of each river between great sandbanks and mud flats. The Maigue and its tributaries drain the area of east Limerick, a flat lightly undulating terrain, broken only by the craggy height on which the ruin of Carrigogunnell Castle stands, and the limestone ridge near the village of Kildimo. The Ferry Bridge over the Maigue close to Kildimo was built in 1792. It has three arches and, in the past, had a swivel span to enable boats go to Adare. A ferry-boat service was operated from the bridge in the last century.

A short distance west of the Maigue is the River Deel with a wide inlet at its mouth. All the rivers west of the Deel are small – the Poulaweala Creek and the Robertstown River surrounding Aughinish Island close by, the White River, or Abha Bán at Loghill, the Glencorbry at Glin, and the creek at Ballylongford. All flow into the estuary with a host of rivulets which drain the countryside, are scenically interesting, and hold fish.

On the Clare shoreline a number of small rivers pour down from the hills of Coonagh, Cratloe and Bunratty, to empty into the upper estuary – the Crompaun, the Cappatteenmore, the Cratloe and the Bunratty, with their tiny tributaries and cargoes of sediment. The shoreline curves smoothly westward for sixteen miles to meet its largest river, that of the Fergus. Rising in County Clare, the Fergus streams to Ennis, the county town, flows south to Clarecastle which has a pier for cargo boats, and a short distance later, pours into the estuary which bears its name.

The Fergus estuary is long and wide. Sandbars and mudflats proliferate on its periphery and land reclamation has been an ongoing process since 1935, when Shannon Airport was first envisaged. This immense group of buildings which includes the airport and its environs, the Shannon Industrial Estate and Shannon Town, is based in the district of Rineanna on the east bank

Though all the streams, creeks and rivulets, tend to deposit sand, clay and pebble at the margins of the estuary, the inlets are invariably narrow, excepting the mouths of the Fergus, the Maigue and the Deel. On the lower estuary, the inlet at Ballylongford on the Kerry shoreline is duplicated by one on the opposite shore, that at Kilrush, the largest town in West Clare, which is sited on a narrow creek. The bays are similarly constricted. Clonderalaw and Poulnasherry Bays, east and west of Kilrush, are small expanses of water, sheltered by promontories, with the wider, more open Bay of Kilbaha on the Loop Head peninsula. Opposite them, on the Kerry side, are the narrow Glencloosagh, Ballylongford and Bunaclugga watercourses, curved and shallow, in the recessed shoreline.

There are many islands in the estuary, some large, some small, some tiny spits of land, the haunts of birds and insects. Much of the soil on the larger islands is fertile. Based on limestone, it is capable of tillage and the growth of nutritious grass. Up to the 1960s and later, they supported a number of families who eventually came to live on the nearby mainland, but retained the islands as grazing land for cattle and sheep, transported to them by boat. A few had monastic foundations like Inis Gad and Inis Catha. Some had military fortifications such as Tarbert and Foynes. Today, only Deer Island and Foynes Island have people living and farming on them.

The first island in the upper estuary, the small grassy Craig Island, with its complement of browsing sheep, stands alone. Many of the islands, however, lie in clusters close to the confluence of rivers, as at the inlet of the River Maigue, where Battle Island, Bush Island, Green Island and Saint's Island, stretch across the channel. In the wide Fergus estuary, islands dot the watercourse, a number of them close to shore - Deer Island at Ballynacally, Inis Corcair and Inis Gad at Killadysert, all on the west shore of the estuary. In the lower estuary, close to the Clare shore at Kilrush, is the small Hog Island and, beside it, the best-known of the estuary islands, Inis Catha, the island of the serpent, also called Scattery Island, of religious and historical fame.

An industrial dimension has been acquired by two islands on the Limerick shoreline. Close to the mouth of the River Deel, in which Greenish Island lies, is the reclaimed Aughinish Island with its large alumina factory and oil jetty. Foynes Island, also with an oil jetty, is nearby. Farther west, on the Kerry shoreline, is Tarbert Island, where the Electricity Supply Board has an oil-fired generating station and an oil terminal.

Some miles farther west in Ballylongford Bay, is the historic Carrig Island, on which the ruins of the old castle of Carrigafoyle still stand.

· · · · ·

A number of villages and small towns, castles and piers, dot the margins and hinterland of the estuary as it streams into the countryside. Its upper section on the Limerick shoreline is one of its narrowest for a distance of up to seven miles. River-like in appearance, its banks are shallow with grasslands rolling to the water's edge at times, its verges often marked by mudflats, sandbars, and clumps of reeds, behind which are areas of trees, scrub and wild vegetation.

In this section the Industrial Estate of Corcanree stretches by the banks of the estuary for over two miles, ending with the huge bulk of Cement Ltd., built in the 1930s. Mungret, the first village of the estuary, is in this area, about a mile inland. A small unassuming village today, with a Jesuit College for boys, it is difficult to believe that its ancient monastery, nothing of which remains, reached a high level of renown between the 5th and 13th centuries, when it was recognised as the most significant seat of learning in North Munster. Close by, is the tiny village of Clarina with a riding school, providing horsemanship, hunting and cross-country rides.

North of Clarina is the highest point of this largely flat terrain – the rocky basaltic height upon which the much-battered shell of Carrigogunnell Castle overlooks the countryside. The name is derived from

The Ferry Bridge

The River Maigue

A section of Foynes Island

Part of the reclaimed Aughinish Island, now a bird sanctuary

A section of the Corcanree Industrial Estate

Mungret Village

Carrig O gConaing, the Rock of the O Conaing, the Gaelic sept that owned the area before the Norman invasion. The original castle was built by the Norman family of the de Burgos and later passed to the strong O'Brien clan to whom they were related by marriage. In the 14th century, the O'Briens built the present castle, now reduced to a shattered if striking ruin. Attacked on several occasions, its walls were

The ruin of Carrigogunnel Castle

Dromore Castle

Pallaskenry

Ringmoylan Quay

Curraghchase Forest Park

The inlet of the River Deel

blown up and the building devastated by the guns of the Williamite army in 1691. Roofless, great irregular holes mar the structure. Rocks clutter its base, others are strewn down the slope. One aspect of the castle, however, escaped the fierce onslaught, the splendid view of the surrounding countryside, a many-hued patchwork of houses, fields and hedges, with the shimmering waters of the estuary in the distance, smoothly flowing past.

Due west of Carrigogunnell is the derelict castle of Dromore, a complete contrast to its wartorn neighbour. Built about a century ago by the Earl of Limerick – the site chosen was a uniquely scenic one, on a height above Dromore Lake with a backdrop of mature trees upon which a building designed in towers and turrets, unusual in the countryside then was erected – it presented in its heyday, a rare and beautiful picture. Unfortunately, it was attacked by the household scourge of dampness, found to be unsuitable as a residence and later abandoned. Yet, it still retains much of its beauty and elegance.

Close to the estuary, is the small pleasing village of Pallaskenry, dating, it is thought, from Cromwellian times and once noted for the occupations of spinning and weaving. Beyond the village on the shores of the estuary, is Ringmoylan Quay. A spacious amenity area with a swimming pool and car park, it offers a clear view of the estuary on a fine day, especially of Shannon Airport on the Clare shore to which boat trips and tours are available in the holiday season. Beside the road, on the approach to the quay, is the remains of a windmill tower. In this area also, is the ruined Beag Castle, built on a low grassy slope close to the shoreline and ringed by a small amenity area and pier, from which a ferry service was operated to Ringannon on the Clare side in the last century. Passenger steamers also called here. A wide expanse of strand is visible when the tide is low, and extensive views may be had across the estuary. The castle, now roofless, is high, with large gaps in its masonry walls. It was owned, originally, by the Knight of Glin of the Norman family of the Fitzgeralds, but was confiscated in 1573.

In the hinterland to the south are the spacious leisure grounds of Curraghchase Forest Park, an area of six hundred acres, acquired by the State in 1957 and developed as an activity centre and camping site. It has numerous forest walks and nature trails. Trees - yew, oak, sycamore, hazel and others, shrubs, wild flowers and small mammals whet the interest. Added to these are small scenic lakes and an arboretum, containing species of trees from all over the world, such as, Sitka spruce, cedar from the Himalayas and redwood from North America.

Curraghchase House, destroyed by fire in 1941 and now a ruin, was once the home of Aubrey de Vere, a well-known poet. He wrote many stirring ballads based on the great military events of Irish history. 'A Ballad of Athlone' and 'The March to Kinsale' are two of his finest. He is buried in the cemetery of St. Mary's Protestant Church at Askeaton, just three miles distant.

From the promontory of Beag Castle, the estuary shoreline swerves in a southerly direction and curls around Greenish Island to make the wide inlet of the River Deel, a river that is tidal and navigable to the small town of Askeaton. The name 'Askeaton' is derived from that of an ancient Celtic tribe – The Géitine who, in earlier times, inhabited the area. Eas Géitine means, the Waterfall of the Géitine.

The Normans, who spread rapidly through North and West Limerick in the 12th century, after the death of Donal Mor O'Brien, occupied those lands and built a castle on an island in the River Deel. Eventually, it became part of the lands possessed by the Norman family of the Fitzgeralds, later the powerful earls of Desmond. In the 14th century, the old edifice was replaced by a fortress-like castle which became the Desmond centre of power. Around it a settlement began to grow. Two centuries later the Desmond overlordship, was destroyed in conflicts with the English Crown, when, in 1579, castle and town surrendered. The 17th century witnessed another spasm of fierce fighting. In 1652, a Cromwellian army captured the castle and reduced it to its present ruined state. The ruin, roofless and tree-ringed, is ninety feet high, and part of it, notably the great Banqueting Hall, has remained in a fair state of preservation.

A short distance downstream, on the east bank of the Deel, close to a modern bridge and highway, is the roofless shell of a Franciscan Friary, founded by the Earl of Desmond in the 14th century. Finely-designed, its outer walls are still intact. It has a nave, chancel and north transept, and its 15th century cloisters, its carved windows and sedilia, remain in a fair state of preservation. Destroyed in 1579, it was rebuilt in the 1620s, but became a victim of the Cromwellian campaign of 1652.

Today, Askeaton is a quiet rural retreat, bypassed by the main highway to Foynes and Tarbert which divides it from the nearby banks of the estuary. All trace of its war-like history has vanished with the exception of the roofless shells of its castle and friary. Its long sinuous street runs downhill to the old stone, five-arched bridge that spans the River Deel, built in the 16th century by the Earl of Desmond. The river is broad here with a busy current in which swans immerse their long necks to peck at aquatic plants. Lower down, it deteriorates into a wide sandy trench at low tide with only a narrow central channel of water, over which birds skim and swivel and flap their wings. An amenity area and swimming pool line its west bank below the bridge.

The Deel, however, was important in past centuries as a trade route to the estuary, when Askeaton had mills and brewing interests. Cargo boats sailed to the quays at high tide to deliver grain, catches of fish, and mounds of seaweed, much used in those days as a fertiliser for the soil. Timber, grain and farm produce were exported. This trade began to decline with the advent of the railways and later of road freight traffic, and eventually fell away altogether. Different interests occupy the town now, the manufacture of baby foods and polystyrene goods, and the production of lime for the alumina factory at Aughinish Island. Along with these, is the small industrial estate in process of development, on the banks of the Shannon estuary nearby.

On the western margin of the inlet of the Deel is the island of Aughinish, or Each Inis, meaning Horse Island, separated from it by the narrow Poulaweala Creek. Much of this island is reclaimed land, lying between the Poulaweala Creek on the east, and Robertstown River on the west, with marshland and brackish pools on the south side where a tarred road joins it to the main highway. The largest industrial complex on the Limerick shore line, it dates from 1983 and consists of major factory installations for the making of alumina from imported bauxite, and a deepwater terminal to which the raw materials may be delivered and unloaded, and from which the alumina can be exported.

A short distance west of Aughinish is Foynes, the only seaport in the county. The name is said to derive from the Gaelic word 'Faing', meaning 'raven' Though small, it has been continually upgraded since the 1960s with the intention of increasing its size and capacity to handle vessels of 35, 000 tonnes deadweight. It first came into prominence during the American Civil War, 1860-64, when it sent a steamship, carrying a cargo of uniforms to the Confederate Army. Towards the end of the century, it had established a busy trade in the export of farm produce from East Limerick, and the import of tools and fertilisers. Close to the port is Foynes Island, part of which is being planted by the Forestry Commission, and on which one household still remains. In the Napoleonic era, it was fortified against a French invasion by the construction of a battery on its westerly perimeter, now called Battery Point.

It wasn't, however, until the Second World War that Foynes achieved dramatic publicity when in July 1937, it became the terminus of the trans -Atlantic seaplane service, which ferried many military and political personnel between North America and Europe during the war years. After the war, when seaplanes and flying boats were no longer viable for the growing upsurge in passenger numbers, the newly-built Shannon Airport replaced it as an air terminus, and Foynes reverted to its normal role as a trading

Ruins of Askeaton Castle

Askeaton Village

The old bridge over the Deel

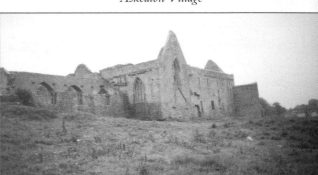

The Franciscan Friary

The alumina factory on Aughinish Island

The port of Foynes

The waterfront at Foynes Island and harbour

The White River flows into the estuary

Foynes Village

An amenity area at Glin

Glin castle

Glin Pier

The village of Glin

port, complemented in the 1960s by the building of an oil jetty on the island close by.

An attractive little town, close to the estuary, Foynes is sited beneath high wooded cliffs where, at the west side, a steep walkway, steps and pathway, lead to the leafy summit where a tall granite Cross, erected to the memory of Edmund Spring Rice by the tenants of his family estate, stands, surrounded by trees and wild flowers, and barely visible from the harbour below. Splendid views of the estuary and the tip of Foynes Island with its oil jetty may be had from this vantage point.

Foynes has many holiday amenities, including yachting, fishing and golf. On its western approach, there is an amenity area with swimming pool and car park. The Yacht Club is sited here and has a jetty for small boats and yachts. In 1989, Foynes opened a Flying Boat Museum in memory of its brief period of war-time glory, fifty years before. The Museum contains many exhibits, a 1940s style cinema and tea room, the original terminal building, radio and weather room, with receivers, transmitters and Morse Code equipment. It shows a video in English and French of the introduction to the first trans-Atlantic passenger service, and a view of Foynes as it was in the war years, 1939-1945.

Not far from the town is the hill of Knockpatrick from which panoramic views of the estuary may be obtained. The ruin of an ancient church surrounded by a large graveyard occupies the top of the hill, and legend has it that St. Patrick visited here and gave a blessing to the County Kerry from its summit. Buried in the graveyard is the poetess, Charlotte Grace O'Brien, daughter of the Young Ireland leader, William Smith O'Brien, exiled for his patriotic efforts. In his later years, he lived in Cahermoyle House some miles to the south and is buried in the nearby Rathronan cemetery.

The estuary shoreline moves gently west from Foynes, skirting the main road, which has a protective tree-topped wall on its left and a low sea wall on the right. Patches of shingle beach lie below; the water is shallow and weedy as it sluices into tiny creeks and inlets. Stands of deciduous trees are frequent, and two headlands, green and fertile, break the smooth contours and stretch into the watercourse. The village of Loghill, or Leamhcoill, the Elm Wood, small and pleasing, and sited on the White River, or Abha Bhán, is perched above a pocket of inlets which divide the shoreline into low green promontories upon which cattle graze. West of Loghill, is the small Kilteery Pier on the brink of the estuary with some amenities - pleasant grassy sections, seating facilities and access to bathing and boating.

Farther west is the larger village of Glin. Situated in one of the most scenic parts of the estuary, it has a shingle beach lying beneath the low coastal wall. An amenity area runs alongside with tennis courts, picnic section, car park and public park. In the shallows combed by the light drifting waves, swans feed and ruffle their heavy wings. Glin, whose ancient name was Gleann Corbrai, the Glen of the Corbrai, a tribe once settled in the area, is designed in the form of a square. It has a long historical background because of its association with the great Desmond family of Askeaton, the Fitzgeralds, a descendant of which, the Knight of Glin, owns the local castle built on lands held by the family for over seven hundred years. The present building, a rectangular mansion within a fine demesne, was erected in the 18th century, and is open to the public at stated times during the tourist season. Two lodges with Gothic-type architecture are built on the roadside in the protective wall of the demesne, one being now used as a craft shop and café.

Standing in the village is the ruined keep of another Fitzgerald stronghold, owned in the past by the Knights of Glin. Solitary and ivy-grown, the narrow Glencorbry stream laps its dark stone walls. In 1600, it was besieged and captured by an English army and wrecked to such an extent that it was later abandoned. Its successor, the present Glin Castle, erected on the west side of the village, has eschewed all warlike emblems and is designed as a gracious and artistic residence, a focus of interest for occupants and visitors alike.

The pier at Glin, on the east side of the village and recently renovated, was at one time a very busy place where fishermen plied their trade daily, landing fish from a number of weirs in the estuary. These were owned by a number of local people, including the Knight of Glin. The fish was packed in ice and exported to the London markets, the ice coming mainly from Norway in cargo ships that unloaded at the pier, though some ice houses in the vicinity maintained a supply as well. On a hillside above the pier, a prominent mansion-type building known locally as Hamilton's Tower, stands alone. Erected in the 19th century by a Doctor Hamilton, it was little used and is now derelict.

From Glin, the shoreline, in one of its most scenic and smoothest stretches, passes into County Kerry to reach the village, the island and the boat ferry of Tarbert. Sited on a steep hill with roads extending to the estuary and the island, Tarbert has the distinction of possessing the only ferry crossing on the entire estuary, south side. The short twenty-minute trip from Tarbert Pier is made to Killimer on the Clare shoreline and caters for passengers and vehicles. The crossings begin at 8 a.m., and are made every hour on the half-hour.

In the last century, the port of Tarbert was busy with local trade, becoming the outlet for agricultural and dairy produce from West Limerick and North Kerry. Sailing ships which plied the estuary routes and brought cargoes to and from the Continent and North America, called here. The first half of the present century saw the decline of this trade due to the competition of road and rail traffic, and its eventual disappearance.

Close to the mainland is Tarbert Island, connected to it by a causeway. A lighthouse stands on its central perimeter. Once known as 'The Battery', the island was garrisoned by the British army for a long period from the 1800s onwards, and equipped with gun emplacements and batteries. At this time, ships of the Royal Navy were a familiar sight in the lower estuary. A few miles to the west, at Fort Shannon, a second garrison was similarly equipped. When the military presence was removed in the present century, Fort Shannon became derelict and its batteries disappeared. Those on Tarbert Island were removed in the 1960s.

At this time, the island found a new industrial role when the Electricity Supply Board bought it as a site for an oil-fired power station. Chosen because of its deepwater facilities and its abundance of cooling water, the 65-acre site was transformed into a complex of office and technical buildings, electrical transmission lines, fuel oil tanks and a jetty to which tankers deliver cargoes of oil. The powerhouse was operational in 1969 and was later enlarged greatly in the 1970s.

The village of Tarbert, forty-eight miles from Limerick and steadily developing into a small town, has many holiday amenities, including angling, water sports and coastal tours through North Kerry. It hosts a music festival and a regatta in the summer months. Tarbert House, a Georgian-type mansion built by John Leslie in 1690 and still in family ownership, is set in woodland and surrounded by fine trees, shrubs and flowers, with an attractive view over the estuary. Open to the public during the holiday season, it exhibits a valuable collection of mirrors, paintings, and items of furniture of the 17th and 18th centuries.

A recent and interesting historical collection has been set up in Tarbert Courthouse and Jail, a well-preserved stone building, now a civic centre. It portrays the court procedures of the Bridewell system of imprisonment in the last century. Three-dimensional displays, pictures, traditional-type furniture and life-size models lend dramatic reality to the various scenes. The centre also contains a tourist office, a coffee shop and gift shop, and is open daily between June and October.

From Tarbert, the shoreline curves into the shallow bay of Glencloosagh, runs north to Ardmore Point

The ruin of Glencorbry Castle

The passenger ferry

A section of Tarbert Island

The ESB Powerhouse

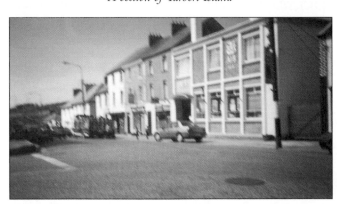

The village of Tarbert

Ballylongford

and then descends steeply into Ballylongford Bay from which a narrow inlet leads to Saleen which has a pier, and then to Ballylongford, a short distance inland. A small pleasant village, it contains historical artifacts and ruined memorials of the once powerful family of the O'Connors of Kerry. Lislaughtin Abbey,

Saleen Pier

Lislaughtin Abbey

Carrigafoyle Castle

Ballybunion

The remains of Ballybunion Castle

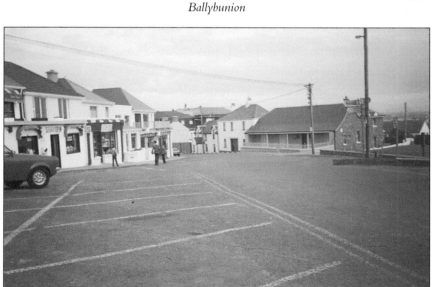

Ballyheigue

a 15th century friary, one mile distant, was built by them for the Franciscan Order. A church with its north transept, and a gateway to the adjoining monastery, are still intact. In the church are a pointed east window, three sedilia, carved in a beautiful and unusual style, and three windows in the south wall of the choir.

A more militant aspect of the O'Connor dominance in this area, is the still-sturdy ruin of Carrigafoyle Castle which was once their centre of power. Two miles to the north-west on the estuary shore, it is built on Carrig Island and in the past, held a commanding position on the lower estuary. The landward side was protected by a strong wall of which a portion still stands. The castle, originally, five storeys high, has a tower eighty feet tall, placed in the centre of an enclosed courtyard which contained a dock for boats. Its outer walls are intact, while inside, a spiral stone staircase to the tower allows visitors to obtain wide and splendid views of the estuary and the surrounding countryside. The castle was attacked many times during the Desmond rebellion in the 16th century, but survived until the Cromwellian campaign in 1649 when it was partially destroyed. In later years, it was abandoned.

The shoreline winds on, past the shallow Bunaclugga Bay to Béal Point, where it turns sharply south on its final stretch to the mouth of the estuary and Kerry Head. A fine sandy beach, long and wide, on each side of the Point, forms Béal Strand, the first of its kind on the south side of the estuary. It is a scenic scene, calm and beautiful. On the watercourse, an oil tanker drifts at anchor, and in the shallows a fisherman trawls for salmon. The opposite shoreline is clearly visible, as is the mouth of the Shannon, stretching from Kerry Head to the Loop Head peninsula. As the shoreline curves abruptly to run south, it leads to the only range of steep cliffs on its long course, the rocky cave-ridden heights on the outskirts of Ballybunion.

The best-known seaside resort in North Kerry, the town is named after the Gaelic form, Baile an Bhuinneanaigh, the Town of the Sapling, and caters exclusively for tourism and sport. Serene and attractive, it provides many facilities and services to woo the visitor. Its sandy beaches, close to the main traffic routes, extend southward for up to two miles. They are fringed by high cliffs, coves, and sand dunes. There are many walks and nature trails. Boats are available for angling and pleasure trips. Some of the caves in the cliffs can only be reached by boat, others can be explored at low tide. Golf, tennis, cinema and summer shows add to the variety of entertainment. An historical and heritage museum provides a focus for more serious moments.

On a narrow headland which juts forward to divide the beach below the town, is the sole remaining wall of Ballybunion Castle. A property of the Norman family of Fitzmaurice, it was destroyed by fire in 1583. From the small green in front of it, one sees a wonderful landscape of sea, land and sky, the central feature of which is the great mouth of the Shannon as the river merges smoothly with the Atlantic Ocean.

The ruined Lick Castle which belonged to the Earls of Desmond, is north of the town, and some distance east is Knockamore Hill, 880 feet high, a landmark in the area, giving a panoramic view of the estuary, the ocean, and the surrounding countryside. South of the town, a coastal path through the sand dunes skirts the local golf course and leads one to Cashen Bay and village, at which the River Feale, which flows from West Limerick and is rich in fish, pours into the sea. The Cashen fishery is located here on the edge of the ocean and is regarded as the finest in the county. In this area also, is the National Monument at Rattoo, which contains the ruins of an ancient church, a graveyard and a Round Tower. Not far away is the Rattoo Museum, which reopens the pages of history to show exhibits from the earliest centuries, warlike, social and religious - the memorabilia of North Kerry.

On the approach to the promontory of Kerry Head topped by the Truskmore and Maulin hills, is the most westerly village in the area – Ballyheigue. Situated, not on the Shannon estuary but on the southern coastline of the promontory, it stands on Ballyheigue Bay. A sheltered arm of the Atlantic Ocean, the bay lies between the small hillside town on the east, and a palisade of rocky and purple peaks on the west, which dominate the seascape as they tower above the waves.

Ballyheigue, a small market centre and seaside resort, is a quiet relaxed place with many tourist amenities - a long spacious strand, a caravan park, a fine esplanade and ample car parking. Sea sports flourish here, surfing and water-skiing, swimming, boating and fishing. Coach tours of the Ring of Kerry, a comprehensive itinerary of the adjacent countryside, to include Kerry Head, historical sites, museums and scenic areas, are also available. A small bird sanctuary lies below the village, close to a sandy stretch of wild vegetation - nettles, grassheads, thistles, dandelions and buttercups, the growth of which helps to firm the soil for the purposes of reclamation. The ruined Ballyheigue castle on the verge of the town was built in the 19th century by the Crosby family.

Three miles northwest of Ballyheigue is the broad summit of Kerry Head, overlooking the mouth of the estuary. It is at the apex of a rising strata of green slopes, moving in spiral fashion to the Truskmore and Maulin hills, with clusters of houses in the valleys and lowlands. Rocks and broken stone are prevalent on and around the thin soil of the summit, interspersed with patches of rough grass, peat and heather. The stones, which are of an off-white hue, streaked with blue, often encase fragments of semi-precious minerals like quartz crystals and ametheysts which can be released by breaking the granite shell. The spongy terrain slopes gradually to the fringe of the estuary on the north shoreline and small fields are cultivated. There is an absence of high cliff, such as occurs at Loop Head on the Clare side, as the land rolls smoothly to the estuary margin and the mouth of the Shannon.

The ruined Ballyheigue Castle

The hills of Kerry Head

A gentle slope to the sea

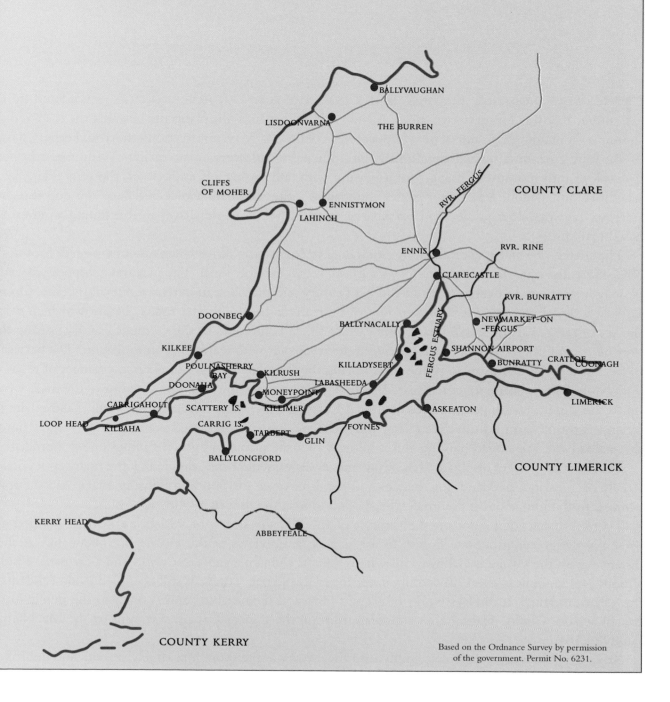

THE SHANNON
ESTUARY

—

CLARE
SHORELINE

BALLYVAUGHAN

LISDOONVARNA

THE BURREN

CLIFFS
OF MOHER

COUNTY CLARE

RVR. FERGUS

ENNISTYMON

LAHINCH

ENNIS

RVR. RINE

CLARECASTLE

RVR. BUNRATTY

DOONBEG

BALLYNACALLY

NEWMARKET-ON
-FERGUS

KILKEE

SHANNON AIRPORT

POULNASHERRY
BAY

KILLADYSERT

BUNRATTY

CRATLOE
COONAGH

DOONAHA

KILRUSH

LABASHEEDA

FERGUS ESTUARY

CARRIGAHOLT

MONEYPOINT

SCATTERY IS.

KILLIMER

LIMERICK

LOOP HEAD

KILBAHA

CARRIG IS.

FOYNES

ASKEATON

TARBERT

GLIN

BALLYLONGFORD

COUNTY LIMERICK

KERRY HEAD

ABBEYFEALE

COUNTY KERRY

Based on the Ordnance Survey by permission
of the government. Permit No. 6231.

Chapter Twelve

THE CLARE SHORELINE, CURVING GENTLY INTO THE TOWNLAND OF COONAGH, is bordered by the public roadway for up to two miles. A wide strip of 'wetland' for plants lies between the road and the shoreline, containing a wealth of trees and saplings - willow, sally, sycamore, whitethorn and others, a mass of soft leafy greenness, sprinkled with early blossom and wildflowers in late spring. As summer advances, it develops into mounds of foliage, interspersing with and setting off each other, those of alder, hazel, hawthorn and willow. Vegetation grows abundantly - the colourful violet buddleja, the dog rose, red valerian, ragwort, cow parsley and blackberry creepers, while scarlet haws are beginning to cram the hawthorn bushes.

The strip is one and a half miles long, stretching to Barrington's Pier where clumps of reeds root in the mire. Here, the open shoreline appears with grassy verges and low bush. The pier was a stopping place for passenger steamers and cargo boats in the last century and provides an extensive viewing point. On the Limerick shoreline opposite, a broken line of bush fronts the Industrial Estate, below which, is a low thicket of reeds. Farther downstream, one can see the tall chimneys of the Cement Factory, issuing thin grey plumes of smoke. A small park surrounds the stone pier with seating accommodation. The barricade of trees peters out downstream of the pier, leaving the shoreline open with deep low fringes of reeds on both banks, cut and harvested each year. A second green area occupies the opposite side of the road, which up to this point, has fringed the Westfield Bird Sanctuary, a wildlife haven with a small shallow lake fed by underground streams from the estuary, and sheltering birds as diversified as the kestrel, the grey heron, the mallard and snipe, reed bunting and swallow. Colourful plants and green saplings line its borders.

There are no villages on this stretch of the estuary. A residential area, divided by the highway, it consists largely of grassland, parkland, low hedges and stands of trees, surrounding housing estates and shopping centres. In the hinterland is the small village of Cratloe at the foot of Woodcock Hill.

There is radio equipment on the summit of the hill, the slopes of which are heavily wooded and presently designated as a State Forest. From it, panoramic views of the estuary are obtainable. A short distance from the village is Gallows Hill where there is a picnic area, forest walks and a car park. Cratloe Woods House, built in the 17th century and fringed by old oak woods, is still occupied by descendants of the O'Brien family. It displays works of art and historical memorabilia and is open to the public in the tourist season. Cratloe Castle, now a desolate ruin on the Limerick road, was built by the MacNamara family in 1610.

Many small streams and rivulets empty into the estuary as the shoreline, largely smooth and unbroken, passes the townlands of Cratloe. The first sizable break is the small inlet through which the Bunratty River joins the estuary. Bunratty Castle, sited on the west bank of the river, is one of the best-known of Irish great houses. It was built in 1277 by the Norman, Thomas de Clare, on an island named 'Tradaree'. Involved in the conflicts of the following centuries, it was destroyed and rebuilt a number of times. Captured by the O'Brien family in the 14th century, it was held by them until the beginning of the 18th century when it passed into the hands of the MacNamaras, a branch of the O'Brien clan, who rebuilt the castle in its present form.

A National Monument since 1954, it has been restored by the Board of Works, and is noted for its collection of furniture, tapestries and works of art from the 14th to the 17th centuries. The castle is open to the public throughout the year, the provision of medieval style banquets being one of its most interesting features. Bunratty Folk Park is located in the castle grounds. In it are recreated aspects of Irish rural life – buildings, traditional crafts and a typical village street of the 19th century. It is open daily and refreshments and entertainment are freely available.

In this part of the estuary, the width of the watercourse has increased dramatically and many small islands dot its expanse. Streams pour in from the hills, as the shoreline curves inward for some miles, and then broadens out again as it reaches the headland of Rineanna and its widest inlet, the estuary of the River Fergus. Here, on the east bank of the Fergus is Shannon Airport, the Shannon Industrial Estate, and Shannon Town.

In 1936, in the swampy district of Rineanna, the foundations of the airport were laid. Five years later, under the name of the Shannon International Airport, it was opened for nonscheduled flights. Commercial passenger flights, however, did not begin, until 1945 with the ending of World War II. Progress was swift. In 1947, it became the first Customs Free Airport with an International Duty-Free Shop. Other activities at this time include its development as a Catering Centre, and as a re-fuelling and maintenance base.

By the mid-fifties, it was winning a sizable share of Atlantic air traffic and a new jet runway was constructed, coming into operation in 1960. New hotels were also being built and plans were made for the creation of a new town as well as an industrial estate. Both projects have undergone continuous development in the following decades, until, in the 1990s, Shannon Town has a population of 8,000 people, and up to one hundred and ten companies located in the Industrial Estate, now known as the Shannon Free Zone. New facilities, such as a large aircraft maintenance firm, more warehousing, an Aviation Park and the Shannon Business Park, have been added. Close to the airport is the Dernish oil jetty, built in 1973, at which tankers supply all the airport's fuel requirements.

To provide full services for the ever-moving procession of passengers through the airport is a gigantic task. It requires restaurants, snack and lounge bars, general shops, rest rooms, banking and car hire facilities, car parks and direct coach connections with other cities. A tourist information office is a necessity and hotel reservation services are in continual demand. Within the precincts of the airport is the Great Southern Hotel, and close by, on the Shannon shoreline, an 18-hole golf course is sited.

A sea wall is built here, enclosing a green marshy area of tall reeds, rushes, grassheads and a variety of other vegetation. Skimming over the watercourse is a flock of seagulls, as an oil tanker draws alongside the Dernish jetty, which stretches from a narrow headland into the estuary, at its widest in this area where it merges with that of the Shannon. Islands and sandy spits are numerous, many of them located on the west and south-west banks.

In the hinterland, north-east of the airport, is the village of Newmarket-on Fergus, small but busy, and

The tree-bordered shoreline

Cow parsley and buttercup

A section of Shannon Free Zone

The Westfield Bird Sanctuary

The ruined Cratloe Castle

Barrington Pier

The Bunratty River

Shannon Airport

Shannon Town

Bunratty Castle

Dromoland Castle

The village of Clarecastle

The River Fergus at Clarecastle Pier

Daingean Castle

Ballynacally Village

Ballynacally Pier with Deer Island

fast becoming popular as a dormitory suburb of Shannon Town and Ennis. Adjacent to it, are many fine houses, now used as hotels and riding centres. Dromoland Castle, the property of the O'Brien family from the 17th century to 1962 – the present well-preserved building being erected about 1826 is now a luxury hotel and international conference venue. Surrounded by scenic grounds, fountains, an ornamental lake and formal flower beds, it includes a golf course, and has extensive views on the Shannon estuary. It retains a patriotic link with the Young Ireland Movement and the aborted rising of 1848, in the person of William Smith O'Brien who was born in the castle in 1803.

The shoreline of the Fergus estuary continues north for some miles, dwindling to a narrow channel at the mouth of the River Fergus which is tidal for twenty miles as it flows through Ennis to Clarecastle, and rolls south to its confluence with the broad watercourse of the Shannon. Clarecastle, a small village, was, in the past, the port for Ennis. At its pier, cargo boats docked to deliver provisions, fuel and fertilisers for the Ennis market, and carried away farm produce for export to the ports of the estuary. This trade has now been replaced by rail and road freight.

The River Fergus is broad and deep as it flows by the now disused Clarecastle pier and streams on to widen enormously as it merges into its estuary. As its western shoreline curves and moves south, narrow shingle beaches appear and islands are very close to the mainland, At Islandavanna, Spartina grass is being grown in an effort to strengthen and impact the mudflats for the purpose of reclamation. At the inlet of the Owenslieve River, one of the many streams that water the shoreline, Horse Island stands close to the land. Nearby, off the main road, is the ruined shell of Daingean Castle, built in the last century by a local landlord. It was later abandoned and became derelict.

The first village on the western shoreline of the Fergus estuary is Ballynacally, or the Town of the Nuns. It is small and pretty, and is steadily being improved by colourful flower borders and beds, new walls, neat houses and a green amenity area. It has a narrow pier, close to which is Deer Island. This island, the only one in the area still inhabited, has a woman resident, maintaining a house and farm and boating ashore for supplies. A short distance farther west is the cattle quay at Crovrahan. A metal pen stands on top of the narrow stone platform. Close by is a sandy cove with wide flat-bottomed boats, having wooden superstructures, to bring cattle and sheep to the nearby islands. The small pier is surrounded by islands, dotting the watercourse in all directions. At Ballynacally, Deer Island and Coney Island, at Crovrahan Quay, Illaunbeg, Shore Island, Inismacowney, Inis Tubrid and the wooded Canon Island, or Inis Gad, at the verge of the Shannon Estuary. The quay is picturesque in summer with wild flowers, oxe-eye daisies, purple thistle, and the distinctive yellow ragwort.

Only a mile farther west is the largest village on the Fergus estuary – Killadysert, or Cill an Disirt, the Church of the Hermitage. In the last century, and in the first half of the present one, Killadysert was a distribution centre as cargo boats from Foynes delivered provisions and goods of all kinds at its pier. Around the harbour, recently dredged and enlarged, are the derelict shops and warehouses of the past, once the scene of brisk buying and selling as the people of the area crowded in to replenish their supplies. Inis Corcair, now uninhabited, is a very short distance from the harbour and can be reached on foot in low water. Green fields upon which cattle graze, and a few old houses stretch behind a skirting of hawthorn, sycamore, and wild vegetation. Beyond Inis Corcair, lies Inis Gad or Canon Island which has the remains of an Augustinian Priory of the 13th century, the founding of which is attributed to Donal Mor O'Brien, King of Munster. Killadysert owes its name, Cill an Disirt, to St. Murthaile who is said to have established a hermitage there. In the harbour area is the remains of an old church set in a graveyard.

From Killadysert the shoreline runs smoothly south, with few inlets or headlands for some distance, and then, making a wide curve, leaves the Fergus estuary and regains that of the Shannon. Strip-like shingle and sandy beaches, lined with seaweed, predominate in this area. The road runs close to the estuary and sections of sea wall divide it from the shoreline.

The width of the estuary narrows considerably opposite Foynes Island on the Limerick side but broadens again as it passes Rinealon Point and curves widely into Labasheeda Bay, making one of the most scenic stretches on the western shoreline. The village of Labasheeda, at the mouth of the bay, consists of one long street. Debilitated by long-term emigration, it has a number of empty houses. A small cement pier and slipway lie on the edge of the village, around which an amenity centre with tennis court, picnic area and seating accommodation, is being developed. The village stands at the north-eastern corner of a long peninsula which juts sharply and broadly into the estuary. At Kilkerin Point, on the western tip of the peninsula is a well preserved Martello tower and military batteries, built there in the Napoleonic era to guard against a French invasion. A circular stone bastion set in a deep ditch in a field, it is surrounded by walled installations, now topped with grass and clay. The wide ditch is also protected by a stone wall. It is sited opposite Tarbert Island on the Kerry shoreline, on which there was also a battery.

On the west side of the peninsula, the shoreline stretches inland for up to four miles. The Cloon River joins it as it turns sharply and curves southwards to form the long, narrow Clonderalaw Bay. Bordered by shingle beaches, it has a remote and rather desolate aspect. With open grassy banks for the most part, and dotted with small creeks and coves, pools and hidden streamlets, it has become a natural haven for wintering wildfowl. Thousands of geese and waders occupy its solitary expanse in the winter months.

The small village of Knock is on the west bank of the bay in a pleasing situation, tucked at the foot of a hill where trees and flowers grow abundantly. The estuary, drifting on to a narrow shingle beach, is curbed here by a sea wall on both sides of a long pier with bollards, stone steps and seating accommodation. The pier is grass-covered and dotted with clumps of daisy while ragwort and brown dock grow on the verges. A flock of wagtails skip and skim over its solitary surface.

Farther to the southwest where Clonderalaw Bay merges with the estuary, is the village of Killimer, or Cill Iomair, the Church of St Iomar of the 6th century, a contemporary of Senan who founded the monastic settlement on Scattery Island. The old church at Killimer is now an ivy-covered ruin, surrounded by grave slabs and headstones which occupy both sides of the road. This graveyard is the burial place of Ellen Hanley, whose death at the hands of a jealous husband, John Scanlon, later sentenced and hanged, inspired three writers to immortalise her memory, novelist Gerald Griffin in the 'Collegians', composer Benedict in the opera 'The Lily of Killarney', and dramatist Boucicault who based a play on the tragic episode, entitled 'The Colleen Bawn'.

Killimer, today, is a small village, in the vicinity of which is a Holy Well with flagstone, associated with St. Senan. Its chief feature, however, is essentially modern. It is the terminal of the ferry-boat service on the Clare shoreline, providing with Tarbert on the Kerry side, a necessary facility much appreciated by tourists and residents alike, and the only one of its kind on the 60-mile estuary. The terminal is a spacious one with ample car parking, and a set of modern buildings, comprising offices, a large, wellstocked shop, a café, an Information Desk, and general facilities. The ferry-boat service begins at 7 a.m. daily, (except on Sunday when it begins at 9 a.m) and runs every hour on the hour until 9 p.m., with two ferry-boats in use in the tourist season.

South-west of Killimer, a few miles distant on the estuary shoreline, is the huge, coal-fired generating station of Moneypoint. Built by the Electricity Supply Board, it is the largest such station in the country. Construction began in 1979 on a 447-acre site, chosen because it had a rock-solid foundation and a

Crovrahan Quay and Illaunbeg

Killadysert Village

Labasheeda Village

Killadysert Harbour

The pier at Labasheeda

Inis Corcair

The Village of Knock

The pier at Knock

Killimer Village

The old church at Killimer

The ferry-boat at Killimer

Moneypoint Generating Station

Kilrush Town Hall

A section of Kilrush Wood

Cappa Pier

deepwater facility. It went into operation in 1985, its supplies of coal being delivered to the newly-built jetty, 380 metres in length, by bulk carriers from all over the world. It can accommodate vessels of 180,000 tonnes deadweight and over. A visitors' facility enables the public to view the complex.

The shoreline swings to the north as it passes the Moneypoint generating station which is a landmark on the estuary. Soon afterwards it rounds Cappa Pier and the narrow inlet upon which the town of Kilrush stands. The chief town of West Clare, it takes its name from Cill Rois, the Church in the Wood, an ancient foundation, said to have been built by monks from the nearby Scattery Island which lies close to Cappa Pier. Around the church of which fragments still remain, a village began to grow. It was not until the l8th and 19th centuries and the enlargement of Cappa Pier, that Kilrush began to develop into a small port. In this process, it was aided by the efforts of the Vandeleur family who were the landlords of the area at that period. Streets and public buildings were progressively added and, by the 1800s, a thriving port, capable of accommodating vessels of up to 2,000 tonnes deadweight, was in operation. Along with these were turf boats, fishing boats and cargo boats crowding the pier, and later on, a passenger steamer service, running twice a week to and from Limerick harbour. British naval craft frequented the lower estuary and a British garrison was located in the town.

The Vandeleur influence died out towards the end of the last century when the family mansion, located in Kilrush Wood was destroyed by fire. The Forestry Division bought the demesne of 420 acres, and in 1973, it was re-named Kilrush Forest Park. It is now an amenity area with nature trails, picnic facilities and a car park, complementing other available sports, golf, tennis, swimming and water sports, and the resources of the Aylevarroo Caravan Park. In the Town Hall a heritage centre has been opened, depicting the history of the town, in exhibits, photographs, and in audio-visual form. Standing in the adjoining street is the Maid of Erin monument – a memorial to the Manchester Martyrs of 1867, Allen, Larkin and O'Brien, with an inscription written in three languages, Irish, English and French.

The Romanesque-style Catholic Church was built in the last century as was the nearby Convent of Mercy, with a school attached. The church's steeple is 230 feet high, and one of the distinctive features of the interior is the row of stained glass windows, eight of which came from the Harry Clarke studio. The older Church of Ireland, erected in 1813, close to the site of the ancient church which gave Kilrush its name, contains plaques to the memory of various members of the Vandeleur family, some of whom are buried in a mausoleum in the adjoining graveyard.

One mile from the town is Cappa Pier. Built in 1764, it was completed in its present form in 1835. Busy in past decades, with passenger steamers plying from Kerry and Limerick, bringing tourists from many areas to the seaside resort of Kilkee on the Clare coast, as well as boats delivering catches of fish, turf boats, and cargo boats exporting the farm produce of the county, Cappa has seen the decline of most of this trade, largely wiped out by road and rail services. Pleasure craft, fishing boats, some cargo boats, and a hovercraft service based in Limerick, use it today.

The most noted of the estuary's islands, Scattery Island, or Inis Catha, of religious and historical fame, is easily reached from Cappa Pier, involving a short boat trip of fifteen minutes which can be arranged at the Interpretive Centre built by the Board of Works close to the marina.

In 1991, Kilrush added a new and interesting project to its amenities, known as the Kilrush Creek Marina. Located in the old disused harbour, it has 120 berths, a set of offices with many facilities, a boatyard equipped to carry out all boat repairs, and a car park. Close by is the Cappa Holiday Village offering excellent holiday homes to complement those at the marina itself, where there is a residential complex, a traditional village street with retail outlets, and a large water sports area for training in the skills of sailing and related activities. Only twenty miles from the mouth of the Shannon, Kilrush can now facilitate Irish and foreign yachts and cruisers desirous of exploring the west coast from Kerry to Galway and Donegal. Operating from within the marina is the Atlantic Adventure Company, which specialises in deep sea fishing and also provides excellent boats and equipment for sea anglers.

From Kilrush, the shoreline runs north to form the triangular Poulnasherry Bay, a haven for wintering wildfowl. In its eastern corner is the tiny village of Moyasta, once known as a 'stop' on the West Clare railway line from Kilkee, serving Kilrush and Cappa Pier, a service that ceased in 1961. The shoreline bites deeply into the terrain here to form the lake but narrows to an inlet as it rejoins the estuary. A coastal road named Sli na Mara runs alongside the shoreline, where it turns sharply south to reach Querrin Point and curls around a grassy headland to form a natural marina. A stone quay with bollards and metal steps provide facilities for boating and fishing, while a large gravel area serves as a car park.

Farther west is the growing village of Doonaha, with a caravan park, and one of the few sandy beaches on the estuary. Short and narrow, flanked by low cliffs on both sides, it is calm and sheltered. An amenity area has been provided above it with concrete pathways and steps, a picnic area and pleasing circular flower beds. A short distance from the village, on the road to Kilkee, is the memorial in honour of Eugene O'Curry, a native of the area, who lived from 1794 to 1862. One of the first Gaelic scholars and philologists, O'Curry became professor of Irish history in the Catholic University of Dublin. His publications on Irish history form source material for research students. The memorial consists of a small railed enclosure off the roadway in which there is a stone-built slated cottage closed by a grille. In the grassy forecourt, through which a stream runs, a large rock stands to which a plaque is attached, containing a metal engraving of O'Curry, and a number of smaller engravings depicting traditional scenes of Irish life.

From Doonaha, the shoreline runs smoothly into Carrigaholt Bay. Sited on the small Moyarta River, Carrigaholt, or Carraig an Chabhaltaigh, the Rock of the Fleet, is almost a small town and has a wide frontage on the estuary. There is a long sea wall and harbour which accommodates boats and larger craft, a pleasant sandy beach, an amenity area and seating accommodation. On the pier, west of the town, is the ruined Carrigaholt Castle, overlooking the estuary. Now roofless, its walls are marked with musket holes. A stone staircase leads to a room on the 4th floor. Built by the MacMahon family, it was captured in 1599 and became the property of the O'Brien family. In 1691, after the Williamite wars, it was confiscated. Carrigaholt, now a holiday resort with a Rent-a-Cottage complex, has boating and water sports. It also has an Irish College for students of the language, established and named in honour of Eugene O'Curry.

From Carrigaholt Bay, where, it is said, a number of ships of the Spanish Armada sought shelter in 1588, the coastline turns abruptly and runs smoothly in a double curve to the most southerly promontory on the lower estuary – Kilcredan Point, close to the mouth of the Shannon. Jutting out into the water-course, it was equipped with a battery and light-house for defensive purposes during the Napoleonic era.

At Kilcredan, the shoreline turns sharply to run west to the small village of Kilbaha, the last village on the estuary. It is sited on a bay of the same name. The bay is a sheltered one with a walled pier, fishing boats and a narrow sandy strip. Overlooking the mouth of the Shannon, spectacular views which reach to the mountains of Kerry may be had from this vantage point. A short distance inland is the village of Moneen, in whose church is preserved 'The Little Ark', a tiny, hut-like mobile chapel, six feet long, five feet wide and seven feet high, set on wheels two and a half feet from the ground. The oppressed Catholics of the village, refused a site on which to build a church by a tyrannical landlord in the 1850s, used The Little Ark to enable a priest to celebrate Mass on the shore at Kilbaha Bay.

While the shoreline moves smoothly with an outward curve to Dunmore Head where there is a Holy Well in honour of St. Senan, the road rises in a series of hills to reach the plateau of Loop Head upon which a lighthouse is built. The plateau rises high above the mouth of the Shannon as it merges with the Atlantic Ocean, while waves pound against its base in thunderous and unceasing rhythm. Cliffs form a fearsome barrier on both sides, with niches and ledges for sea birds. The highest point of the estuary and the most westerly on the Clare coastline, it provides grand all-round views of land and sea, from the Kerry

Scattery Island

Kilrush Creek Marina

Querrin Point

Doonaha Village

Doonaha Beach

The O'Curry Memorial

Carrigaholt Beach and Village

mountains in the south to the Aran Islands and the Connemara hills in the north.

Loop Head is a corruption of Leap Head, deriving from the Gaelic description – Léim Chon Chulainn, or Cuchulann's Leap. Legend provides two versions of the ancient and mysterious 'Leap'. It is said that Cuchulann jumped from the mainland cliff to a precipitous crag nearby to escape the spells of a local witch named 'Mal'. A second version

Carrigaholt Pier and Castle

Kilbaha Village and Beach

Kilbaha Pier

The Little Ark

Cliffs at Loop Head

Diarmaid and Gráinne's Rock

The Lighthouse at Loop Head

claims that the fugitive lovers, Diarmaid and Gráinne, made the leap in order to escape from their pursuers, the Fianna, a warrior group of pre-historic times. The crag, high and rugged, is a fragment of the mainland, close to it, but divided from it by a deep cleft, wild and wavebeaten by the in-rushing sea. It is popularly known as 'Diarmaid and Gráinne's Rock', in memory of the beleaguered lovers whose adventures have passed into folklore and are now celebrated in song and in story.

The cliffs on both sides of Loop Head rear tall and

forbidding above the mouth of the Shannon and invite comparison in height and ruggedness with the well known Cliffs of Moher, some miles to the north. Despite its isolated westerly position and craggy wildness, Loop Head, in common with West Clare, has a mild cool climate due to the influence of the Gulf Stream. Fish are plentiful in the clear waters that lap its coastline. From its summit, spectacular views of the vastness of the Atlantic Ocean may be obtained. It is a fit gateway for the great river that has, here, reached its natural end and passes into the depths of the sea.

The passage of the Shannon into the Atlantic Ocean has been an inevitable natural and physical event, revealing a vast and beautiful expanse of sea and global distance. But in practical and industrial terms it is a non-event. It does not connote a spreadway of docks, piers and harbours on one or both banks, a large maritime fleet or even a fishing fleet. It is not marked by a bustling town or a growing village, by a glut of factories, large or small, by shipyards, repair depots, seamen, and the accompaniments of a busy existence, dictated by the needs of a live import/export trade. The mouth of the Shannon is, instead, the centre of a panorama of sea and sky, cliffs and waves and green fields.

The Atlantic Ocean, however, is one of the great oceans of the world and also one of the best known. Since the days of Columbus, ships have been crossing and re-crossing its vast expanse. The development of the United States and Canada in the last two centuries has turned it into one of the busiest of maritime waterways. But the various merchant fleets have largely bypassed the mouth of the Shannon, with the exception of a small number of cargo boats which has slipped up its long channel. Similarly with the passenger steamers and ocean-going liners of the midcentury, they called at Cobh on the south coast and Galway in the west.

It is interesting to recall that in the history of the Shannon estuary only one group of people is known to have invaded the country successfully, by using the mouth of the Shannon as a gateway to and from the Atlantic Ocean. These were the Vikings who, in their crudely made boats , mastered the terrors of the sea and in doing so, came and went at will, and had established a settlement at Limerick before the 10th century A.D. The lower estuary does not figure again in history until the 16th century, when a remnant of the ill-fated Spanish Armada limped into Scattery Island, seeking food and shelter.

The Atlantic Ocean at and around the mouth of the estuary is a quiet expanse of water. Fishing boats ride the waves in season and fill their nets with sea fish, but there is no large fleet at anchor here and few cargo boats to pollute its waters.. Oil tankers and bulk carriers may be seen at present, supplying the needs of the recent industrial units sited on the banks of the estuary but these come at intervals and have not materially altered the historical character of the estuary as a scenic and rural retreat, a place for walking, climbing and boating, a calm haven for birds, flowers and wildlife.

In the last century, the estuary has been described as sheltering an enormous number of birds, especially in the marshes, the mudflats, the spits, rocks and islands, not only the native species but also migratory geese and ducks – curlew, teal, barnacle geese, snipe, shoveller and widgeon. The number of birds has decreased since then, though not the great variety. This remains,not only in the native species but also in the huge wintering flocks that invade the bays and mudflats. The reclamation of much of the marshlands and the erection of new buildings and installations have contributed largely to bring about this decrease, coupled with the growing activity in the industrial units on the estuary's banks and the heavy road traffic.

• • • • •

Side by side with the human presence and its myriad activities, the estuary provides suitable habitats for birds, and 'wetlands' for overwintering wildfowl as they fly in from the frozen wastes of Greenland, Iceland, Canada and the Baltic States. In that respect, it compares well with Loch Ree, the Little Brosna, and the Wexford slobs which, between them, supply winter feeding grounds for thousands of migratory birds.

In the spring and early summer, numerous native species flit and skim over the shoreline and islands. The clamorous blackheaded gulls nest on the islands as do a host of other birds, such as, skylark, magpie, blackbird, robin and wren. The coot, waterhen, mallard and shelduck, teal and lapwing frequent the hummocks of grass and the tussocks of wild vegetation close to the shorelines. On or near the water, the mute swan constructs a raft of sticks and grass. Rustling in the thickets of reeds are the great-crested grebes, the water rails and moorhens, the sedge and reed warblers. And in the fertile sandy shallows, flocks of birds feed ceaselessly – curlew, redshank, tufted duck, grey heron and ringed plover.

There is a bird sanctuary by the estuary, at Westfield Park on the Clare shoreline, close to Limerick City, and a second one at Ballyheigue beside the Kerry coast. Both are small and are frequented by an assorted group of waders, gulls and small birds such as, the blue tit, the wagtail and the swallow, and less often, by the larger birds, the grey heron, the mute swan and the kestrel.

From October onwards, wildfowl in their thousands descend on the estuary, more specifically, on the intertidal mudflats, sand bars and spits, mounds of clay and loam deposited by the streams and rivers upon the shorelines. A multitude of migratory 'visitors' feed on those areas, moving instinctively with the rhythms of the twice-daily tides – Brent and Grey-lag geese, White-fronted geese, widgeon and scaup, black-tailed godwits, Whooper and Mute swans, dunlin and shoveller.

All of these birds feed on the unlimited range of organisms to be found on the shoreline grass, in the sand and mud, and the aquatic plants in the estuary. Plankton, diatoms, protozoa and crustacea form the basis of the freshwater food chain and each type of bird hunts ceaselessly for its own specific diet. Geese and widgeon graze on the moist nearby fields and patches of eel-grass. Swans search the water for aquatic plants. Waders with long powerful beaks penetrate the sand and mud layers to find rag and lug worms, beetles and snails, while the ducks trawl the watercourse for insects, shrimps, stickleback and mussel.

The many areas of sand and mud shelter myriads of burrowing worms, tiny shrimps, snails and shellfish. Minute organisms grow between the grains of sand and the particles of mud. Long strands and clumps of seaweed and bladderwort line the shingle beaches, providing cover for numbers of organisms unable to bear exposure to the air. But the ever-hungry birds, chiefly the turnstone and the dunlin, quickly find and devour them, and thus they join the great natural food chain which makes the estuary such a rich and bounteous 'wetland'.

Only the movement of the tides, as a rule, disturbs this incessant hunt for finding and ingesting food. Sections of the feeding grounds are continuously washed over by the non-stop march of wave and wavelets, while other sections laden with fertility, are gradually uncovered. Then the flocks erupt, sweeping across the sky in lines and V-shapes, to plummet and skim and twist, until they reach their preferred feeding zones.

Thousands of birds haunt the Fergus estuary with its plethora of sand banks, mud spits, islands and solitary, reed-choked inlets. The area around Shannon Airport is a favourite habitat, the birds seemingly unaffected by the large complex of buildings, the clamour and swoop of the planes, the ceaseless movement of people and cars. In the lower estuary, on the west side of the Labasheeda peninsula is the secluded stretch of Clonderalaw Bay. A quiet undisturbed locale of calm streamy water, pools, islets, and grassy verges, this watercourse which has all the features of an inland lake, proves an ideal habitat for the thousands of

The Coot

Waders

White-fronted Geese and Swans

Poulnasherry Bay

Tufted Duck

Clonderalaw Bay

Mullet

Brill and Turbot

Hawthorn Blossom

Red Valerian

Ferns

Fuschia

Sea Pink

The Cabbage White

wildfowl that converge on it in the winter months – widgeon, teal, Whooper swan, golden plover and lapwing. Similarly, Poulnasherry Bay, close to Kilrush and west of the town, a lake rather than a bay, shelters many more.

The Limerick shoreline has also many areas favoured by native and migrant wildfowl – the stretch from Limerick Harbour to the inlets of the Rivers Maigue and Deel with their islands and mudbanks, Aughinish Island, which has a bird sanctuary with a colony of birds which include the redshank, dunlin, curlew, shelduck, oyster-catcher, widgeon and turnstone. Added to these, are Tarbert's sheltered pools and coves, and the inlets and creeks of Ballylongford Bay, each with its own complement of wildfowl. It is estimated that the winter habitats of the estuary are frequented by up to 20,000 waders and 10,000 other wildfowl, giving it a high international status as a 'wetland'. The estuary is also a great wild fishery throughout its length. Both shorelines are noted angling waters, particularly in the vicinity of bays, pools and inlets to rivers. Eels are numerous in the mid and upper estuary. The mouths of the rivers, Maigue and Deel, and the rivers, themselves, have salmon, sea trout and brown trout. The River Fergus is similarly rich in salmon and grilse, brown trout and eels. Sea trout and salmon may be fished for throughout the estuary, while coarse fish – bream, tench, roach, pike and perch – frequent the small lakes in the hinterland and the streams that flow into it on both sides.

The lower estuary, however, from Kerry Head to Foynes, forty miles upstream, is an especially promising area. The water here is deep and provides unlimited food for a large and exotic array of fish not found in the upper Shannon and its lakes. Their names conjure up the space and power of the ocean, beating against the sea cliffs not far distant, gurnard, shark, ray, monkfish, skate, conger eel, turbot, mullet, whiting and bass. On the surface of the watercourse, they feed on plankton, crustacea and water flies, while, in the bottom mud, a feast of minute organisms await – snail and shrimp, stickleback, minnow, clam and sand eel.

The vicinity of bays like Kilbaha, Poulnasherry and Clonderalow are favourite habitats of these fish. There is shore angling at Carrigaholt for dogfish, and at Cappa Pier for conger eel. Querrin Point can be fished for tope, bass, monkfish and ray, while angling for shark, tope and skate is available in the deep waters off the Kilrush shore.

It is mainly in the lower estuary that these fish congregate, making sea angling a major sport in this area. To facilitate people desirous of taking up the sport, the Atlantic Adventure Company, operating from Kilrush Marina, provides boats and yachts, fully outfitted for charter and hire, whether for fishing trips, tours or deep sea fishing, making it possible to cruise along the West Coast from Cork to the Aran Islands and Galway Bay, or farther north, if required.

The flora of the estuary is largely a replica of that of the upper Shannon and its lakes, chiefly Loch Ree and Loch Derg though not so varied or so abundant. Three factors tend to inhibit the growth of wild flowers – the open unprotected shorelines at the mercy of storms and the twice-daily tides which affect the salinity of the atmosphere, their pastoral nature because of which animals graze them constantly and so prevent the development of flowers, and the quality of the surrounding terrain which, in the west on both shorelines, changes to a large proportion of shale and sandstone rather than limestone, and makes for a limited flora.

This is particularly true in south-west Clare, where the land is flat and marshy with patches of bog and fen. It does not have the astonishing wealth of flora that characterises the area of the Burren in North Clare, scarcely thirty miles distant. Similarly, the Kerry shoreline lacks the distinctive flora of its south-west uplands, cliffs and valleys.

Many of the islands, however, have a strong limestone content which supports tillage and abundant grass. In early summer, they flare brilliantly with yellow gorse, heavy white clusters of hawthorn blossom, red valerian, and the small flowers of the fields and copses – the familiar primroses, daisy and bluebell, cowslip, buttercup and cuckoo flower, and a multitude of weaving grasses. As the summer months progress, meadow sweet and yellow iris appear on both banks, the long green pennants of the latter weaving a background to the host of other colourful flowers and plants that surround them – purple loosestrife, ferns, red and white clover, marguerites, willowherb and yellow ragwort. In the sand spits and ooze of the shallows, water plantain, cattails and bulrush, clubrush and clumps of tall reeds compete for space.

Wild grasses, the brown dock, nettles and briars, grow profusely in the watery ditches and in untrimmed corners of the grasslands. Solitary discs of red betray the presence of the field poppy. On the surface of the shallows are pennywort, duckwort and spike rushes, while beneath the streamy current, hornwort and stonewort develop a small watery forest of weed.

The narrow shingle beaches that quarter the shorelines have long oily strands and mounds of seaweed and bladderwort, and growing in niches among the crevices in the background rocks are moss, lichen and tufts of grass. More unusual plants are squinancywort, madder and scale fern which flourish on the limestone rock. The three-angled bulrush is to be found only in the shallow waters of the Limerick shoreline.

The hedges are thick and luscious in summer and autumn. Lichen, moss and ivy cling to the old gnarled trunks of hawthorn and sycamore. Cow parsley, cleavers and docks, nettles and plaintain shelter the small mammals, the frogs, mice and rabbits, while an attractive array of foxglove, wild rose and fuschia lures the bees and wasps. Butterflies hover and skip endlessly from flower to flower, the Cabbage White, the Orange Tip and Brimstone.

The plants on the outer verges of the watercourse give shelter to numerous insects. A myriad of flies, such as, the alder fly, sawfly and mayfly, hide in waterside vegetation and feed on it. Biting midges ascend into the air in clouds. Snails and leeches crawl on leaves and stems, food for the ever-hunting birds. On the surface of the watercourse are the pondskaters, while sticklebacks, tadpoles and diving beetles stream with the current.

On the cliffs and sand dunes sea pink grows, with sea aster and samphire, couch and marram grass, thyme and violet. The sand dunes have their own types of insect - mites and beetles, moths and butterflies, spiders, digger wasps, and incessant swarms of flies. Marram grass, its stems, leaves and flowering tops, provides shelter and food for many insects as does couch grass, particularly for moths and butterflies and their larvae.

The waterside plants also give shelter to small mammals like the frog and the grasshopper. Other residents of the shoreline, the brown rat, the otter, a nocturnal hunter of fish, the rabbit, the bank vole and the pigmy shrew are rarely seen.

Chapter Thirteen

A S WITH THE LANDS SURROUNDING THE HEADWATERS OF THE SHANNON rather more than other areas of its long course, those adjacent to the estuary contain notable artefacts and symbols of pre-historic times and attest to the periods and strength of the two colonizations - those of the Mesolithic and Neolithic Stone Ages.

Archaelogical research has uncovered megalithic residues at Loch Gur in County Limerick, twelve miles from the estuary, which indicate the period, about 6,000 B.C., as a significant date, from which the presence of people in the area can be deduced. Stone Age habitations – ring and stone forts, standing stones, foundations of crannóga, or lake dwellings, caves, wedge-shaped gallery and other type graves have been excavated. Complementary to these are numerous objects, primitively made, such as, pottery shards, flint arrowheads, stone axes, boring tools, and scrapers – the implements and dwelling places of fishermen and farmers.

Bolin Island in the lake is a man-made construction of a crannóg, or lake dwelling. Rising above its waters, the hill of Knockfennell contains a grave in which the bones of animals, now extinct, were discovered, while on a low hill, on the approach road to the lake, are two large stone structures, now overlaid with grass, one oval, the other circular, named the Carraig Aille forts. Silver objects, belonging to the Norse invasion period, it is thought, were found in the oval fort. Farther south, near New Church

Loch Gur and Knockfennel Hill

A reconstructed crannóg

A Carrig Aille fort

Stone circle at Grange

is the Giant's Grave, a wedge-shaped gallery grave divided into two chambers by a stone slab. A few miles away at Grange, is the largest stone circle in the country, dating probably, from about 2,000 B.C. Some miles distant, at Kilfinnane, is Treada an Ri, the Kilfinnane Moat, a raised ring fort, surrounded by three circular banks and fosses. Farther east, near Galbally, the hill of Dún Tri Liag is topped by a large, well-preserved tomb with a chamber and long entry passage said to date from 3,500 B.C.

In County Clare, the northern boundary of the estuary, similar artefacts have been found, especially in the area of the Burren. Here, too, are wedge tombs and gallery graves, dolmens and cairns. At Poll an Bhaic is an ancient cemetery, containing the remains of human skeletons, metal fragments and primitive tools. A short distance north, at Poll na Bron, is a large dolmen which dates from about 2,500 B.C. Here, too, are ring forts and raths, or earthen forts. One of these is at Rathborney, while a well-preserved ring fort is at Caherconnell.

The Celts, who colonised the country from about 300 B.C. were skilled workers in the use of metals. The Turoe Stone, a standing stone ornamented with a subtle pattern of carved design, dates from about 200 B.C., and is an example of early Celtic geometric art. Craftsmanship began to develop throughout the country, and new ranges of tools and other objects were being made, examples of which, are daggers, rapiers and shields, axes and hammers. Pottery. Discs and gorgets, bracelets, rings and pendants. Ornaments in gold were being fashioned at this time in the area of the lower Shannon – beads, brooches, collars and

The remains of Mooghaun Fort

Diggings at Mooghaun

torques. The Celts were especially skilled in the use of iron. Close to the estuary, near Newmarket-on-Fergus, is a large hill fort, dating from the Iron Age, Mooghaun Fort, the most extensive of its kind in the country. In this area, a significant 'find' of gold ornaments, crafted in pre-historic times, was discovered in the last century.

During the 5th century, A.D., Christianity spread from Europe to Ireland and gradually overlaid the nature cults of the Celts, the worship of fire, water, trees, animals and statuary, but did not extinguish them. The shorelines and islands of the estuary became identified as a notable part of the development of the Christian era, known as the 'Golden Age', which lasted for up to four hundred years. Churches, large and small, monastic foundations, including chapels, schools and workshops, were built on both shorelines, in the hinterland, and on some of the estuarine islands. Each monastic settlement created its own cultural activities, its crafted artefacts in stone, copper, gold and bronze, ornaments and church vessels, literary work in writing manuscripts of the Gospels, along with the artistic task of illuminating them. The developing church became noted for its craftworkers, scribes and illuminators. The Tara Brooch, the Ardagh Chalice and a number of High Crosses belong to this period.

One of the first and greatest of monastic settlements was that at Mungret on the Limerick shoreline, just three miles from the city. Founded by St. Nessan in the 5th century, it enjoyed growth and prosperity throughout the 'Golden Age', and was described in the Psalter of Cashel, as having six churches and up to fifteen hundred monks in its heyday. This era of peace, however, ended calamitously with the invasion of the Norsemen in the 8th century, their continual fierce raids on church property, and later on, their making a permanent settlement upstream on Inis Sibhtonn in the River Shannon. Their longboats enabled them to penetrate where they pleased, while their skill and ferocity in battle, terrorised the unprepared native population. For the following two centuries, the monastery at Mungret was raided, plundered and despoiled on several occasions, until Brian Boru broke the Viking power in the estuary in the 10th century. Mungret, surviving these attacks, continued to progress and expand its cultural influence into the 12th century when Limerick City was made a bishopric, a decision which proved fatal to the future of the monastery. The King of Munster at that time, Donal Mor O'Brien, who had made Limerick his centre of power, granted the monastic foundation and the lands it occupied to the See of Limerick in perpetuity.

Today, the site of the ancient monastery is covered by a cluster of cemeteries, medieval and modern, secular and religious. The cemeteries are collectively known as Mungret Graveyard and occupy both sides of a narrow road. The older and larger graveyard is unkempt and neglected, with loose graveslabs and mounds of vegetation. Some of its headstones date from the early 1800s. Although no trace of the 5th century monastic settlement remains, the ruined shells of three roofless churches still exist, two in the larger graveyard, and the third in a smaller burial place across the road.

The biggest of these ruins, standing among grave mounds and granite slabs, has its walls and gables still intact. Known as 'The Abbey', it is a medieval church, dating from the 13th century, or later. Some distance from it, at the end of the long graveyard, is a fragmented and ivied ruin, considered to belong to the same period. The third, standing in a small graveyard across the road, and consisting of a doorway and gable, is the oldest, and is said to date from the 12th century.

Another very famous foundation was that established in Inis Catha, the Island of the Sea Serpent, one and a half miles from Kilrush and only twenty from the unprotected mouth of the estuary and the Atlantic Ocean. It is also called Scattery Island, the word 'Scattery' said to be a Norse version of 'sea serpent'. In the 6th century, St. Senan founded a monastery on the island and is credited with banishing the serpent which had been regarded as an object of terror in the area. Even more so than the settlement at Mungret,

Scattery Island suffered continuously and severely from Norse raids and depredations, and from their conflicts with each other, and with native tribes to obtain possession of the island because of its strategic position near the mouth of the estuary. Eventually they occupied the island and held it for a century, until the year 970 A.D., when they were forced to abandon it by Brian Boru.

Periods of peace had alternated with bouts of warfare and the religious community had remained on the island. With the elimination of the Viking onslaughts, the monastery began to consolidate its position and, in the 12th century, became the See of a diocese which, however, lasted only a short time. The Normans took over the island in the 13th century, and for the next two hundred years, it became an important collegiate church with a number of buildings. It lasted until the coming of the Reformation in the 16th century, when it was dissolved and the island granted to the then Corporation of Limerick.

The remains of the monastic site today consist of the Cathedral of St. Senan, Senan's Well, a small nave and chancel church, fragments of a pre-Romanesque church on the Hill of the Angels, a graveyard and a Round Tower. The Tower is one hundred and twenty feet high, with its door on ground level, instead of in the usual raised position. On the most southerly tip of the island is a military battery of the 1800s, and beside it, a lighthouse, built in 1872. Close to the pier is the remains of an old castle of the O'Cahan clan, once caretakers of the monastery.

In the 1840s, a number of river pilots and other personnel on the estuary settled with their families on the island which has one hundred and sixty seven acres of land, mainly fertile. They built a village and supported themselves by farming and fishing. This period of habitation lasted until 1978, when the residents moved to the mainland and settled there. The island is now administered by the Board of Works.

Inis Gad, or Canon Island, in the estuary of the Fergus, is the third, great religious settlement of the area, but stems from a later period. It holds the ruins of a priory, dating from the 13th century, belonging to the Augustinian Order, and is said to have been founded by Donal Mor O'Brien, King of Munster. The ruins consist of an abbey, cloisters, kitchen and refectory with dormitory overhead. In 1543, with the advent of the Reformation, it was dissolved, and the island granted to the O'Brien family. Later, it passed into other hands but is now uninhabited.

In the 12th century, the Norman Invasion began. With superior weapons, more skilful methods of warfare and a fierce determination to occupy and conquer, they overran the country quickly. By 1200, they had reached Limerick, occupying the south shoreline of the estuary and adjacent lands, and had taken over the small Viking settlement on Inis Sibhtonn at which, after their military defeat, the Norse had settled down, developing it into a progressive trading post.

The Norman method of penetration and gaining possession was drastically different from that of the Vikings. Instead of making sporadic raids for plunder and loot, they occupied the areas which they succeeded in taking, built strong stone castles, fortified them, maintained garrisons and so withstood the attacks of native tribes. They built bridges and eventually roads. By the beginning of the 13th century, the first castle and bridge on the lower Shannon were built close to the Viking settlement - King John's Castle and Thomond Bridge. At Askeaton, the Fitzgeralds, the ruling Norman family on the south bank of the estuary, erected a castle on an island in the River Deel. On the Clare shoreline, the O'Brien family, still powerful, remained in place. On both shorelines, and in the hinterland, the building of castles, churches and monasteries, Irish and Norman, continued. Prime examples of these are the Franciscan Friaries at Askeaton and Lislaughtin, the Carrigafoyle Castle, the Abbey on Canon Island, and the resurgence of the monastery on Scattery Island.

For two centuries, the estuary enjoyed a period of relative peace during which fishing boats and cargo

Mungret Graveyard – The Abbey   *The oldest church*

boats replaced the old warlike craft, and trading became an established occupation on the watercourse. A small harbour was built just below Thomond Bridge, in the area of the present Merchants Quay and became the forerunner of the modern Limerick Harbour. From here, boats laden with wheat, grain and farm produce plied the estuary and sailed to Britain and the continent, bringing back tools, agricultural implements, textiles and sundry other goods. Small ports were developed at Askeaton, Foynes and Tarbert, to form a busy local trade, sailing to and fro on the estuary, supplying both shorelines with fish, provisions and tools.

This period of growing commercial activity was suddenly broken by the Elizabethan wars, the first of which, the Desmond rebellion, involved the entire south bank of the estuary for six years, ending in 1580 with the destruction of the powerful Fitzgerald family of Askeaton, and hitting the small town and port a disabling blow from which it did not recover for a long period. In the following century, two campaigns, the Cromwellian in 1651, and the Williamite in 1690-'91, in which Limerick City, now many times larger than its original settlement, suffered three rigorous sieges, having finally to capitulate. This sequence of misfortunes disrupted the town's trading ventures, ravaged its fleet of boats and brought loss and impoverishment to the farms supplying goods to the harbour. It was to be another half-century before the estuary recovered its former flow of commercial activity and began to attract ships from abroad, in

Scattery Island Old Church and Graveyard   *Scattery Island Old Church and Round Tower*

Derelict cottages on Scattery Island

The battery and lighthouse on Scattery Island

The ruined Beag Castle

Beag Pier

The battery at Kilkerin Point

A section of Corcanree Industrial Estate

order to establish itself as an international trade route.

In 1764, a pier was built at Cappa in the lower estuary, close to Kilrush. The latter, only twenty miles from the mouth of the estuary had a short flash of notoriety in 1588, when seven ships of the Spanish Armada, battling against storms on the west coast, sailed into the estuary and anchored briefly off Scattery Island, little more than a mile distant. With a new pier, it would now make progress as a small fishing port.

In Lloyd's Tour of Clare, published in 1780, it is mentioned that 'numbers of vessels from various parts of the Globe are daily trading up and down the Shannon'. Complementary to these were the local cargo boats and the large turf boats, often up to seventy of them, bearing turf to the Limerick markets and the villages on both shorelines. Cargoes of grain, beef, eggs and butter were brought up the Fergus estuary to the piers at Killadysert and Clarecastle, the latter supplying the market at Ennis, while boats, similarly laden, sailed down the Kerry coast to the market at Tralee.

During the Napoleonic wars from 1796 onwards, the estuary gained a political dimension as one of the suitable invasion points selected by the French Directory. Two others considered were Bantry Bay and Galway Bay. The estuary had sheltered harbours on its low shorelines and anchorages at ports and islands convenient for landing troops, stores and artillery. A defensive system was then planned. Coastal batteries were installed in the lower estuary. On the Clare shoreline they were placed at Kilkerin Point, at the tip of the Labasheeda peninsula opposite Tarbert Island, at Kilcredan Point south of Carrigaholt, and at Kilbaha in the Loop peninsula, both of these covering the mouth of the estuary. The batteries on the Limerick/Kerry shoreline were – on Foynes Island, on Carrig Island in Ballylongford Bay, on Tarbert Island and on the most southerly point of Scattery Island, covering the centre of the lower estuary. All of the batteries have now disappeared, except those at Scattery Island and at Kilkerin Point.

Tarbert Island became a fortress in those years, and up to a thousand military personnel manned the batteries there, giving such a warlike aspect to the area, that the island was known locally as 'The Battery'. The western tip of Foynes Island is also known as Battery Point. Kilrush too, had a garrison, though on a smaller scale. British naval units patrolled the estuary and, though normal commercial trading was allowed to continue, ships and boats were routinely searched.

In the event, the invasion did not take place and with the relaxation of military and naval surveillance, trade began to flourish again. In 1849, a wet dock was built at Limerick Harbour. The port of Tarbert, small and sheltered, grew busy, becoming the main outlet for agricultural produce from the areas of North Kerry and West Limerick. Sailing ships called here, to and from Limerick Harbour, bringing cargo from the Continent and North America. Foynes, some miles upstream of Tarbert, had begun to develop its port, having a very favourable deepwater anchorage, and by 1890, was busily exporting the farm produce of East Limerick and distributing goods to the villages of the estuary. Glin, a fishing village on the shoreline between Tarbert and Foynes, used its pier to develop its own form of trading. With various weirs owned by local people, the catching and landing of fish became highly profitable, most of the catch being exported to the London markets. To do this successfully, ice was needed and, although some ice houses were constructed near the village, the chief source of supply was Norway, and Norwegian cargo boats were a familiar sight at the pier.

Kilrush, on the West Clare shoreline, had also become a busy port, its pier at Cappa having been enlarged in 1835. It was the venue for numerous fishing boats and turf boats, and had begun an export trade, sending corn to Britain and the Continent. The piers at Killadysert, Clarecastle and Barrington were used mainly for unloading supplies – coal and turf, provisions, fertilisers and medicines.

The scourge of the Famine towards the middle of the century had a calamitous effect on Clare as a whole, and on West Clare in particular. The population was decimated both by death and by emigration, and only of late years are attempts being made to lift this shoreline and its hinterland, out of the torpor induced by the happenings of that disastrous period.

In the 1850s, a passenger steamer service was inaugurated between Limerick and Cappa Pier and operated twice a week. It called at Beag Castle, which had at that time a ferry service to Ringannon Point on the Clare shoreline, and also at Foynes, Glin and Tarbert, putting down and taking up passengers at these points. In the summer months, many people travelled to Kilkee on the Clare coast, then becoming a fashionable seaside resort. The steamer service continued until the first World War and began to decline afterwards. The development of the railway in West Clare contributed greatly to this decline. The service was discontinued in the 1920s.

The growth of rail and road traffic had a damaging effect on the boat trade of the estuary in general. At the same time, manpower was being attracted by industrial schemes and other forms of employment which were being made available, such as, the hydro-electric scheme on the River Shannon from 1925 to 1929, and later on, in the thirties, the building of Shannon Airport and the emergence of Foynes as a Flying Boat Centre. By the end of World War II, trading in the estuary had dwindled, the chief sufferers being the ports of Tarbert and Kilrush. Limerick Harbour and that of Foynes remained in operation, but on a declining economic level.

• • • • •

After 1946, the Board of Commissioners of Limerick Harbour, with the support of the Government, set out to modernise the two main ports of the estuary, Limerick and Foynes. New dramatic developments were taking place across the world in regard to maritime trade. The fleets of cargo boats and merchant shipping, once the mainstay of oceanic transport, had suffered grievously during the war. It was not considered economic to rebuild them. In their places came the bulk tankers and the super-carriers, ferrying huge volumes of commodities to the hungry, battlescarred countries of Europe and Asia. Far-reaching changes were also occurring at the docks and quays, in the loading and unloading of cargo, and in the machinery and handling equipment. Containerisation, the roll-on, roll-off, and the lift-on, lift-off systems necessitated new methods and new mechanical gear which resulted in a quicker turn around of ships and a reduction in dock labour crews.

Major dredging operations deepened and extended Limerick Harbour, the greatest depth of which is twenty feet. In this respect, it is disadvantaged by comparison with other ports and bays in the estuary, the deep channel of which reaches from sixty to one hundred feet at its mouth, and sixty two feet in the lower Fergus estuary, forty miles upstream. The docks were also deepened and improved. New machinery was put in place and the work of reclamation continued. The value of these operations became evident in the 1960s when the Industrial Estate of Corcanree was built on the south side of the harbour. A wide diversity of goods manufactured here, includes wire products, electrical goods, engineering components, animal feedstuffs, fertilisers, and cement.

Twenty miles west of Limerick Harbour is Foynes, a deepwater port. It handled vessels of 22,000 tonnes deadweight normally, at depths of thirty two feet, but with renovation — with dredging, deepening and reclamation, more warehousing and the up-dating of handling equipment it increased its capacity to vessels of 35,000 tonnes, deadweight. The port has the advantage of being connected with the National Rail System, and can provide services for the transport of bulk commodities. In the 1960s, a new jetty was built at Foynes Island which has a depth of fifty feet, and in 1967, the highest tonnage ever recorded in the estuary was carried by a tanker, discharging at the jetty — it delivered 38,000 tonnes deadweight of fuel oil, imported by Cement Ltd.

From this point on, developments in the facilities for larger vessels, went ahead rapidly. In 1969, an oil-

Askeaton Industrial Estate

Aughinish Alumina

Cement Ltd.

Loading at Foynes

Moneypoint Power Station

fired power station, built by the Electricity Supply Board on Tarbert Island, came on stream. With it was a fuel oil jetty, having a low water depth of forty eight feet, which accommodates tankers of up to 80,000 tonnes deadweight. This was followed by a similar, though smaller operation at Dernish in the Fergus estuary in 1973. An oil jetty was constructed here to supply fuel oil to nearby Shannon Airport. With a low water depth of twenty five feet, it normally caters for tankers of 6,000 tonnes deadweight, but is designed to take vessels of twice that size if need be.

By 1974, the existing facilities on the estuary were listed as – ports at Limerick, Foynes, Tarbert and Kilrush, piers at Glin, Tarbert, Saleen at Ballylongford, and Clarecastle on the River Fergus, the second category being capable of handling small coastal vessels only. It was clear that additional deep water berths and services to complement those at Foynes and Tarbert would be required if the middle and lower estuary were to be fully utilised. Significant developments began to follow. The construction of the hugh alumina plant on Aughinish Island beside the port of Foynes began in 1978 and became operational in 1983. Aughinish has its own bulk-handling facility and at its jetty vessels of up to 70,000 tonnes deadweight can be catered for. Bauxite, the main raw material of alumina, is delivered by ore-carriers of this magnitude from West Africa. Other necessary commodities, such as, oil and liquid caustics are supplied by tanker, while the industrial product, alumina, is exported. Following Aughinish, came the building of a coal-fired power station by the Electricity Supply Board at Moneypoint on the Clare shoreline. At its jetty, bulk carriers of up to 180,000 tonnes deadweight can be accommodated. It became operational in 1985. This rapid development over thirty years has given a tremendous boost to the trade of the estuary. With three industrial estates presently operating on its shorelines - Corcanree, Shannon Free Zone and, on a lesser scale, Askeaton, as well as large industrial units, an increase from 450,000 tonnes of cargo in 1966 to six million tonnes in the 1990s, has occurred. The sizes of vessels in use have also grown dramatically.

Future projections for the estuary are ambitious and far-reaching, based as they are on three major factors – firstly, that the present water depths are sufficient to allow vessels of 200,000 tonnes deadweight sail to the Fergus estuary, forty miles upstream; secondly, that the Atlantic sea routes off the west coast remain largely free of general shipping; and thirdly, that the physical potential of the estuary, if fully and wisely developed, can be made to compare favourably with that of great ports, such as, Rotterdam in Holland, and Milford Haven in Wales. It is being envisaged as an international trade depot between the markets of North and South America, and those of Europe and Asia. A transhipment port for ores, oil and oil products, grain and other bulk commodities. A harbour which could accommodate ships of up to 400,000 tonnes deadweight, or even greater volume, and provide berthage for similar large vessels. All of this would entail deepwater facilities of up to seventy nine feet and over, and the removal of a sandbar at the mouth of the estuary which, at present, inhibits the entry of carriers of such magnitude. It would also require the upgrading of facilities and services throughout the estuary, new port and backup industries, such as, heavy engineering and ship repairing, smelting plants, steel works, oil refining and ore processing, the making of new roads in the hinterland, and the improvement of those already there.

The industrialisation of the estuary has not proceeded without fears being expressed for its effect on tourist potential, on the safety of the wildlife habitats, as well as on the quality of the environment. Despite its pastoral and scenic features and its mild climate, the estuary has never achieved a 'tourist significance', with the single exception of Ballybunion on the Kerry shoreline, a factor which may explain why most of its villages are so small. Tourists have tended to bypass its long expanse in favour of the seaside resorts of the Clare and Kerry coastlines, and the scenic areas of the Burren and Killarney. A study of the estuarine shorelines has pin-pointed some areas as more scenic than others, the villages of Glin and Carrigaholt, the woods of Kilrush and Labasheeda and the spacious strands at Béal Point. Into this category also, come the settings of National Monuments, such as, Scattery Island, the Franciscan Friary at Askeaton, Lislaughtin Abbey and Carrigafoyle Castle. It is intended that these areas will be excluded from industrialisation and developed for tourism.

The bird havens, sanctuaries and wetlands are rather more difficult to cater for, especially as the largest of them, the Fergus estuary, its islands and mudflats, is a favourite wintering place for thousands of waders, ducks and geese. The proximity of Shannon Airport on the east side of this estuary, and the busy port of Foynes just opposite on the Limerick shoreline, have not affected the bird population adversely to any great extent. In only one instance has this happened. During the heavy construction work on Aughinish Island, a colony of migratory geese abandoned the wetlands there. Now a protected bird sanctuary awaits their return. In general, it is intended that safeguards will be applied to ensure the immunity of the birds' feeding grounds on both shorelines.

Pollution, in the wake of industrial development, is the chief enemy of both human and bird populations, and of the fish stocks also. It can occur in different forms - fuel ash from the coalburning station, dust from the cement factory, oil slicks in the vicinity of fuel tankers, gases from oil, coal and chemical usage, effluent and waste debris. Moneypoint power station, the largest complex on the estuary, has established its own monitoring system in regard to fuel ash and emissions of gas, and maintains constant watch on the quality of the air in its local environment. At Aughinish Alumina, a water treatment plant has been installed. The quality of the water used is routinely analysed, particularly waste water which is not returned to the estuary unless it reaches anti-pollution requirements. The results of all such private efforts are supervised and assessed by the Research Unit of the Department of the Environment.

The maintenance of standards of air and water quality will become of paramount importance in the development of the estuary if future industrial projects, spear-headed by Shannon Development and the IDA, go ahead as envisioned. But with so many of these under consideration, all allied to heavy industry and requiring fuel in bulk to operate them, how far the policy of protecting the environment will stretch, remains to be seen.

One thing seems certain. The Shannon estuary is in the process of being prepared for a major development which, if carried through, will transform its largely historical and passive role into one of vital commercial importance. The most westerly maritime seaway in Europe, opening on the Atlantic Ocean, it is in the central area of world trade – between North and South America and Europe on the one hand, and between Europe and the countries of the Far East on the other. If full advantage can be taken of this position and the necessary facilities and services be installed, the 21st century may well see the estuary reaching a continuous industrial growth, hitherto unknown, which will benefit, not only itself and its environment, the Shannon region as a whole, but the entire country as well.

Acknowledgements

I am indebted to the following organisations for providing information in the form of reports, booklets and papers relevant to the preparation and writing of this book.

Aughinish Alumina, Ltd. Public Relations Office, for the
booklet – *Bauxite to Alumina at Aughinish*;
Bord na Mona for the Information Sheet on the
Mountdillon(Cnoc Dioluin) Works;
Central Fisheries Board for regional maps of the Shannon;
Electricity Supply Board (ESB) for booklets on –
Ardnacrusha, Moneypoint and Tarbert;
Electricity Supply Board(International) for the booklet on the reconstruction
of the Ballinamore/Ballyconnell Canal (Shannon/Erne);
Foynes Harbour Office for the booklet on the Port of Foynes;
The Interpretative Centre Kilrush, for Information Sheets on Scattery Island;
Kilrush Creek Marina Office for leaflets on the Marina;
Office of the Limerick Harbour Commissioners for leaflets and
Shannon Shipping News, December, 1992;
Ordnance Survey, Dublin, for Sheets 7 and 17;
Ordnance Survey, N. Ireland, for Sheet 26;
Shannon Development for Information Sheets on the estuary.

To the staffs of the public libraries in Cavan, Carrick-on-Shannon and Drumshanbo, I am most grateful for being enabled to read collections of papers on the local history of the Shannon in these areas. Also to the staff of Limerick public library for providing reports, booklets and papers on Limerick Harbour and the Shannon estuary. I thank the people I have met, local inhabitants, naturalists and fishermen, who freely added to my knowledge and made my journey along the Shannon shorelines more stimulating and interesting than it otherwise might have been.

I am particularly indebted to Tony Moreau for his thorough preparation of the MS.

Maeve Henry
The Conna Press,
P.O. Box 5097,
Dublin, 7.
July 1996

Bibliography

HISTORY

Evans, E.E.	*Prehistoric and Early Christian Ireland*. London. Batsford. 1966
Harbison, P .	*Guide to the National Monuments of Ireland*. Dublin. Gill and MacMillan. 1975
Harbison, P	*Archaelogy of Ireland*. London. Bodley Head. 1976
Hayden,M and Moonan, G.	*Short History of the Irish People*. Dublin, 1921.
Herity,M and Eogan,G.	*Ireland in Pre-History*. London. Routledge and Keegan Paul.1977.
MacNeill, E.	*Celtic Ireland*. Dublin. The Academy Press. Reprint,1981
MacNeill, Maire.	*The Festival of Lughnasa*. Oxford, 1962.
Ó'Riordain, S.P.	*Antiquities of the Irish Countryside*. London. Methuen and Co. 1942.

LANDSCAPE, FLORA AND FAUNA

Angel, Heather.	*Natural History of Great Britain and Ireland*. London. Michael Joseph. 1981.
de Buitlear, E.	*Wild Ireland*. Dublin. Amac Faoin Aer. 1984
de Buitlear, E.	*Irish Rivers*. Dublin. Country House. 1985.
Delany, Ruth.	*The Canals of the South of Ireland*. Newton Abbot. David and Charles. 1966
Delany, Ruth.	*Ireland's Inland Waterways*. Belfast. Appletree Press. 1986.
Freeman, T.W. A	*General and Regional Geography of Ireland*. London. Methuen. 1960
Gillmor, D.(ed)	*The Irish Countryside*. Dublin. Wolfhound Press. 1989.
Hutchison, C.	*Ireland's Wetlands and their Birds*. Dublin. Irish Wildbird Conservancy. 1977.
John, Moody and Rolls.	*Geology and Landscape in Britain and Western Europe*. Oxford University Press. 1983.
Mitchell, F.	*Irish Landscape*. London. Collins. 1976.
Mitchell, F.(ed.)	*The Book of the Irish Countryside*. Belfast. Blackstaff. 1987
O'Reilly, P.	*Trout and Salmon Rivers of Ireland*. London. Unwin Hyman. 1987.
O'Reilly, P.	*Trout and Salmon Loughs of Ireland*. London. Revised ed. Collins Willow, 1992.
Praeger, R.L.	*Natural History of Ireland*. E.P. Publishing Ltd. 1950.

GENERAL

Delany, Ruth..	*By Shannon Shores*. Dublin. Gill and MacMillan. 1987.
Doyle, Doirin.	*Clonmacnois*. Dublin. Kamac Publications. 1972.

Feehan, J.M.   *The Magic of the Shannon*. Cork. Mercier. 1980.

Fitzpatrick, Margaret.   *The Kingdom of Glan*. Glangevlin. I.C.A. Guild. 1983.

Harvey, J.R.   *The Shannon and its Lakes*. Dublin. Hodges Figgis. 1896.

Hayward, R.   *Where the River Shannon Flows*. Dundalk. Dundealgan Press. 1940.

Hayward, R.   *This is Ireland – Connacht*. London. Barker. 1952.

Kierse, S.   *Historic Killaloe*. Killaloe. Boru Books. 1983

Lloyd, J.   *Tour of Clare, 1780*. Whitegate. Reprint, Ballinakella Press. 1986.

MacMahon, M.   *Portumna Priory*. Shannon Books. 1975.

MacNamara, T.V.   *Guide to Holy Island*. Mountshannon. Reinhold. 1978.

O'Brien, G.(ed.)   *Athlone Tourist Trail*. Athlone Chamber of Commerce. 1991.

Owen, E.   *The Church and Parish of Tuamgraney*. Publisher unnamed. 1964.

Rice, H.   *Thanks for the Memory*. Athlone Printing Works. 1955.

Seoighe, M.   *Portrait of Limerick*. London. Hale, R. 1982.

Trodd, V.   *Banagher on the Shannon*. Publisher Unnamed. 1985.

GUIDES

AA   *Illustrated Road Book of Ireland*.

Bord Failte.   *Ireland: A Guide.1993*. Official county guides.

Clear, J.K.   *Shannon Guide*. Dublin. 1970.

Delany, Ruth.   *Shell Guide to Shannon*. Dublin. Gill and MacMillan. 1989.

IBRA, IWAI & ERA-MAPTEC Ltd.
              Navigational Guide to the Shannon. Dublin. 1991.

Killanin,M. and Duignan,M.V.
              Shell Guide to Ireland. London. Ebury Press. 1962.

Loch Allen Region Community Development Co Ltd
              Guide to the Loch Allen Region. Drumshanbo. 1993.

Shannon Development   *Shannon Region Visitors Guide*. Shannon. 1994

Tipper, Bernadette.   *The River Shannon. A Boater's Guide*. Dublin. Town House. 1987.

Weaver, J.   *Shell Guide to Shannon (Navigational)*. Dublin. 2nd edition.

184

Index